Published in 2018 by Rockridge edu. enterprise & services. inc.
ALL RIGHTS RESERVED.
COPYRIGHT @2016
BY SAN YOO

NO part of this book may be reproduced in any form, by phtosat, Microfilm, PDF or any other means, or incorporated into any information retrieval system, electronic or mechanical, without the written permission of the copyright owner

All inquiries should be addressed to:
Rockridge edu. enterprise & services inc.
869 SEYMOUR BLVD. NORTH VANCOUVER B.C. CANADA V7J 2J7
satvancouver@gmail.com

Video animation aids, go to Youtube and type | ssat absolute patterns |

HOW TO USE THIS BOOK

Chapter 1

15 Hidden Patterns in the Analogy Section

The entire Analogy Section uses these 15 Absolute Patterns.

The official SSAT creates the questions based on these patterns.

Instead of practicing each individual question endlessly without knowing the patterns and logic behind it, please work with these hidden patterns.

Memorize 15 Absolute Patterns in this chapter and check to see if you are following the patterns.

Practice until every pattern becomes natural to you.   To obtain a FREE SSAT ABSOLUTE Vocabulary with picture book, please send a simple email request: satvancouver@gmail.com

15 Hidden Patterns in the Analogy Section

Absolute Pattern 1. Production (Cause-Effect) Pattern

Q1. Fire is to heat as

A) job is to money

B) waiter is to restaurant

C) lamp is to bulb

D) shower is to bathroom

E) meal is to chef

The correct answer is A.

San: Fire produces heat as job produces money. No other choices meet this pattern

Donny: What about E? Chef produces meal, doesn't he?

San: I know. There's always a catch, right? Patterns can be shown in the opposite order, which can make your decision even harder. But you should know that choice (A) follows the same order as shown in the question. You can't pick (E), which is flipped over and say (A) is wrong. Besides, the question and (A) are nonhuman concept—the same non-human category, while (E) is a human category.

Video animation aids, go to Youtube and type $\boxed{\text{ssat absolute patterns}}$

HOW TO USE THIS BOOK

Chapter 2.

8 Absolute Reading Patterns

8 Absolute Patterns in the Reading Section

The entire 40 questions in the reading section, both literary and informational passages, can be categorized into two parts: Category A: Content Question; Category B: Technique Question. These two categories can be subcategorized into eight Absolute Patterns.

The eight Absolute Patterns—mostly one pattern per question —plus incorrect option patterns will be absolutely the most effective and systemic way to improve your scores.

Category A: Content Question has five patterns:

▶ Pattern 1: Local Question

▶ Pattern 2: Main idea Question

▶ Pattern 3: Summary Question

▶ Pattern 4: Relationships Question

▶ Pattern 5: Word-in-Context Question

Pattern 1 Local Question has three major types.

　◆Type 1: Example Question

　◆Type 2: Inference Question

　◆Type 3: Analogy Question

Local question— either with the line reference number or without it—normally asks detailed information from only one or two sentences in the passage. The question may ask explicitly stated keywords in the sentences, or, in more complex level, implicitly analogous situations. Neither of the cases requires a holistic understanding of the entire passage.

UNAUTHORIZED COPYING OR REUSE OF ANY PART OF THIS PAGE IS ILLEGAL

Video animation aids, go to Youtube and type | ssat absolute patterns |

HOW TO USE THIS BOOK

20 Common Patterns for *In*correct Options

You—now armed with more enthusiastic and strategic understanding with the reading questions by employing 8 Reading Patterns—will be ready to isolate the dusty three incorrect options with less wrinkles on your face using the following 20 incorrect common patterns.

1 | Positive-Negative Tone (value)

Over 50 percent of the reading questions can be solved using this simple but powerful tool.

All you need is to identify the keywords in each multiple choice, and pick one of them that matches the reading passage's keyword (s) based on positive-negative value. This rule will lead you to the concrete prediction to the answer than any other rules.

3 | Active-Passive Value

We can observe how securely and predominately this pattern is anchored in the vast majority of the questions alongside the positive-negative value.

*Please note that this active-Passive value is not the same thing as the active-passive voice in Grammar.

Video animation aids, go to Youtube and type | ssat absolute patterns |

HOW TO USE THIS BOOK

Chapter 3. **Reading Test**

Eight Complete Tests

Eight Reading and Verbal Tests in this book are designed with the same level of difficulties and methodologies as used in the real SSAT Middle & Upper Level.

Test 1 Reading Section
Time: 40 Minutes, 40 Questions

Directions: Each reading passage is followed by questions about it. Answer the questions that follow a passage on the basis of what is stated or implied in that passage.

Questions 1-6 are based on the following passage.

Line
"I am afraid, Watson, that I shall have to go," said Holmes, as we sat down together to our breakfast one morning.

"Go! Where to?"

"To Dartmoor; to King's Pyland."

1

In line 5, "mixed up" most nearly means

A) confused with
B) associated with
C) obsessed with
D) united with
E) put together

2

Line 9 (absolutely deft to my question) suggests that the narrator

A) observes another character paying little attention to any of his question
B) worries another character's physical condition
C) sees another character's degree of contemplation
D) regards the extraordinary case is not important
E) argues the extraordinary case requires a high level of attention

CONTINUE ▶

UNAUTHORIZED COPYING OR REUSE OF ANY PART OF THIS PAGE IS ILLEGAL

Video animation aids, go to Youtube and type | ssat absolute patterns |

HOW TO USE THIS BOOK

Chapter 3. Verbal Test

Eight Complete Tests

Eight Reading and Verbal Tests in this book are designed with the same level of difficulties and methodologies as used in the real SSAT Middle & Upper Level.

Test 1 Verbal Section   30 MINUTES, 60 QUESTIONS

Directions: the synonym questions ask you to find the most appropriate synonym to the question.

The analogy questions ask you to find the most appropriate analogy to the question.
Select the answer that best matches to the question.

Synonym Sample Question:

Q: SUPERIOR

   A higher rank

   B inferior

   C considerable

   D supermarket

   E supper

A) is the best answer because the synonym for superior is higher rank.

B) is incorrect because it applies the 'opposite concept.

C) and E) are irrelevant words.

D) is incorrect because it applies physical concept to mental concept

---

Test 1 Synonym questions 1 to 30

1. LATER
(A) subsequent
(B) latent
(C) earlier
(D) lament
(E) durable

2. EXPLOIT
(A) explore
(B) utilize
(C) help
(D) expunge
(E) brave

3. ACCOUNT
(A) perjury
(B) report
(C) countenance

CONTINUE ➡

Video animation aids, go to Youtube and type | ssat absolute patterns |

HOW TO USE THIS BOOK

How to Read the Reading Patterns

When you were entering the SSAT for the first time, you would probably rely heavily on your own strategy to tackle the questions. Inside the mechanism of the SSAT, however, is just a little bit more complex so that it requires not only <u>how much time </u>you deal with the problems but also <u>how systematically </u>you can handle them.

To thoroughly understand the patterns, please solve one question at a time and check the answer using the step-by-step pattern explanations without time limit.

▶ Identify the question category

▶ Question Pattern & Keywords

▶ Keywords from the text

▶ Keywords from the answer

▶ Cross-match Tone/Concept

Incorrect Choices

Evidence

Incorrect Choice keywords

Incorrect Tone or Concept

▶ **STEP 1: Identify the Question Category**

Q1. Pattern 5: Word-In-Context Question

Question 1 asks the meaning behind the word "mixed-up, which can be categorized as the Word-In-Context in the Content Category.

▶ **STEP 2: Question Pattern & Keywords**

Question Pattern: most nearly means
Question Keyword (s): In line 5, "mixed up"

After identifying the question category, you should separate the question into two major parts: the question pattern and the question keywords.

▶ The **Question Pattern** is the main frame of the question.

This frame never changes. The number of these unchanging question patterns is very limited. In fact, there are only 8 of them. These patterns will appear in your test by slightly modifying some words—if not exactly written as appeared in this book.

By understanding these patterns, you will be rewarded several advantages:

√ you will be familiar with tricky terms within the questions so that you can save time in the actual test.

√ you will be able to guess what the question is basically seeking even without reading the passage.

√ you can avoid possible confusion or mistakes such as "EXCEPT" or "Unlike"

UNAUTHORIZED COPYING OR REUSE OF ANY PART OF THIS PAGE IS ILLEGAL

Video animation aids, go to Youtube and type | ssat absolute patterns |

HOW TO USE THIS BOOK

Reading Section Absolute Patterns

The entire Reading Section tests have been analyzed by 8 ABSOLUTE PATTERNS that enable you to approach each question systemically and logically.

Q1. Pattern 5: Word-In-Context Question		
Question Pattern: most nearly means	**Question Keywords:** In line 5, "mixed up"	
Step 1	Step 2	Step 3
Keywords from the Passage	Keywords from Answer	Tone & Concept
L5: one topic of conversation, with his chin upon...	C) obsessed	Positive, mental concept
Incorrect Choices & Common Patterns		
Evidence	Incorrect keywords	Tone & Concept
he had not already been mixed up in this extraordinary case, which was the one topic of conversation...For a whole, had rambled about the room with his chin upon his chest	A) confused	Negative
	B) associated	too weak implication
	D) united	too literal implication
	E) put together	Physical concept

The word-in-context question normally use the following paradigm:

1> physical vs. mental concept   2> Positive vs. Negative concept

3> Literal vs. Figurative concept   4> Active vs. Passive concept   5> Too weak vs. Too extreme implication

Q2. Type 2: Inference Question [Pattern 1: Local Question] {Category A}		
Question Pattern: suggests that the narrator	**Question Keywords:** Line 9 (absolutely deft)	
Step 1	Step 2	Step 3
Keywords from the Passage	Keywords from Answer	Tone & Concept
L9: absolutely deaf to any of my questions	C) degree of contemplation	Synonym, positive
Incorrect Choices & Common Patterns		
Evidence	Incorrect keywords	Tone & Concept
absolutely deaf to any of my questions implies the	A) little attention	Negative
	B) worries physical	Negative, physical ......

Video animation aids, go to Youtube and type | ssat absolute patterns |

HOW TO USE THIS BOOK

Analogy Section Absolute Patterns

The entire Analogy Section tests have been analyzed by 15 ABSOLUTE PATTERNS that enable you to approach each question systemically and logically.

Q31. Absolute Pattern 2: Part-Whole Pattern

B is the best answer

Cattle (Whole) is to cow (Part); star (part) is to constellation (whole)

Although the order is flipped over, there is no other selection available except B.

*Constellation = a group of stars

Q32. Absolute Pattern 7: Association (Characteristic) Pattern

A is the best answer

1> Doctors give pills; baseball coaches give signs.

2> Both doctors and baseball coaches use (give) pills and signs respectively to operate their works.

3> Pills and signs, underpinning such a characteristic, are similar and provide the similar function in their unique purpose or existence.

4> They are both human concept

Q33. Absolute Pattern 7: Association (Characteristic) Pattern

D is the best answer

Both motel and stadium reserve guests and crowd respectively.

1> Choice A is wrong because coffee is a non-human concept although cups reserve coffee.

2> Choice E is wrong

3> Although (E) police station reserve police, its characteristic is different from that of the question and (D)

4> Guest and crowd are visitor-concept, while police is the host concept.

5> Therefore, (E) is less associated with the question

UNAUTHORIZED COPYING OR REUSE OF ANY PART OF THIS PAGE IS ILLEGAL

Video animation aids, go to Youtube and type | ssat absolute patterns |

HOW TO USE

At the end of each test, you will review the most important concept we discussed in the patterns.

Test 1 Recap

Word-in-Context Questions

Word-in-context (WIC) in the reading passage can be either literal or figurative. For instance, the word "fire" has several definitions: it could be fire with heat and flame, or it could be "love" between lovers.

WIC question despises options inhabit too literally. What is very normal in literal meaning does not fit in the psychology of WIC. That's why those who are desperately seeking the correct answer while struggling with the inner voice: *"why it should be so unusual for picking literal"* often choose an awful option.

The quintessential point is to understand the psychology of WIC.

To get to the right point, we should categorize WIC first:

Interpretation of Word
As seen in the Test 1, question 1 "mixed up"—relies on the qualification of emotion rather than literal meaning of the word.

While the answer (C) presents the qualification of emotion, options (A), (B) ,and (D) adopt the degree of literal meaning "mixed up"

Active vs. Passive Mental Concept
Imagine your loved one is dying in bed in front of you, you may feel terribly sad. That's the (pro) active mental concept".

The same degree of active emotional involvement goes with the feeling of rage or humiliation.

On the contrary, if you see an actor dying in bed while you are watching a movie that you have no idea why this actor is dying, your sad feeling is transformed to mere sympathy or passive mental concept.

Rhetoric Underpinning the Tone, Style and Meaning.
The tone often accompanies with negative-positive tone.

Video animation aids, go to Youtube and type ‖ ssat absolute patterns ‖

HOW TO USE THIS BOOK

Almost all students preparing for the SSAT put enormous intellectual effort to achieve their goals. However, when they receive the test reports, they soon find themselves disappointing scores. Most often than not, the main culprit is the Verbal and Reading.

That is what delays the improvement of your scores.

This book focuses mostly on Verbal section and the Reading.

Please practice with the ABSOLUTE PATTERNS until you thoroughly understand the logic behind each question. You will get the score you want on your upcoming test!

CAN THIS BOOK GUARANTEE MY SCORE?

Yes. If you understand all the ABSOLUTE PATTERNS in the reading and verbal section and maintain the minimum vocabulary level. But remember! There's no overnight scheme. You should work very hard to memorize vocabulary first.

WHAT IS THE MINIMUM VOCABULARY AND IS IT IN THIS BOOK?

For the students aiming the 99% on the reading and Verbal section, I recommend:

SSAT Upper Level: ....1500 vocabulary

SSAT Middle Level: ....1000 vocabulary

The vocabulary list is not in this book. Please request the ABSOLUTE VOCABULARY e-book at: satvancouver@gmail.com

WHAT IF I FAIL ON MY SSAT, WHAT CAN I DO? SUPPOSE I MEMORIZED ALL THE VOCABULARY YOU RECOMMENDED AND UNDERSTOOD ALL THE LOGIC IN THIS BOOK, BUT STILL FAILED.

If you failed on your SSAT, you should try again! In fact, there are eight chances to try again every year! Nobody reaches to the goal in one shot!

If you believed in yourself that you had memorized all the vocabularies I recommended, you are wrong! It took me many years to store all the vocabularies into my long-term memory.

Try to review the vocabularies up to the point that you feel comfortable. You will soon forget what you memorized, but keep going, don't stop.

Your reward won't stop at the SSAT, but you will reach your goal beyond the SAT.

CONTENTS

CONTENTS

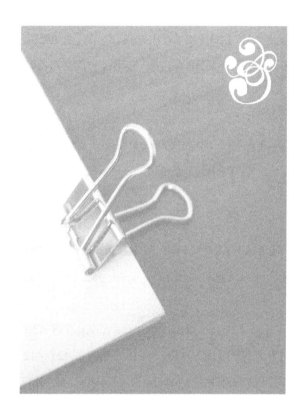

Chapter 1

15 ABSOLUTE PATTERNS IN VERBAL SECTION

15 Absolute Patterns in the Analogy Section

Absolute Pattern 1. Production (Cause-Effect) Pattern

Q1.Fire is to heat as

    A) job is to money

    B) waiter is to restaurant

    C) lamp is to bulb

    D) shower is to bathroom

    E) meal is to chef

    The correct answer is A.

San: Fire produces heat as job produces money. No other choices meet this pattern

Donny: What about E? Chef produces meal, doesn't he?

San: I know. There's always a catch, right?

    Patterns can be shown in the opposite order, which can make your decision even harder.
    But you should know that choice (A) follows the same order as shown in the question.
    You can't pick (E), which is flipped over and say (A) is wrong. Besides, the question
    and (A) are nonhuman concept—the same non-human category, while (E) is human
    category.

Donny: Then, if the words were flipped over, would that choice always be wrong?

San: Yes and No. In this question, yes, because Choice E can't beat Choice A.
    If choice A were not in this question, which one would you choose?

Donny: E.

San: That's right. Inevitably you should choose E because there's no other alternative, but
    to choose E.

15 Absolute Patterns in the Analogy Section

Absolute Pattern 2. Part-Whole Pattern

Q2.Rose is to flower as

A) ant is to insect

B) dinosaurs is to extinct

C) electronics is to T.V.

D) student is to school

E) happiness is to money

The correct answer is A

San: Rose is a part of flower as ant is a part of insect.

Donny: How about B)? dinosaurs is a part of extinct animals....

How about C)? electronics is a part of T.V...

How about D)? student is a part of school...

How about E)? happiness is a part of money...,or money is a part of happiness....

San: For choice B), the word "extinct" does not automatically include "animals" Donny!

You can't just add or remove a word!

Choice C) is incorrect. The word orders are flipped over.

For choice D) "Student is a part of a school" is the true statement but incorrect because "student" is the human concept, while the question and choice A) are nature concept. Make sure if the pair of the words belongs to the same category.

Donny: I learned from Jesus that we are all part of nature.

San: You're right ! You are no more than an insect.

15 Absolute Patterns in the Analogy Section

Absolute Pattern 3. Antonym (Positive-Negative) Pattern

Q3-1. Antipathy is to sympathy as love is to

    A) abhor

    B) dislike

    C) friendship

    D) illusion

    E) magic

Q3-2. Evil is to God

    A) Bible is to Satan

    B) lion is to zebra

    C) dark is to light

    D) medicine is to poison

    E) man is to woman

The correct answer is A

San: Q3-1: Antipathy is the antonym for sympathy; Love is antonym for abhor.

Donny: I didn't know what the "abhor" was, so I chose B. why not B, San?

San: If you have no idea what the "ABHOR" is, don't worry. Just divide it into meaningful fractions like ab/hor. (Oh! Horror) So, next time, when you spot some difficult, never-heard-of word, don't be shy, just divide it.
By that way, you can at least see if the word is a negative type of word or a positive type of word.

Choice B is wrong because "love" is NOT the antonym for "dislike," but "like" is.
You can't kiss a girl because you like her. She will smack you on your face flat.
You should love her to earn her kiss.

San: Do you know the answer for the Q3-2, Donny?

Donny: Just as Evil is negative and God is Positive, so is the dark and light.

San: Not bad! Antonym can be Negative vs. Positive or Tangible vs. Intangible too!

UNAUTHORIZED COPYING OR REUSE OF ANY PART OF THIS PAGE IS ILLEGAL

15 Absolute Patterns in the Analogy Section

Absolute Pattern 4. Synonym Pattern

Q4. Chronicle is to history as

    A) dance is to choreography

    B) businessman is to entrepreneur

    C) dancer is to choreography

    D) ending is to beginning

    E) inform is to reform

The correct answer is A

San: Chronicle is the synonym to history as dance is the synonym to choreography.

Donny: Isn't an entrepreneur a fancy word for a businessman?

San: Make sure a pair of words belongs to the same category.
Choice B is wrong because the question is a non-human concept, while B is the human
For choice C, Dancer is a human, while choreography is non-human. The choreography
is the act performed by a dancer.

Donny: How about D)?

San: Choice D is an Antonym Pattern. Choice E is assonance or homophony.

Donny: I have a quick question, San! Why is your answer always A? Is the next question also A?
If then, why should I even bother to study if the entire universe is A?
I suspect it's because you are a part of nature too.

15 Absolute Patterns in the Analogy Section

Absolute Pattern 5. Degree Pattern

Q5. Dime is to cent as

    A) yard is to area

    B) meter is to centimeter

    C) sea is to sky

    D) phone is to communication

    E) big is to great

The correct answer is B

San: As Dime is to cent, so is meter to centimeter.

        Here in this question, the degree is shrinking. Therefore, you should find a choice that has a degree concept moving from big to small.

Donny: How about A)?

San: It's an Association Relationship. I will explain it later.
        Bye the way, did you notice E) has also the degree but moves from small to big?

Donny: No, I didn't. But I noticed the you changed your answer from A) to B) right after I mentioned about it. A little man with a big ear!

15 Absolute Patterns in the Analogy Section

Absolute Pattern 6. Purpose (Tool) Pattern

Q6-1. Painter is to paint as

    A) love is to marriage

    B) teacher is to school

    C) menu is to restaurant

    D) exam is to pass

    E) gambler is to win

Q6-2. Biologist is to microscope

    A) architect is to hammer

    B) taxi driver is to car

    C) teacher is to lesson

    D) employer is to bonus

    E) pilot is to passenger

The correct answer is E

San: Q6-1: The Purpose (Job) of the painter is to paint so is the gambler to win.

Donny: How about A)?

San: Choice A is incorrect. the purpose of love is not necessarily marriage or vice versa. Choice A is Cause-Effect Relation or Association Relation.

Donny: What about B)?

San: Choice B is wrong because it is Association Pattern. Teacher is associated with a school, but the purpose of a teacher is to teach students. He/she can't teach school.

Donny: The purpose of taking an exam is to pass the test, isn't it?

San: Yes. but the category is conflicting. You should prioritize the same human category as in the question.

Donny: Q6-2: Just as biologist uses a microscope, so does taxi driver a car.

San: Good!

Donny: How about A) architect is to hammer ?

San: architect uses a blueprint or drawings. Carpenter use hammer

15 Absolute Patterns in the Analogy Section

Absolute Pattern 7. Association Pattern

Q7. Lottery is to luck as

    A) student is to school

    B) doctor is to white

    C) keyboard is to language

    D) moon is to solar

    E) construction is to noise

    The correct answer is E

Donny: I don't get it! How is Association Pattern different from the Purpose (Tool) Pattern? They are all the same isn't it?

San: You're right! Just trying to make it look more sophisticated because it looks cool. No! Compared to the Purpose (Tool) Pattern, Association Pattern has some broader concept. It often involves an intangible, nonhuman concept such as love, happiness, or sense nouns and sense verbs like the answer E) "noise".

Donny: Lottery is associated with luck; construction is associated with noise. that's cool!

San: The question and the answer are both non-human concept. Therefore, Choice A and B are wrong because 'student' and "doctor" are human concept.
In other words, If the question were Choice A, then the answer should be B. No doubt.

Donny: Choices C is too vague. It is just so ambiguous to associate how the keyboard is related with a language.

San: Choice D has to be 'Sun is to solar' or 'moon' is to 'lunar.' to make it a Synonym Pattern.

Donny: Hitting jackpot and construction noise seem very unassociated with each other though.

San: No, you've missed the point, Donny! It is the relations between the question as a whole group and the answer as a whole group.

UNAUTHORIZED COPYING OR REUSE OF ANY PART OF THIS PAGE IS ILLEGAL

15 Absolute Patterns in the Analogy Section

Absolute Pattern 8. Shape Pattern

Q8. Round is to bottle as

    A) bottle is to glass

    B) indication is to sign

    C) coffee is to caffeine

    D) monitor is to square

    E) monitor is to flat

    The correct answer is D

San: Just as the round is the shape of a bottle, so is the monitor to a square.

Donny: How about Choice E)?

San: It's wrong because the compatible shape with "round" is a 'square', not a 'flat'

Donny: That is hard one!

15 Absolute Patterns in the Analogy Section

Absolute Pattern 9. Quantity-Quality Pattern

Q9. Book is to knowledge

    A) business is to happiness

    B) dime is to ten cents

    C) friend is to fight

    D) centennial is to 100 years

    E) boiling point is to 10 degree

The correct answer is C

San: Book is quantity and knowledge is quality, so is friend and fight.

Donny: I am still confused!

San: A book is a material and can be quantified (counted). However, knowledge is not a material and can't be counted.

This logic can be applied to choice C. friend can be counted like two friends or 100 friends.

However, fight can't be counted or measured. Therefore, it is quality.

Donny: Are there any patterns in choice B), D), E)?

San: Choice B and D are Synonym Pattern.

Choice E is the Characteristic (Association Pattern).

Choice B "ten cents," D and E "100" are all numbers that can be quantified.

Therefore, you can't relate these choices to the question because they have no qualified entities like the question does.

15 Absolute Patterns in the Analogy Section

Absolute Pattern 10. Subjective-Objective Pattern

Q10. Today's temperature is Fahrenheit 10 degree as

    A) Jane is tall

    B) the movie was good

    C) girl is to woman

    D) last year was 2016

    E) happiness is to money

    The correct answer is D

San: Data, numbers, money, years… all these values can be quantified. That is, objective. On the other hand, the mental concept such as tall, fast, cheap, quick, expensive, beautiful is the subjective concept.

Fahrenheit 10 degree is number, therefore, objective.

Only choice D has number value, therefore, objective.

Donny: That's easy.

San: Just one more thing!

Subjective, mental value can be further divided into the passive-active value.

For example, sympathy is weak mental concept compared to worry.

This question will be combined to the Degree Pattern.

15 Absolute Patterns in the Analogy Section

Absolute Pattern 11. Homophony Pattern

Q11. Seven is to Sandwiches

    A) sunny is Sunday

    B) rainy is to umbrella

    C) study is to lazy

    D) dig is to tunnel

    E) supermarket is to grocery

The correct answer is A

San: It is all about sound. That's all there is to it. No meaning or logic is involved. Just as seven and sandwiches make the same sound or rhythm, so do sunny and Sunday.

Donny: Okay!

          if the question does not make sense at all, then I should suspect it to be the Homophony Pattern.

15 Absolute Patterns in the Analogy Section

Absolute Pattern 12. Active-Passive Pattern

Q12. Spider is to web as

A) zebra is to stripe

B) beaver is to dam

C) mosquito is to insect

D) caterpillar is to butterfly

E) bee is to sting

The correct answer is B

San: Spider builds its web to live and catch preys; Beaver builds its dam to live and catch preys. If you compare them with Choice E, you will see how active the bee sting is, and on the contrary how passive both the spider and beaver are.

Donny: How about A? Bee, spider, beaver, and zebra, all of which use their own unique tools for the survival mechanism.
Then, how come A) can't be the answer?

San: The key concept in the analogy is to classify a pair of words into the minimal level.
To the maximum level, the entire words in the question 12 can be classified (called) as the parts of nature.
That's not the way to find the answer, Donny!

Donny: Oh! I see....

San: For choice A, you might have confused because "Zebra is to stripes" can be conceived as the passive action like B).
However, it can't be the answer because the stripe is natural, while beaver's dam or spider's web are creations.
That's the way you can classify and re-classify them to the minimal level.

15 Absolute Patterns in the Analogy Section

Absolute Pattern 13. Physical-Mental (Tangible-Intangible) Pattern

Q13. Church is to prayer as

    A) chapel to cathedral

    B) priest is to sermon

    C) believer is to non-believer

    D) religion is to Buddhism

    E) Christmas is to elf

The correct answer is B

San: Church and prayer are the combination of physical-mental concepts.

Donny: This one is confusing!
           They are all related to religion.

San: We should break them down further and further by categorizing and sub-categorizing them to the minimal level.
           You should employee all the Absolute patterns you have learned in the process.

Donny: What I've found was this: A) is small and big, the Degree Pattern
           B) is the Purpose Pattern, C) is Antonym Pattern, D) is Part-Whole Pattern
           E) is Association Pattern
           Then, the question can be both the Purpose and Association Pattern.

San: If you apply the association pattern here, the entire choices will be the answer!

Donny: Then what is it? Quantity-Quality Pattern, maybe?

San: Both Church and feast are physical concept, while both prayer and Christmas are mental concept.
           Only B) "priest is to sermon" has the combination of physical-mental concept.
           So, next time, imagine if the entities are tangible (physical) or intangible (mental).

15 Absolute Patterns in the Analogy Section

Absolute Pattern 14. Human-Nonhuman Pattern

Q14. Baby is cute as battery is

A) dead

B) discharged

C) gone

D) deceased

E) lifeless

The correct answer is B

San: Baby is cute; battery is discharged

We more often use the word "dead" when the battery is discharged.

We also often say like "Hey, San! You need to recharge your battery.

You look awful today."

We, however, should distinguish the proper words before we use only to human and

to nonhuman concept.

Donny: But, then, San! We have euphemism or metaphor

San: No! We don't.

The entire words that you see from the verbal section use the first definition from the

standard English dictionary.

As an example, If you see the phrase "Fire is to flame" in the question, It means the

literal fire ignited by the chemical reaction that produces flame.

You should never interpret the fire euphemistically like "I'm in love" or metaphorically,

unless the question itself contains the euphemism or metaphor.

15 Absolute Patterns in the Analogy Section

Absolute Pattern 15. Syntax (Grammar) Pattern

Q15-1. Departure is to go as computer is to

    A) calculate

    B) calculator

    C) electronics

    D) expensive

    E) fast

Q15-2. He's is to he is as there's is to

    A) there was

    B) there are

    C) theirs

    D) there is

    E) there has

The correct answer is B

Donny: What is syntax anyway?

San: Syntax is linguistic elements (such as words) that are put together to form phrases or clauses.
It's a fancy word for grammar, but we are only dealing with the analogy part of the grammar in the SSAT Verbal. So, it becomes the Syntax pattern.

    Q15-1: Departure is the noun form of the verb "go" as a computer is the noun form of the verb "calculate"

San: Do you know the answer for Q15-2?

Donny: Sure. It's D)

San: Yes. He's is the contraction of he is as there's is the contraction of there is.
A) "there was" is incorrect because it's the past tense. the question is the present tense.
B) "there are" is incorrect because it's the plural. the question is the singular.
C) "theirs" incorrect because it's the possessive pronoun.
E) "there has" is incorrect because the question specifies its contraction to "it is", not "it has".

SSAT Analogy Absolute Pattern Summary

Absolute Pattern 1. Production (Cause-Effect) Pattern

Absolute Pattern 2. Part-Whole Pattern

Absolute Pattern 3. Antonym (Positive-Negative) Pattern

Absolute Pattern 4. Synonym Pattern

Absolute Pattern 5. Degree Pattern

Absolute Pattern 6. Purpose (Tool) Pattern

Absolute Pattern 7. Association (Characteristic) Pattern

Absolute Pattern 8. Shape Relations

Absolute Pattern 9. Quantity-Quality Patterns

Absolute Pattern 10. Subjective-Objective Patterns

Absolute Pattern 11. Homophony Patterns

Absolute Pattern 12: Active-Passive Patterns

Absolute Pattern 13: Mental-Physical Pattern

Absolute Pattern 14: Human-Nonhuman Patterns

Absolute Pattern 15: Syntax Pattern

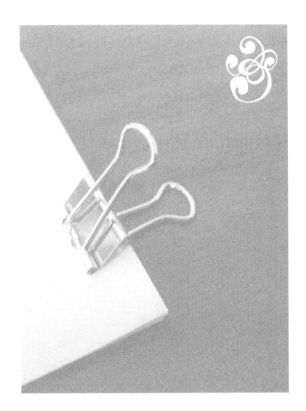

Chapter 2

8 ABSOLUTE PATTTERNS IN READING SECTION

Chapter 2

8 Absolute Patterns for Reading Test

The entire 40 questions in the reading section, both literary and informational passages, can be categorized into two parts: Category A: Content Question; Category B: Technique Question. These two categories can be subcategorized into eight Absolute Patterns.

The eight Absolute Patterns—mostly one pattern per question —plus incorrect option patterns will be absolutely the most effective and systemic way to improve your scores.

To obtain a FREE SSAT ABSOLUTE Vocabulary with picture book, please send a simple email request: satvancouver@gmail.com

Category A: Content Question has five patterns:

▶ Pattern 1: Local Question

▶ Pattern 2: Main idea Question

▶ Pattern 3: Summary Question

▶ Pattern 4: Relationships Question

▶ Pattern 5: Word-in-Context Question

Pattern 1: Local Question

Local Question has three major types.

 ◆Type 1: Example Question
 ◆Type 2: Inference Question
 ◆Type 3: Analogy Question

The local question— either with the line reference number or without it—normally asks detailed information from only one or two sentences in the passage. The question may ask explicitly stated keywords in the sentences, or, in more complex level, implicitly analogous situations. Neither of the cases requires the holistic understanding of the entire passage.

Reading only the target sentence will save your precious time and mental horse power. The typical technique applied in the local question can be found in Type 1: Example type question.

The example sentence is almost certainly identifiable through a specific name or idea used within a sentence.

However, the example sentence itself rarely contains any value nor the answer.

It merely supports the main idea.

The answer for this type of questions is normally located right above or right below the example sentence because that's where the main idea should be presented.

That's the quintessential concept of this pattern.

Sometimes, the last sentence in a paragraph can be the example sentence. In that case, the topic sentence in the following paragraph can produce the answer because that's where the main idea starts—although many students overlook this fact.

Pattern 2: Main Idea Question

The main idea question asks either the main idea of the entire passage (the universal type question) or the central idea in a specific paragraph or even a couple of sentences within a paragraph (the local type question)

First, the main idea question—especially when it asks the main idea of the entire passage—quite often appears at the very beginning, preceding other questions. In that case, you should skip and save it for last until you have solved all the other questions because the main idea questions highly likely reveal the answer at the concluding paragraph. A holistic approach should, therefore, be the crux of your technique.

For instance, if option (A) originates from the middle of the second paragraph while option (B) is from the concluding paragraph (e.g., the fifth paragraph), the answer will be more likely (B) than (A) due to the unique characteristic of this question.

And also, the frequency does matter in the main idea question. As an example, if option (A) has the keywords that appeared for three times throughout the passage while option (B) has the keywords that appeared six times, then (B) has the greater chance to be the answer because (B) appeared twice more.

Finally, there's a technique called "amplifier."

The amplifier is located right after the main idea sentence starting with a pronoun such as "It" or "This"

The amplifier sentence often emphasizes—or de-emphasizes—the main idea, hence the answer.

Should the central idea in a specific paragraph be the question, the main idea can be found after the transitional words or a phrase such as "because", "but", "however", "with all due respect", etc.

Please make sure that you read the first sentence in the following paragraph, where you very often neglect.

UNAUTHORIZED COPYING OR REUSE OF ANY PART OF THIS PAGE IS ILLEGAL

Pattern 3: Summary Question

The basic technique to find the answer is almost the same as pattern 3: Main Idea Question. The major difference, however, —especially in literary passage—can be seen in its focusing on the manner of voice, tone, and style.

In literary passage, summary question often carries more subjective and polarized words, such as "criticize", "emphatic", "celebrate"—contrary to the main idea pattern that maintains a neutral tone and objective view.

The summary question in informational passage is quite similar to the main idea question. They both tend to apply broad and neutral tone in the keywords, so do the multiple choices.

The process of creating the general and neutral keyword is simpler than we think: the best option (answer) can simply cut-off the significantly important part of the information. This concept, however, should not be confused with insufficient information that will be discussed in the following page.

Pattern 4: Relationships Question

This pattern can be identified in various ways:

   (1) The relationships between the cause-effect situation, normally carried out by subordinating conjunctions such as "because…" (or similar perception).

   (2) The relationships within comparison-contrast, flagged by "more", "better", "never", often" ,"if."

   (3) The relationships between historical events

   (4) The relationships between characters, ideas, and arguments.

Common—but preventable—mistakes we quite often make is that we forget to remember the question were two or more events, things, theories, or people compared (related).

For instance, when question asks "compared to the paragraph 1, paragraph 2…is?"

Very effective way is crossing out irrelevant information using your pencil.

(e.g., "compared to the paragraph 1, paragraph 2…is?" .)

To sum up, the keywords should be located at/near the:

   √ coordinating conjunction "but (or similar perception),

   √ correlative conjunction such as "more ~ than"

   √ transition words/phrase for supporting detail, contrast, consequence such as "on the other hand",
      "in fact,", "Consequently".

Pattern 5: Word-in-Context Question

This pattern employs two methodologies: (1) Finding the precise meaning of the word—normally high-level vocabulary and its synonym. (2) Identifying the nature of the word in passage—normally figurative and metaphorical meaning, not a synonym. The multiple choices employ the literal meanings with only the very first definition from the dictionary, not the second or third one.

When the word-in-context question asks the figurative word, you must find a clue word (s) from the sentence. The sentence in the passage should provide the clue word (s). You should find and apply the clue word in each option. Never skip this process and rely on your memory.

The Word-in-Context question is not a piece-of-cake because it's a short question.

Most importantly, you must distinguish between the clue word and the key word in question.

To illustrate, a clue word can be a flamboyant adjective or adverb, sitting pretty next the keyword that can be as simple as "it" (the singular pronoun).

Your job is to find the answer for the keyword "it," not the answer for the pretty clue word.

Category B: Technique Question

Category B: Technique question has three patterns:

▶ Pattern 6: Understanding the Structure of the Passage

▶ Pattern 7: Understanding the Attitude (Point of view) of the Author/Narrator/Character

▶ Pattern 8: Understanding the Purpose

Typical patterns under this category use broad techniques. Metaphorically speaking, if category A: Reading Content is about understanding the interior of the building, Category B: Technique question is about understanding the foundation and frame of the building.

Pattern 6: Understanding the Structure of the Passage

This pattern can be subdivided into three types:

◆Type 4: Structural Characteristics

◆Type 5: Part-Whole Relationships

◆Type 6: Overall Structural Relationships

◆Type 4: Structural characteristic question has little to do with the content of the passage.

Typical question statement are "What is the primary function of the first paragraph?"

If you have two competing choices (e.g., "(A) to discuss the harmful impacts of mutation to protein,"

and "(B) to introduce certain scientific thesis.), the answer should be (B) because the major function

of the first paragraph is to introduce things.

◆Type 5: Part-whole relation question asks the role of partial information in line X in the passage.

The answer might start with (e.g., "to raise cause of action concerning the main issue x", "to argue

against the main issue x", or "to set aside from the main issue" etc.)

◆Type 6: Overall structural relationships question is the most complex type in this pattern.

The question normally asks relationships between paragraphs. Therefore, the answer presents more

than two significances between the paragraphs. (e.g., "(A) paragraph 2 presents added details from

the paragraph 1 while paragraph 3 foreshadows the critic's evaluation that the author later opposes")

Pattern 7: Understanding Attitude (Point of view) of the Author/Narrator/Character

The author, narrator, or character in passage should give a certain impression to the reader, the other

characters, or events. You should figure out the primal perspective (or concern) from his/her expression.

The attitude question often contains subjective arguments such as positive-negative, active-passive,

mental-physical tone and style that are more likely to be qualified than quantified.

Pattern 8: Understanding Purpose

The main procedure to reach to the answer is very similar to that of Pattern 3: Main ideas. The major

difference is the scale of the reading scope. While the main idea question requires the overall

understanding of passage, the purpose question (except for the question statement such as "the main

purpose of the passage") isolates the answer based on a single or two lines of expression made by a

character, narrator, or author.

Unlike pattern 7: The attitude question, the purpose question looks into the construction of the message

and tends to be more objective and neutral in tone, and style because it represents the view of narrator or

the author, instead of character's private emotion.

Imagine the narrator or author is an umpire in baseball game.

The trickiest part of this pattern is that it does not give you the clear keywords, just like the way that you

find difficulty from the inference question or analogy question.

Paradoxically, a true statement written in the passage can be incorrect option because that won't be the main purpose we should understand.

For instance, if you are so hungry that you need to go home, your primary purpose is not going home or reminding yourself that you are hungry. These two true premises should definitely be the incorrect options.

Absolute Pattern Summary for the Reading Test

Category A: Content Question

➡ Pattern 1: Local Question

◆ Type 1: Example Question

◆ Type 2: Inference Question

◆ Type 3: Analogy Question

➡ Pattern 2: Main ideas Question

➡ Pattern 3: Summary Question

➡ Pattern 4: Relationships Question

➡ Pattern 5: Word-in-Context Question

Category B: Technique Question

➡ Pattern 6: Understanding Structure of the Passage

◆ Type 4: Structural Characteristics

◆ Type 5: Part-Whole Relationships

◆ Type 6: Overall Structural Relationships

➡ Pattern 7: Understanding Attitude (Point of view) of the Author/Narrator/Character

➡ Pattern 8: Understanding Purpose

Chapter 2
8 Absolute Patterns in Reading Test

20 Common Patterns for *In*correct Options

20 Common Patterns for *In*correct Options

1 Positive-Negative Tone (value)

Over 50-60 percent of the reading questions can be solved using this simple but very powerful tool. All you need is to identify the keywords in each multiple choice, and pick one of them that matches the reading passage's keyword (s) based on positive-negative value. This rule will lead you to the concrete prediction to the answer than any other rules.

Practically majority of the questions were solved using this single pattern.

2 Antonym or Opposite Perception

This pattern, next to the positive-negative value, appears most frequently. The vast majority of incorrect options, including "EXCEPT", "NOT" questions—known as "the negative type"—apply antonym or opposite perception. So readily applicable is the usage of antonym as an incorrect choice that almost all questions apply this option.

3 Active-Passive Value

By simply skimming through the Test Pattern Analysis, we can observe how securely and predominately this pattern is anchored in the vast majority of the questions alongside the positive-negative value.

*Please note that this active-Passive value is not the same thing as the active-passive voice in Grammar.

20 Common Patterns for *In*correct Options

4 Not stated in the passage (incl. Future Prediction)

Some incorrect choices use keywords that did not appear in the passage at all but familiar with our common sense. One representative example is exploiting our prediction that lets the reader predict for the future, using a word such as "likely to be", "will", "appear" "seem".

Unless it is written as it is, the prediction based on our common sense cannot be the answer.

Again, new information, however tempting it is, should not be an answer.

5 Minor or Unrelated Example

This type appears frequently with the question **Pattern 3: Main idea Question**. The answer for the main idea question contains a relatively general and therefore neutral keyword so that it could amalgamate and be fit into every keyword in the passage while maintaining the objective tone.

On the contrary, were the keyword too specific, it becomes a minor idea or a mere example.

*Please note that "unrelated example" here is not the same thing as "Not Stated in the Passage"

6 Insufficient Information

Some multiple choices could be both correct and incorrect at the same time. "What does that mean?"

For instance, if option (A) contains one correct keyword while (B), two, Option (A) is incorrect because information is insufficient or only partially correct.

This type is the main culprit that put you in a quandary situation between two options.

UNAUTHORIZED COPYING OR REUSE OF ANY PART OF THIS PAGE IS ILLEGAL

20 Common Patterns for *Incorrect* Options

7 | Unrelated Word or Issue

The question Pattern 6: Word-in-Context Question [Category A: Content Question] employs this incorrect choice pattern most often. Common incorrect choice patterns usually employ the followings:

(a) Switch the word in figurative meaning with the one in literal meaning.

(b) Place an impressive flamboyant adverb or adjective right next the plain keyword as simple as the pronoun "it" so that you can focus on the unrelated pretty baits instead of the keyword.

(c) Show a difficult vocabulary that requires your vocabulary knowledge.

8 | Inconsistency with Question

This pattern employs the inconsistency trick.

It often distracts the nature of the question by writing a true statement from somewhere else in the passage, which has little relations with the question.

As an example, when the concessional phrase such as "although" is in a question and a true statement from the concluding paragraph is presented as an option, you should not pick the option because the question asks the relations between the concessional phrase and the result of it. .

9 | Unknown Prediction

Some incorrect choices include a verb in future tense or adverb such as 'likely to be' or regular verb or noun that contains the future meaning such as 'seem', 'will', 'anticipation'.

It is not your job to predict the future without having a logically written cause-effect situation in the passage. Even inference question is anchored in the cause-effect logic.

Those unknown choices already have congenital defects when they were born.

20 Common Patterns for *Incorrect* Options

10 Too Specific Example

Universal question types like Pattern 2: Main Idea Question [Category A: Content Question] do not seek out the answer from too specific example. If you must choose the best one between too general and too specific, choose the former option.

Type 1: Example Question [Pattern 1: Local Question], on the other hand, seeks this specific example.

11 Too Objective Word Usage

Some options stop short at explaining the fact, making the phrase too objective and vague.

Pattern 7: Understanding Attitude (Point of View) Question requires a keyword that illustrates a decisive, subjective, and positive-negative tone, not too broad and objective word.

12 Extreme Word Usage

Compared to other patterns, extreme word usage pattern is relatively easy when it involves adverbs such as "always", "only", "never", etc. However, this pattern does not often appear with a sweeping assertive word. Can you instantly compare the nature of the words like "dwindling", "compromised", "extinct", or "failed"? Please practice with this book.

13 Shifting the Argument

Argument can change within paragraphs. For example, in paragraph 1, critics will argue with one thing, for which the author will later oppose in paragraph 2 or 3.

In more complex question, the author himself suddenly changes his opinion, known as "setting aside".

20 Common Patterns for *Incorrect* Options

14 Repeating the Question

Fooling students can never be easier when options paraphrase the question instead of answering it. Some questions that look extremely easy at first sight can turn into super tough one.

15 Synonym or Similar Perception

If you look at the test pattern explanations, you will be surprised by how dominantly this pattern is employed, a situation where the keywords from the text and the keywords in the correct answer are the same or similar to each other.

Virtually, the majority of the correct answers rely on the synonym pattern.

Although this pattern has some limited applications in incorrect choices—such as the inconsistency with the question—it is pivotal to be reminded.

For instance, some options simply combine the synonym with a word like "least", in which case, all those synonyms appear in the options become default.

16 Concept Comparison

This pattern is applied dominantly in Type 3: Analogy Question.

Concept comparison pattern normally presents two opposing concepts.

This pattern can be subcategorized into several sub-conceptions such as the "Physical-Mental", "Negative-Positive", "Passive-Active", "Part-Whole", "A single individual involvement-Two individuals involvement", etc.

20 Common Patterns for *Incorrect* Options

17 Quantity-Quality Concept

Some keywords contain quantity concept, while others are quality.

SSAT official test applies this concept for about 20 percent.

18 Personal-Social Perspective

Personal perspective is usually represented by the first person 'I'.

More often than not, however, you will see the passage employing an anecdote discusses a social, metaphysical, national, historical, political, or global issue. You may call it "A big and small scope question" Based on the holistic approach, a personal statement at least becomes a low-key concept, making incorrect choice.

19 Part-Whole Relations

Imagine one paragraph made of one long compound-complex sentence.

In textual evidence question, this single sentence is often broken down into all four options.

Please remember you are assigned to read only the corresponding segment of the sentence, not the whole chunk of it. The textual evidence gives you the exact line that you're supposed to read.

Please do not read beyond the line provided for you.

20 Characteristics

You should be ready to translate abstract concepts using our five senses. Some keywords characterize the idea or object with visual, auditory or olfactory. For instance, instead of saying "onion", the option will write "an edible bulb plant with a pungent taste and smell." Some options revolving around this pattern simply die without having such a sensory element.

How to Read the Reading Patterns

▶ Identify the question Category

▶ Question Pattern & Keywords

▶ Keywords from the text

▶ Keywords from the answer

▶ Cross-match Tone/Concept

Incorrect Choices

Evidence

Incorrect Choice keywords

Incorrect Tone or Concept

▶ **STEP 1: Identify the Question Category**

Q1. Pattern 5: Word-In-Context Question

Question 1 asks the meaning behind the word "mixed-up, which can be categorized as the Word-In-Context in the Content Category.

▶ **STEP 2: Question Pattern & Keywords**

Question Pattern: most nearly means
Question Keyword (s): In line 5, "mixed up"

After identifying the question category, you should separate the question into two major parts: the question pattern and the question keywords.

Question Pattern is the main frame of the question, and the frame never changes. The number of these unchanging question patterns is very limited. In fact, there are only 11 of them. These patterns will appear in your test by slightly modifying some words-if not exactly written as shown in this book.

By understanding these 11 patterns, you will be rewarded several advantages:

√ you will be familiar with tricky terms within the question so that you can save time in the actual test.

√ you will be able to guess what the question is basically seeking even without reading the passage.

√ you can avoid possible confusion or mistakes such as "EXCEPT" questions.

Question Keyword (s): Question keyword (s) is the most important word (s) in the question.

Test creators look for keywords from the passage first and then plug the keywords into the question patterns to create each question.

The most common question keywords in the reading passage and the question are nouns and verbs.

Adjectives and adverbs seldom provide an answer, although they provide some clues for the answer. (except for the coordinating conjunction and conjunctive adverbs with negative connotation).

With the keywords that you underlined from the question, you should remind yourself what you have to seek out even before start reading the passage. For example, the PSAT question #3, seeks out the words that represent personality based on positive-negative meaning, or active-passive connotations.

How to Read the Reading Patterns

Q1. Pattern 5: Word-In-Context Question		
Question Pattern: most nearly means	**Question Keywords:** In line 5, "mixed up"	
Step 1	Step 2	Step 3
Keywords from the Passage	Keywords from Answer	Tone & Concept
L5: one topic of conversation, with his chin upon...	C) obsessed	Positive, mental concept

Identify the question category

Question Pattern & Keywords

▶ Keywords from the text

▶ Keywords from the answer

▶ Cross-match Tone/Concept

Incorrect Choices

Evidence

Incorrect Choice keywords

Incorrect Tone or Concept

▶ **STEP3: Identify the Keywords & Tone and Concept**

Step 3 can be subcategorized into three groups.

(1) Keywords from the Passage

Once the target sentence or paragraph from the passage is decided, you should find the most meaningful keywords from the sentence.

(2) Keyword from the answer

Find the keywords from all four options and compare them with the keywords that you found from the text.

(3) Cross-match the Tone / concept

For question 1, for example, choice (C) keywords "one topic," "with his chin upon"....is the matching keywords " from the text because they are positive and mental concept.

How to Read the Reading Patterns

▶**STEP 4: Incorrect Choices & Their Common Patterns**

Incorrect Choices & Common Patterns		
Evidence	Incorrect keywords	Tone & Concept
he had not already <u>been mixed up in this extraordinary case, which was the one topic of conversation</u>...For a whole, had rambled about the room with his chin upon his chest	A) confused	Negative
	B) associated	too weak implication
	D) united	too literal implication
	E) put together	Physical concept

STEP 4: Incorrect Options & Their Common Patterns

Identify the question type

Question Pattern & Keywords

Keywords from the text

Keywords from the answer

▶Cross-match Tone/Concept

▶Incorrect Choices

▶Evidence

▶Incorrect Choice keywords

▶Incorrect Tone or Concept

For the remaining four options, you should prove yourself the reasons for their defects before you move on and fill in the bubble.

Please remember you have only 20 percent chance in each option.

It is not a good start to assume each option is correct when 80 percent of them are wrong. Treat all five choices are basically wrong and pick one keyword terribly hard to understand, which will be the correct answer.

A keyword immune to this process is always the answer.

Let's get back to the above question.

The Word-In-Context question normally uses the following paradigm:

1> physical vs. mental concept

2> Positive vs. Negative concept

3> Literal vs. Figurative concept

4> Active vs. Passive concept

5> Too weak vs. Too extreme implication

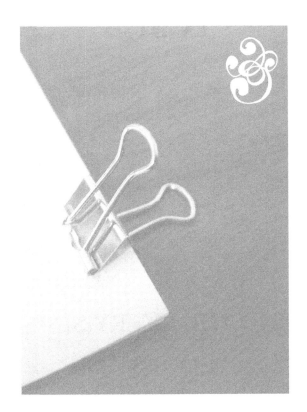

Chapter 3

SSAT MIDDLE & UPPER LEVEL
8 PRACTICE TESTS

SSAT
Reading & Verbal Practice
Test 1

ALL THE LOGIC AND RULES
BEHIND THE EVERY SINGLE
SSAT QUESTION

Test 1 Reading Section
Time: 40 Minutes, 40 Questions

Directions: Each reading passage is followed by questions about it. Answer the questions that follow a passage on the basis of what is stated or implied in that passage.

Questions 1-6 are based on the following passage.

Line

"I am afraid, Watson, that I shall have to go," said Holmes, as we sat down together to our breakfast one morning.

"Go! Where to?"

"To Dartmoor; to King's Pyland."

5 I was not surprised. Indeed, my only wonder was that he had not already been mixed up in this extraordinary case, which was the one topic of conversation through the length and breadth of England. For a whole day my companion had rambled about the room with his chin upon his chest and his brows knitted, charging and recharging his pipe with the strongest black tobacco, and absolutely deaf to any of my questions or remarks.

10 Fresh editions of every paper had been sent up by our news agent, only to be glanced over and tossed down into a corner. Yet, silent as he was, I knew perfectly well what it was over which he was brooding. There was but one problem before the public which could challenge his powers of analysis, and that was the singular disappearance of the favorite for the Wessex Cup, and the tragic murder of its trainer. When, therefore, he suddenly announced his

15 intention of setting out for the scene of the drama it was only what I had both expected and hoped for.

1

In line 5, "mixed up" most nearly means

A) confused with
B) associated with
C) obsessed with
D) united with
E) put together

2

Line 9 (absolutely deft to my question) suggests that the narrator

A) observes another character paying little attention to any of his question
B) worries another character's physical condition
C) sees another character's degree of contemplation
D) regards the extraordinary case is not important
E) argues the extraordinary case requires a high level of attention

CONTINUE

UNAUTHORIZED COPYING OR REUSE OF ANY PART OF THIS PAGE IS ILLEGAL

3

In describing Homels, the narrator emphasizes his

A) vicious temperament

B) humility

C) innate pessimism

D) obsession with one issue

E) intelligence

4

The "extraordinary" mentioned in line 6 is most likely

A) uneasy feeling of one character

B) sensitive relations between the characters

C) difficult issue at hand

D) irritable traveling itinerary

E) supernatural experience

5

It can be inferred from the passage that Waton's role with Holmes is most similar to that of

A) a critic

B) a reporter

C) the king from Dartmoor

D) a writer

E) a co-worker

6

The primary purpose of the passage is to

A) highlight the supportive relationship between the characters

B) reveal one character's excitement to an extraordinary case

C) note the mystical aspect of an extraordinary case

D) show one character's preoccupation with an extraordinary case

E) display the revelation of mystery

Questions 7-12 are based on the following passage.

Line

All boys are nature lovers. Nothing appeals to them more than a summer vacation in the woods where they can escape from the restraints of civilization and live a life of freedom. Now, it may appear to be a bit of presumption to attempt to advise the boy camper how to spend his time. Surely the novelty of outdoor life, the fascinating charm of his surroundings,

5 will provide him plenty of entertainment.

But, after all, a camp generally affords but two major amusements, hunting and fishing. These have been fully covered by a vast number of books. However, there is another side of camp life, particularly in a boys' camp, which has been very little dealt with, namely, the exercise of one's ingenuity in creating out of the limited resources at hand such devices and

10 articles as will add to one's personal comfort and welfare.

It is, therefore, the aim of my advice to suggest certain diversions of this character for the boy camper which, aside from affording him plenty of physical exercise, will also develop his mental faculties, and above all stimulate that natural genius which is characteristic of every typical American boy.

15

CONTINUE

7

Which generalization about "All boys" in line 1 is supported by the author?

A) They display self-control

B) They experience a constant stress from the woods

C) They are fascinated by civilization

D) They have a certain degree of expertise in playing outdoor

E) They have shown the ability to live without the restraints of civilization

8

The description in line 7 ("there is another side of camp life") most directly emphasizes that the author

A) values boys' personal comfort and welfare

B) loves exercising ingenuity in the wildness

C) is aware of all the boys need to develop mental faculties

D) is aware of all the boys are nature lovers

E) believes reading a vast number of books expands boys' creativity

9

Which statement best describes the primary purpose of the passage?

A) It presents a lighthearted view of civilized boy campers

B) It illustrates the author's exciting view on creating ingenuity in the wilderness

C) It compares the advantages between physical and mental exercise

D) It provides the reason to have a summer vacation in the woods

E) It describes all boys are nature lovers.

10

In the context, the phrase "It may appear to be a bit presumption," (line 3) acknowledges that the boy campers

A) are usually sensitive to advice

B) do not generally spend time playing

C) surely understand the novelty of outdoor life

D) are usually associated with entertainment

E) are less fascinated by hunting than reading books

11

The characteristic of every typical American boy refers to

A) a way of thinking within civilized life

B) a sudden burst of inspiration in nature

C) a research based on book

D) instinct to hunting and fishing

E) a spiritual composure in the wilderness

12

According to the passage, which of the following boys processes the most desirable characteristics?

A) A boy versatile at both hunting and fishing

B) A boy accompanied by his parents at camping

C) A boy bringing books about camping at camping

D) A boy setting a fire without a match to keep himself warm in the wild

E) A boy displaying emotion to the animals in the wild

CONTINUE

Questions 13-18 are based on the following passage.

Line   It was either very careless or very astute of Nature to leave the entire length of the American continent without a central passage from ocean to ocean, or, having provided such a passage at Nicaragua, to allow it to be obstructed again by volcanic action. This imperviousness of the long American barrier had, as we shall see, important economic and political results, and the eventual
5   opening of a waterway will have results scarcely less important.

The Panama Canal will achieve, after more than four centuries, the object with which Columbus spread his sails westwards from the port of Palos--the provision of a sea-route westwards to China and the Indies. The capture of Constantinople in 1453 by the Turks interrupted the ancient trade routes between East and West.
10   Brigands held up the caravans which plodded across the desert sands from the Euphrates and the Indus, and pirates swarmed in the Mediterranean and Red Sea, intercepting the precious cargoes of silks and jewels and spices consigned to the merchants of Italy. The eyes of all Europe were turned to the Atlantic, and an ocean route westwards to India and the Orient, the existence of which had been fabled from the days of Aristotle, became an economic necessity.
15

13

In line 3, the author refers "Nicaragua" to indicate

A) both American continent and Nicaragua lack the central passage way

B) the country has oceanographic benefits

C) America's distrusts of nature

D) Panama Canal created the similar ocean passage eventually

E) the volcanic action as another obstacle

14

In line 3, "imperviousness" most nearly mean

A) not allowing water to pass

B) protected by water

C) unrestricted by water

D) unprotected from the flood

E) the technical limitation to control water

15

The author 's overall tone in this passage is best described as one of

A) jubilation

B) anticipation

C) qualified curiosity

D) uncertainty

E) melancholy

16

In lines 10-14 (Brigands held up...an economic necessity), the author primarily draws attention to

A) the extent to which desire for the canal is not new

B) the distinctive position that America enjoyed for four centuries

C) the possibility of another obstacle in the future

D) the likelihood that East and West will rebel again

E) the historical fact noted by Aristotle

CONTINUE

17

The word "fabled" (line 14) best conveys the meaning of the

A) unreliable rumors
B) ancient truth
C) written historical records
D) reliable opinion
E) words of wisdom

18

As described in line 14, "Aristotle" refers to the

A) commercial aspects of Panama Canal
B) preservation of historical importance
C) parallel perspective in history
D) distortion of cultural treasures
E) philosophical aspect of the Panama Canal

Questions 19-24 are based on the following passage.

Line

It is said that we are aiming at carrying education too far; that we are drawing it out to an extravagant length, and that, not satisfied with dispensing education to children also have attained what in former times was thought a proper age, we are now anxious to educate mere infants, incapable of receiving benefit from such instruction.

5 In the first place, it should be observed, that the objection comes from those very persons who object to education being given to children when they arrive at a more advanced period, on the ground that their parents then begin to find them useful in labor, and consequently cannot spare so much of their time as might be requisite: surely, that, the education of the children should commence at that time when their labor can be of value to their parents.

10 It is found even at the early age of seven or eight, that children are not void of those propensities, and I can give no better illustration of this, than the fact of a child only eight years old, being convicted of a capital offence at our tribunals of justice; when, therefore, I find that at this early period of life, these habits of vice are formed, it seems to me that we ought to begin still earlier to store their minds with such tastes, and to instruct them in such a

15 manner as to exclude the admission of those practices that lead to such early crime.

CONTINUE →

19

In lines 1 –4, the author suggests that

A) modern education is indifferent toward
   infant education.

B) we should lament the decline of educational value

C) some people offend the early education

D) infant education is costly

E) there should not be an age limit to education

20

In line 2, "dispensing" most nearly means

A) dishing out

B) providing

C) omitting

D) working with

E) explaining

21

The primary purpose of the first paragraph (lines
1-4) is to

A) introduce the concept of early education

B) illustrate the trend toward infant education

C) explore the connection between education
   and age limit

D) present the opinion that the author will
   later oppose

E) show even infant can learn at a rapid rate

22

In lines 8-9 ("surely, ...parents.") the author's
tone conveys

A) cynicism

B) appeal to emotion

C) exaggeration

D) humor

E) deference

23

The reference to " capital offence" (line 12), is
used to

A) illustrate the importance of education

B) reveal that even at early age child can be instructed

C) persuade the reader to exclude a capital
   Punishment to children

D) debunk a myth about early education

E) warn against those parents criticizing early
   education

24

At the end of the passage, the author suggests that

A) the issue should be reviewed to avoid the critical
   consequence

B) child labor is less valuable than education

C) there's no age limit as far as education is concerned

D) every child processes the possibility to commit
   a crime

E) all children should exclusively receive an infant
   education

CONTINUE

Questions 25-30 are based on the following passage.

Line   If you were asked, "What did Columbus discover in 1492?" you would have but one

answer. But what he discovered on his second voyage is not quite so easy to say. He was

looking for gold when he landed on the island of Hayti on that second trip. So his eyes were

blind to the importance of a simple game which he saw being played with a ball that bounced

5   by some half-naked Indian boys on the sand between the palm trees and the sea.

    Instead of the coveted gold, he took back to Europe, just as curiosities, some of the strange

black balls given him by these Indian boys. He learned that the balls were made from the

hardened juice of a tree.

    The little boys and girls of Spain were used to playing with balls made of rags or wool, so

10 you may imagine how these bouncing balls of the Indians must have pleased them. But the

men who sent out this second expedition gave the balls little thought and certainly no value.

Since Columbus brought back no gold, he was thrown into prison for debt, and he never

imagined that, four hundred years later, men would turn that strange, gummy tree juice into

more gold than King Ferdinand and Queen Isabella and all the princes of Europe ever

15 dreamed of.

25

The question in line 1 ("what did...1492?")
implies that some historical events

A) are intentionally ignored

B) are less profound

C) enjoy privileges

D) have only one answer

E) are revolutionary

26

In line 4, "blind" most nearly means

A) unable to see clearly

B) uninterested

C) disinterested

D) physically impaired

E) obsessively entertained

27

Which of the following was particularly important
for "the men" In line 11?

A) conquering the island of Hayti

B) finding a new route to East

C) valuable minerals

D) anything that can please their children

E) reclaiming the Spanish heritage

28

The author describes "the little boys and girls of
Spain" (lines 9-10), in order to

A) reveal the frustration of Columbus failed to bring
   gold

B) disparage the less developed Spain

C) parody the play with balls made of rags

D) show the zealotry that bouncing balls brought in

E) analyze the source of a modern soccer game

29

The author implies that Columbus would have never imagined that

A) he would be thrown into a prison

B) a gummy ball would bring an immediate popularity in Spain

C) a gummy ball would be more valuable than gold

D) he brought a model that could be a major popular activity in the future

E) a gummy tree juice ball was better than balls made of rags

30

"Indian boys" in line 5 and "The little boys and girls" in line 9 were alike in that they both

A) were the ancestors of modern soccer game

B) indulged in the similar entertainment

C) had a significant influence on later sports

D) didn't realize their play would become a popular sports several hundred years later.

E) realized a gummy tree ball was better than balls made of rags

Questions 31-35 are based on the following passage.

Line   In shape Egypt is like a lily with a crooked stem. A broad blossom terminates it at its upper end; a button of a bud projects from the stalk a little below the blossom, on the left-hand side. The bud is the Fayoum, a natural depression in the hills that shut in the Nile valley on the west, which has been rendered cultivable for many thousands of years by the introduction

5   into it of the Nile water, through a canal known as the "Bahr Yousouf." The long stalk of the lily is the Nile valley itself, which is a ravine scooped in the rocky soil for seven hundred miles from the First Cataract to the apex of the Delta, sometimes not more than a mile broad, never more than eight or ten miles. No other country in the world is so strangely shaped, so long compared to its width, so straggling, so hard to govern from a single centre.

10   At the first glance, the country seems to divide itself into two strongly contrasted regions; and this was the original impression which it made upon its inhabitants. The natives from a very early time designated their land as "the two lands," and represented it by a hieroglyph in which the form used to express "land" was doubled. The kings were called "chiefs of the Two Lands," and wore two crowns, as being kings of two countries.

15

CONTINUE

31

The primary purpose of the passage is to

A) display the early Egyptians' belief.

B) debunk the false belief about the divided lands

C) explain the shape of a country

D) describe characteristics that are essential to understand ancient Egypt

E) explain the impressive landscape

32

The phrase "The kings were called "chiefs of the Two Lands" (lines 13) refers to

A) Egypt that was originally controlled by two kings

B) the symbol of power

C) a sort of misconception of the early inhabitants

D) the early inhabitants' tendency to boast

E) one of the many theories related to the shape of Egypt

33

The primary literary device used in the passage is

A) Metaphor

B) Allusion

C) Personification

D) Simile

E) Oxymoron

34

The author's geographical references to Egypt is underscored by the

A) barren landscape in the Nile Valley

B) exquisite lily-like landscape

C) advanced hieroglyph

D) impressive cooperation between two lands

E) difficulty to govern the country

35

The central tone of the author in the last paragraph is best described in which term?

A) Idealism

B) Speculation

C) Disappointment

D) Anticipation

E) Fascination

CONTINUE

Questions 36-40 are based on the following passage.

Line

About two o'clock the following day a calash, drawn by a pair of magnificent English horses, stopped at the door of Monte Cristo and a person, dressed in a blue coat, with buttons similar color, a white waistcoat, over which was displayed a massive gold chain, brown trousers, and a quantity of black hair descending so low over his eyebrows as to leave it
5   doubtful whether it were not artificial so little did its jetty glossiness assimilate with the deep wrinkles stamped on his features – a person, in a word, who, desired to be taken for not more than forty, bent forwards from the carriage door, on the panels of which were emblazoned the armorial bearings of a baron, and directed his groom to inquire at the porter's lodge whether the Count of Monte Cristo resided there, and if he were within.

10   His glance was keen but showed cunning rather than intelligence; his lips were straight, and so think that, as they closed, they were drawn in over the teeth; his cheek-bones were broad and projecting a never failing proof of audacity and craftiness: while the flatness of his forehead, and the enlargement of the back of his skull, which rose much higher than his large and coarsely shaped ears, combined to form a physiognomy anything but prepossessing, save
15   in the eyes of such as considered that the owner of so splendid an equipage must needs be all that was admirable and enviable, more especially when they gazed on the enormous diamond that glittered in his shirt, and the red ribbon that depended from his button-hole.

36

The statement in lines 6-7 (a person...forty,) functions primarily to

A) show vivid imagery of a character

B) provide the evidence of a character's mood

C) describe a reason for the conflicting view

D) show a humorous outfit

E) reveal a character's anxious to be young

37

As used in line 9 "glossiness," author views that Dangles attempts to

A) reveal shiny feature

B) cover up the incongruity

C) show a form gesture

D) bring unaffected manner

E) show his preferred hairstyle

CONTINUE

38

Which of the following situations is analogous to the image on lines 4-6 (black hair....on his features)

A) The police who restrains a violent criminal

B) The teacher performs a sophisticated experiment

C) The woman hides her donations to the charity

D) The criminal who pretends to be innocent at the scene of a crime

E) The gentleman who maintains his hairstyle

39

In line 5, "assimilate" most nearly means

A) introduce

B) associate

C) resemble

D) make familiar to

E) make shiny

40

In lines 10-14, the narrator illustrates the physical characteristic of a person in order to reveal the

A) cunning character of a person

B) social status

C) stylish attire

D) actual age and desire to be seen

E) truthful nature of a character

Test 1 Verbal Section   30 MINUTES, 60 QUESTIONS

Directions: the synonym questions ask you to find the most appropriate synonym to the question.

The analogy questions ask you to find the most appropriate analogy to the question.
Select the answer that best matches to the question.

Synonym Sample Question:

Q: SUPERIOR

A higher rank

B inferior

C considerable

D supermarket

E supper

A) is the best answer because the synonym for superior is higher rank.

B) is incorrect because it applies the 'opposite concept.

C) and E) are irrelevant words.

D) is incorrect because it applies physical concept to mental concept

---

Test 1 Synonym questions 1 to 30

1. LATER
(A) subsequent
(B) latent
(C) earlier
(D) lament
(E) durable

2. EXPLOIT
(A) explore
(B) utilize
(C) help
(D) expunge
(E) brave

3. ACCOUNT
(A) perjury
(B) report
(C) countenance
(D) defy
(E) harsh

4. ABUNDANCE
(A) lack
(B) dearth
(C) abusive
(D) inundation
(E) plentiful

5. CONSEQUENCE
(A) frustrate
(B) publish
(C) result
(D) cause
(E) reason

CONTINUE ➤

6. PREVAIL

(A) dominant

(B) defeat

(C) avail

(D) trample on

(E) lift

7. SUBSTANTIAL

(A) submissive

(B) insignificant

(C) heave

(D) delayed

(E) significant

8. VAST

(A) extensive

(B) minute

(C) convincing

(D) origin

(E) promote

9. COMPELLING

(A) impelling

(B) boring

(C) final

(D) huge

(E) disoriented

10. DISPERSE

(A) distribute

(B) start

(C) enormous

(D) gather

(E) forceful

11. INITIATE

(A) first

(B) in the end

(C) accurate

(D) through

(E) progress

12. ADVOCATE

(A) dissuade

(B) promote

(C) ultimate

(D) in the end

(E) greatly

13. INADVERTENT

(A) unintentional

(B) ironic

(C) premeditated

(D) in time

(E) retard

14. INTRIGUE

(A) flaw

(B) fascinate

(C) bland

(D) without interest

(E) chance

15. ULTIMATE

(A) consequential

(B) ultimatum

(C) initiate

(D) ready

(E) willing

CONTINUE ➤

16. PROLIFERATE

(A) surprise

(B) wizen

(C) constant

(D) increase

(E) attentive

17. SUSTENANCE

(A) food

(B) hunger

(C) favor

(D) sublime

(E) suspense

18. VIRTUALLY

(A) fabricated

(B) artificially

(C) multiple

(D) nearly

(E) numerously

19. ADJACENT

(A) neighboring

(B) far

(C) distant

(D) attentive

(E) adverse

20. DURABLE

(A) long-lasting

(B) worn-out

(C) complete

(D) dubious

(E) draconian

21. PROMINENCE

(A) pivotal

(B) standout

(C) less-known

(D) notorious

(E) dangerous

22. COMPRISE

(A) convene

(B) disassemble

(C) be made of

(D) outstanding

(E) heterogeneous

23. DECIMATE

(A) decree

(B) decisive

(C) liberate

(D) destroy

(E) reach

24. INDUCE

(A) bring about

(B) complicate

(C) industrious

(D) consider

(E) feed

25. INTACT

(A) broken

(B) taciturn

(C) tactile

(D) unaffected

(E) stimulate

CONTINUE

26. MODIFY

(A) mode

(B) fashion

(C) fix

(D) change

(E) prosper

27. PHENOMENAL

(A) extraordinary

(B) philistine

(C) extremely normal

(D) wired

(E) appearance

28. UNIQUE

(A) heterogeneous

(B) distinct

(C) ubiquitous

(D) similar

(E) union

29. EXCLUSIVELY

(A) sharing

(B) inclusively

(C) exalt

(D) entirely

(E) separately

30. FLOURISH

(A) flower

(B) shrink

(C) flow

(D) prosper

(E) revolutionary

Analogy Sample Question:

Q: River is to Ocean as:

A better is to good

B rain is to cloud

C father is to mother

D city is to country

E fork is to spoon

D is the correct answer. Just as the river is smaller than the Ocean, the city is smaller than the country. The pattern applied in this question is the Degree Pattern (small to big)

A) is incorrect because the word order is flipped over.

B) is incorrect because it applies the production pattern (cloud produces rain)

C), E) are incorrect because they apply the Antonym patterns.

Test 1 Analogy questions 31 to 60

31. Cattle is to cow as

(A) dancing is to dancer

(B) star is to constellation

(C) pencil is to pen

(D) cat is to mice

(E) fingers is to gloves

CONTINUE

UNAUTHORIZED COPYING OR REUSE OF ANY PART OF THIS PAGE IS ILLEGAL

32. Pill is to doctor

(A) signs is to baseball coach

(B) eraser is to pencil

(C) water is to thirsty

(D) bullet is to gun

(E) pastor is to preach

33. Motel is to guests as

(A) cup is to coffee

(B) register is to university

(C) announcer is to microphone

(D) stadium is to crowd

(E) police station is to police

34. Stanza is to line as

(A) alcohol is to drink

(B) fight is to setting

(C) paragraph is to sentence

(D) word is to grammar

(E) comma is to punctuation

35. Sadness is to anguish as

(A) dog is to poppy

(B) adult is to infant

(C) joy is to exultation

(D) punch is to kill

(E) bear is to cub

36. Lunar is to Moon as

(A) star is to constellation

(B) Solar is to Sun

(C) Planet is to satellite

(D) Rain is to Snow

(E) Air is to water

37. Adherent is to follower as

(A) boss is to demagogue

(B) chairman is to employee

(C) apology is forgiven

(D) split is to fissure

(E) criminal is to lie

38. Ambition is to achieve as

(A) Court is to appeal

(B) politician is to election

(C) school is to graduation

(D) money is bank

(E) lazy is to fail

39. Arid is to desert as

(A) friend is to loyal

(B) priest is to patience

(C) apprehension is to determination

(D) humid is to swamp

(E) oasis is to desert

40. awe is to celebrity as

(A) calf is to cry

(B) cat is to rat

(C) firefighter is to fire

(D) pen is to pencil

(E) milk is to cow

41. Wound is to heal as malfunction is to

(A) ignore

(B) repair

(C) diagnose

(D) build

(E) finish

CONTINUE

42. Handcuff is to arrest as

(A) ripe is to pick

(B) fun is to laugh

(C) late is to scold

(D) tame is to train

(E) lamp is to light

43. Arrogant is to humble

(A) fragile is to break

(B) King is to mercy

(C) vocabulary is to memorize

(D) fruit is to abundant

(E) forget is remember

44. Legible is to articulate

(A) Teacher is to teach

(B) leg is to art

(C) evolve is to demolish

(D) excel is to good

(E) speak is to write

45. Newspaper is to typo as personality is to

(A) psycho

(B) extrovert

(C) introvert

(D) perfect

(E) flaw

46. Discrepancy is to difference as equivalent is to

(A) equanimity

(B) equestrian

(C) similar

(D) equal

(E) ambiguous

47. Equivocal is to equal society as egalitarian is to

(A) clear

(B) noise

(C) equal

(D) unclear

(E) suitable

48. Eruption is to volcano

(A) building is to explosion

(B) pioneer is to cultivate

(C) water is to river

(D) dynamite is to danger

(E) spring is to well

49. Faction is to union as

(A) cold is hot

(B) helmet is to protect

(C) chilly is to frozen

(D) element is to problem

(E) habitat is to oyster

50. Futile is to harvest as

(A) bathroom is to bedroom

(B) disaster is to flood

(C) dam is to water

(D) arid is to plantation

(E) fertile is to fruit

51. Goods is to factory as

(A) Painting is to art center

(B) school is to student

(C) farm is to produce

(D) sauna is to sweat

(E) heat is to fire

CONTINUE

UNAUTHORIZED COPYING OR REUSE OF ANY PART OF THIS PAGE IS ILLEGAL

52. Habit is to innate as

(A) Practice is to talent

(B) GPS is to compass

(C) river is to stream

(D) forward is to backward

(E) wind is to sun

53. Genre is to romance as Organism is to

(A) base

(B) cell

(C) body

(D) physical

(E) health

54. Gentle is to praise as

(A) hoax is to fake

(B) knowledge is to wisdom

(C) good is to quality

(D) diligent is to success

(E) Lady is to charm

55. Ignite is to abrasion as

(A) disease is to cancer

(B) plan is to success

(C) practice is to win

(D) failure is to mistake

(E) idiom is to word

56. Ink cartridge is to printer as

(A) candle is to cake

(B) seat is to theater

(C) employee is to staff

(D) tomato is to banana

(E) cellphone is to battery

57. Immense is to narrow as

(A) exercise is to healthy

(B) dancing is to cheer

(C) sad movie is to parody

(D) cure is to healing

(E) princess is to Royal

58. Improvisation is to preparation as

(A) improvement is to goal

(B) hostility is to sympathy

(C) handsome is to growth

(D) formula is to equation

(E) steal is to kill

59. Unique is to original as

(A) manipulate is to lie

(B) makeshift is to stopgap

(C) strong is to weak

(D) radio is to T.V.

(E) elegant is to attractive

60. Marvel is to myth as

(A) history is to fact

(B) true story is to biography

(C) idea is to develop

(D) anecdote is to personal

(E) letter is to journal

STOP

If you finish before time is called,
you may check your work on this section.

Do not turn to the next section.

Test 1

ABSOLUTE PATTERNS

For your Score Interpretation Resources, please use the official SSAT Guidebook or visit:
https://ssat.org/scores/read-score-report/score-interpretation-resources

TEST 1
READING SECTION ANSWER KEYS

Please refer to the Reading Section Absolute Pattern Analysis next page

THE SYNONYM QUESTIONS
TEST 1 NO.1 ~ 30.

1	A	16	D
2	B	17	A
3	B	18	D
4	E	19	A
5	C	20	A
6	A	21	B
7	E	22	C
8	A	23	D
9	A	24	A
10	A	25	D
11	A	26	D
12	B	27	A
13	A	28	B
14	B	29	D
15	A	30	D

THE ANALOGY QUESTIONS TEST 1 NO. 31 ~ 60

Please refer to the Analogy Section Absolute Pattern

Test 1

ABSOLUTE PATTERNS for the Reading Section

Q1. Pattern 5: Word-In-Context Question

Question Pattern: most nearly means		Question Keywords: In line 5, "mixed up"	
Step 1		Step 2	Step 3
Keywords from the Passage		Keywords from Answer	Tone & Concept
L5: one topic of conversation, with his chin upon...		C) obsessed	Positive, mental concept
Incorrect Choices & Common Patterns			
Evidence		Incorrect keywords	Tone & Concept
he had not already <u>been mixed up in this extraordinary case, which was the one topic of conversation</u>...For a whole, had rambled about the room with his chin upon his chest		A) confused	Negative
		B) associated	too weak implication
		D) united	too literal implication
		E) put together	Physical concept

The word-in-context question normally use the following paradigm:

1> physical vs. mental concept   2> Positive vs. Negative concept

3> Literal vs. Figurative concept 4> Active vs. Passive concept   5> Too weak vs. Too extreme implication

Q2. Type 2: Inference Question [Pattern 1: Local Question] {Category A}

Question Pattern: suggests that the narrator	Question Keywords: Line 9 (absolutely deft)	
Step 1	Step 2	Step 3
Keywords from the Passage	Keywords from Answer	Tone & Concept
L9: <u>absolutely deaf</u> to any of <u>my questions</u>	C) degree of contemplation	Synonym, positive
Incorrect Choices & Common Patterns		
Evidence	Incorrect keywords	Tone & Concept
<u>absolutely deaf</u> to any of <u>my questions</u> implies the character's degree (obsessed) of contemplation	A) little attention	Negative
	B) worries physical	Negative, physical
	D) case, not important	Negative, Opposite
	E) argues extraordinary case	Inconsistency

E) is incorrect because such a statement should be made by Holmes, not the narrator as the observer.

Therefore, it is Inconsistent with the question.

Q3. Pattern 7: Understanding Attitude

Question Pattern: the narrator emphasizes his, describing   **Question Keywords:** Homels,

Step 1	Step 2	Step 3
Keywords from the Passage	Keywords from Answer	Tone & Concept
Line 7: For a whole...absolutely deaf to any	D) obsession	Synonym, Active

Incorrect Choices & Common Patterns		
Evidence	Incorrect keywords	Tone & Concept
For a whole day my companion had rambled about the room with his chin upon his chest and his brows knitted, charging and recharging his pipe with the strongest black tobacco, and absolutely deaf to any	A) vicious temperament	Negative
	B) humility	Passive
	C) innate pessimism	Negative
	E) intelligence	Shifting the argument

E) could have been the correct answer if the question were to ask "In describing the extraordinary case,

   Holmes was…"

Q4. Pattern 3: Summary Question

Question Pattern: mentioned in line 6 is most likely **Question Keywords:** "extraordinary"

Step 1	Step 2	Step 3
Keywords from the Passage	Keywords from Answer	Tone & Concept
which was the one topic	C) difficult issue	Logical Conclusion

Incorrect Choices & Common Patterns		
Evidence	Incorrect keywords	Tone & Concept
this extraordinary case, which was the one topic of conversation	A) uneasy feeling	unrelated items
	B) sensitive relations	unrelated items
	D) irritable traveling	unrelated items
	E) supernatural	unrelated items

UNAUTHORIZED COPYING OR REUSE OF ANY PART OF THIS PAGE IS ILLEGAL

Q5. Pattern 4: Relationship Question

Question Pattern: It can be inferred   **Question Keywords:** Waton's role with Holmes is most similar to

Step 1	Step 2	Step 3
Keywords from the Passage	Keywords from Answer	Tone & Concept
my companion	E) a co-worker	Synonym
Incorrect Choices & Common Patterns		
Evidence	Incorrect keywords	Tone & Concept
For a whole day my companion had rambled about the room. 1> Throughout the passage, Watson appears to be a character who knows very well about the Holmes' inner mindsets. 2> There is no other indication referring his job other than this information	A) a critic	Not Supported by the passage
	B) a reporter	
	C) king from Dartmoor	
	D) a writer	

Q6. Pattern 2: Main Idea Question

Question Pattern: The primary purpose of the passage is to

Step 1	Step 2	Step 3
Keywords from the Passage	Keywords from Answer	Tone & Concept
L7: For a whole day my companion had...	D) preoccupation	Synonym
Incorrect Choices & Common Patterns		
Evidence	Incorrect keywords	Tone & Concept
The overall passage is about Watson's description of one character (Sherlock Holmes) and his contemplation on an extraordinary case.	A) highlight relationship	minor information
	B) character's excitement	Opposite
	C) mystical aspect	Not stated
	E) revelation of mystery	Opposite

1> Unlike the tone question, which relies mostly on the emotional state of a person, the primary purpose question relies mostly on the volume of information.

2> Therefore, you should seek which idea or words appear most often throughout the passage, and then, find the word or synonym from the multiple choice

Q7. Pattern 3: Summary Question

Question Pattern: Which generalization   **Question Keywords:** All boys" in line 1

Step 1	Step 2	Step 3
Keywords from the Passage	Keywords from Answer	Tone & Concept
boy camper how to spend his time	D) playing outdoor	Synonym, positive

Incorrect Choices & Common Patterns		
Evidence	Incorrect keywords	Tone & Concept
it may appear to be a <u>bit of presumption to attempt to advise the boy camper how to spend his time.</u> Surely the novelty of outdoor life, the fascinating charm of his surroundings, <u>will provide him plenty of entertainment.</u>	A) self-control	Not stated
	B) stress	Negative
	C) fascinated by civilization	B), C) and E) are opposite to the author's statement.
	E) live without restraints	

Q8. Pattern 3: Summary Question

Question Pattern: The description emphasizes **Question Keywords:** ("there is another side of camp life")

Step 1	Step 2	Step 3
Keywords from the Passage	Keywords from Answer	Tone & Concept
exercise of one's ingenuity in creating	B) ingenuity in the wildness	Synonym

Incorrect Choices & Common Patterns		
Evidence	Incorrect keywords	Tone & Concept
<u>However,</u> there is another side of camp life, ...<u>exercise of one's ingenuity in creating out of the limited resources</u> at hand such devices and articles	A) personal comfort and welfare	Opposite
	C) develop mental faculties	Too broad concept
	D) boys are nature lovers	Too broad concept
	E) reading books	Opposite

Finding a contradicting conjunction (adverb) such as but or however is integral process to deal with the summary question.

Q9. Pattern 2: Main Idea Question

Question Pattern: the primary purpose of the passage

Step 1	Step 2	Step 3
Keywords from the Passage	Keywords from Answer	Tone & Concept
...exercise of one's ingenuity	B) creating ingenuity	Synonym, positive

Incorrect Choices & Common Patterns		
Evidence	Incorrect keywords	Tone & Concept
It is, therefore, <u>the aim of my advice to</u> <u>suggest...</u> and <u>above all stimulate that natural genius.</u>	A) lighthearted view	Negative
	C) physical and mental exercise	C), D), E) are all too broad concept so can't be the primary concept
	D) a summer vacation	
	E) nature lovers.	

The primary concept (purpose) question can often, if not always, be found in the concluding paragraph, especially in the concluding sentence.

Q10. Pattern 3: Summary Question

Question Pattern: acknowledges that
Question Keywords: "It may appear to be a bit of presumption," (line 3) the boy campers

Step 1	Step 2	Step 3
Keywords from the Passage	Keywords from Answer	Tone & Concept
plenty of entertainment.	D) associated with entertainment	Synonym, Active

Incorrect Choices & Common Patterns		
Evidence	Incorrect keywords	Tone & Concept
it may appear to be a bit of presumption ... plenty of entertainment.	A) sensitive to advice	Negative
	B) do not, playing	Negative
	C) understand outdoor life	Repeating the question
	E) are less fascinated	Negative

C) "the novelty of outdoor life" is a part of a suggestion from the author; therefore, it should be considered as a part of the question.

Q11. Type 2: Inference Question [Pattern 1: Local Question] {Category A}

Question Pattern: The characteristic boy refers to   **Question Keywords:** of every typical American

Step 1	Step 2	Step 3
Keywords from the Passage	Keywords from Answer	Tone & Concept
stimulate, natural genius	B) a sudden burst of inspiration	synonym

Incorrect Choices & Common Patterns		
Evidence	Incorrect keywords	Tone & Concept
above all <u>stimulate</u> (a sudden burst) that <u>natural genius (inspiration)</u> which is characteristic of every typical American boy. a way of thinking within civilized life	A) civilized life C) on book D) hunting and fishing E) a spiritual composure	A) this is what the author wants boys to avoid. D) the author categorizes hunting and fishing as an entertainment C), E) are Not stated

Q12. Type 3: Analogy Question [Pattern 1: Local Question] {Category A}

Question Pattern: which of the following characteristics?

Question Keywords: boys processes the most desirable

Step 1	Step 2	Step 3
Keywords from the Passage	Keywords from Answer	Tone & Concept
<u>stimulate, natural genius (inspiration)</u>	D) setting a fire without a match	similar concept

Incorrect Choices & Common Patterns		
Evidence	Incorrect keywords	Tone & Concept
<u>above all stimulate that natural genius natural genius (inspiration)</u> which is characteristic of every typical American boy. Choice D, will be the most desirable boy from the author's view.	A) hunting and fishing B) by his parents at camping C) bringing books E) displaying emotion	A) The author claims that it is entertainment. C), D) The author is pessimistic about civilized education

UNAUTHORIZED COPYING OR REUSE OF ANY PART OF THIS PAGE IS ILLEGAL

Q13. Type 1: Example Question [Pattern 1: Local Question] {Category A}

Question Pattern: In line 3, the author refers to indicate   **Question Keywords:** "Nicaragua"

Step 1	Step 2	Step 3
Keywords from the Passage	Keywords from Answer	Tone & Concept
having provided a passage at Nicaragua	B) oceanographic benefits	Similar concept

Incorrect Choices & Common Patterns		
Evidence	Incorrect keywords	Tone & Concept
It was either very careless or very astute of Nature to leave the entire length of the American continent without a central passage from ocean to ocean, or, having provided such a passage at Nicaragua,	A) Nicaragua lack C) America's distrusts D) Panama Canal E) the volcanic action	A) is Opposite C) Too broad conception D), E) are true statements but do not respond to the question; therefore, they are inconsistent with the question

Q14. Type 1: Example Question [Pattern 1: Local Question] {Category A}

Question Pattern: most nearly mean   **Question Keywords:** In line 3, "imperviousness"

Step 1	Step 2	Step 3
Keywords from the Passage	Keywords from Answer	Tone & Concept
This imperviousness of the long American barrier	A) not allowing water	barrier is the synonym

Incorrect Choices & Common Patterns		
Evidence	Incorrect keywords	Tone & Concept
Imperviousness = im/per/vi/ousness = im (not), per (through), vi (way) *As you can see, the answer to the WIC question always carries a clue word within the sentence.	B) protected by water C) unrestricted by water D) flood E) technical limitation	B), C) are opposite. D) is not only opposite but also extreme

Q15. Pattern 7: Understanding Attitude

Question Pattern: The author 's overall tone

Step 1	Step 2	Step 3
Keywords from the Passage	Keywords from Answer	Tone & Concept
Canal will achieve, after, four centuries,	B) anticipation	Positive

Incorrect Choices & Common Patterns		
Evidence	Incorrect keywords	Tone & Concept
The Panama Canal will achieve, after more than four centuries, the object with which Columbus spread his sails westwards …	A) jubilation	A), E) are Not proper word usage for this sort of essay C) "qualified" means limited, which is negative D) is negative
	C) qualified curiosity	
	D) uncertainty	
	E) melancholy	

Q16. Type 1: Example Question [Pattern 1: Local Question] {Category A}

Question Pattern: In a series of historical analogies, the author primarily draws attention to
Question Keywords: in lines 10-14 (Brigands held up...an economic necessity),

Step 1	Step 2	Step 3
Keywords from the Passage	Keywords from Answer	Tone & Concept
from the days of Aristotle, became...necessity	A) not new	Logical Conclusion

Incorrect Choices & Common Patterns		
Evidence	Incorrect keywords	Tone & Concept
The eyes of all Europe were turned to the Atlantic, the existence of which had been fabled from the days of Aristotle, became an economic necessity.	B) America enjoyed	The author states that the importance of the ocean route is not new, and goes a long way back to the days of Aristotle.
	C) obstacles, future	
	D) rebel against, future	
	E) Aristotle	

C), D) Predicting the future that is not stated in the passage is always incorrect

UNAUTHORIZED COPYING OR REUSE OF ANY PART OF THIS PAGE IS ILLEGAL

Q17. Pattern 5: Word-In-Context Question

Question Pattern: The word best conveys the meaning of   **Question Keywords:** "fabled" (line 14)

Step 1	Step 2	Step 3
Keywords from the Passage	Keywords from Answer	Tone & Concept
the existence , fabled from, Aristotle	D) reliable opinion	Similar concept

Incorrect Choices & Common Patterns		
Evidence	Incorrect keywords	Tone & Concept
the existence of which had been fabled from the days of Aristotle	A) unreliable rumors	A) should be "reliable", not "unreliable"
	B) ancient truth	B), C) fable has no truth or written records
	C) written historical	
	E) words of wisdom	E) "wisdom" is not a related word

Q18. Type 2: Inference Question [Pattern 1: Local Question] {Category A}

Question Pattern: As described refers to   **Question Keywords:** in line 14, "Aristotle"

Step 1	Step 2	Step 3
Keywords from the Passage	Keywords from Answer	Tone & Concept
existence, had been fabled from the days of Aristotle	C) parallel, in history	similar concept

Incorrect Choices & Common Patterns		
Evidence	Incorrect keywords	Tone & Concept
The eyes of all Europe were turned to the Atlantic, and an ocean route westwards to India and the Orient, the existence of which had been fabled from the days of Aristotle, became an economic necessity.	A) commercial aspects	Material concept
	B) preservation, historical	Unrelated word usage
	D) distortion	Negative
	E) philosophical aspect	Unrelated word usage

The author states that the importance of the ocean route is not new, and goes a long way back to the days of Aristotle. Therefore, it suggests a historical parallel.

Q19. Type 2: Inference Question [Pattern 1: Local Question] {Category A}

Question Pattern: the author suggests that		**Question Keywords:** In lines 1 –4,
Step 1	Step 2	Step 3
Keywords from the Passage	Keywords from Answer	Tone & Concept
It is said that	C) some people offend	similar concept, Negative
Incorrect Choices & Common Patterns		
Evidence	Incorrect keywords	Tone & Concept
It is said that we are aiming at carrying education too far... we are now anxious to educate mere infants, incapable of receiving benefit from such instruction.	A) indifferent	Too extreme word usage
	B) we should lament	
	D) costly	Not stated
	E) should not be age limit	Opposite

1> "It is said that" implies that the author is delivering other people's opinion. Therefore, the author's opinion such as B or E) are incorrect.

2> It should be "some people" as in (C)

Q20. Pattern 5: Word-In-Context Question

Question Pattern: most nearly means		**Question Keywords:** In line 2, "dispensing"
Step 1	Step 2	Step 3
Keywords from the Passage	Keywords from Answer	Tone & Concept
not satisfied	B) providing	similar concept, figurative
Incorrect Choices & Common Patterns		
Evidence	Incorrect keywords	Tone & Concept
not satisfied with dispensing education to children	A) dishing out	A), D) are too literal.
	C) omitting	C), E) are Unrelated word usage
"not satisfied" implies "dispensing" should be the positive word.	D) working with	
	E) explaining	

UNAUTHORIZED COPYING OR REUSE OF ANY PART OF THIS PAGE IS ILLEGAL

Q21. Pattern 6: Understanding Structure of the Passage

Question Pattern: The primary purpose   **Question Keywords:** first paragraph (lines 1-4) is to

Step 1	Step 2	Step 3
Keywords from the Passage	Keywords from Answer	Tone & Concept
L5: it should be observed	D) author later oppose	Negative

Incorrect Choices & Common Patterns		
Evidence	Incorrect keywords	Tone & Concept
It is said that we are aiming Line 5: In the first place, it should be observed,	A) concept	A),B),C),E) are all minor information, not the primary
	B) trend	
	C) connection	
	E) learn rapid rate	

1> When the question asks the entire paragraph, it is asking the relations between the following paragraphs, not the content within the paragraph.

2> Therefore, the answer should be normally found in the first sentence of the following paragraph.

3> The first paragraph is the opinion of the others whom the author disagrees.

4> We can see the relations by reading " It is said that we are aiming" (line 1) and "it should be observed" (line 5)

Q22. Pattern 7: Understanding Attitude / Tone

Question Pattern: the author's tone conveys   **Question Keywords:** In lines 8-9 ("surely, ...parents.")

Step 1	Step 2	Step 3
Keywords from the Passage	Keywords from Answer	Tone & Concept
their parents them useful in labor, not spare...	A) cynicism	Logical Conclusion

Incorrect Choices & Common Patterns		
Evidence	Incorrect keywords	Tone & Concept
education being given to children when they arrive at a more advanced period, ...their parents then begin to find them useful in labor, and consequently cannot spare so much of their time as might be requisite: surely, that, the education of the children should commence at that time when their labor can be of value to their parents.	B) appeal to emotion	The underlined portion of the sentence contains the hypocritical view of the parents. Therefore, the author's tone should be cynical.
	C) exaggeration	
	D) humor	
	E) deference	

Q23. Type 1: Example Question [Pattern 1: Local Question] {Category A}

Question Pattern: The reference to...is used to   **Question Keywords:** capital offence (line 12)

Step 1	Step 2	Step 3
Keywords from the Passage	Keywords from Answer	Tone & Concept
L: It is found even at the early age of seven	B) child can be instructed	The main idea

Incorrect Choices & Common Patterns

Evidence	Incorrect keywords	Tone & Concept
It is found even at the early age of seven or eight, that children are not void of those propensities, and I can give no better illustration of this, than the fact of child only eight years old, convicted of a capital offence	A) importance, education	Too broad concept
	C) capital Punishment	Not related issue
	D) debunk a myth	Negative
	E) warn, those parents	Too extreme word usage

1> capital offence (line 12) is one of the examples that the author uses to emphasize the topic sentence. "It is found even at the early age of seven…

2> The answer for the example type question should be found in the topic or concluding sentence.

D) debunk a myth about early education means that there is a myth to be disclosed of in early education. That is, early education is not the right one, which is opposite to the author's opinion.

Q24. Pattern 3: Summary Question

Question Pattern: At the end of the passage, the author suggests that

Step 1	Step 2	Step 3
Keywords from the Passage	Keywords from Answer	Tone & Concept
we ought to begin still earlier	A) should be reviewed	Similar concept

Incorrect Choices & Common Patterns

Evidence	Incorrect keywords	Tone & Concept
therefore, I find that at this early period of life, these habits of vice are formed, it seems to me that we ought to begin still earlier to store their minds with such tastes, and to instruct them in such a manner as to exclude the admission of crime	B) child labor	Minor issue
	C) there's no age limit	Too extreme
	D) to commit a crime	Minor issue
	E) all children	Too extreme .

The author maintains the parents should teach their children at an early age to avoid the terrible consequence. Therefore, the issue (early education) needs to be reviewed.

UNAUTHORIZED COPYING OR REUSE OF ANY PART OF THIS PAGE IS ILLEGAL

Q25. Type 2: Inference Question [Pattern 1: Local Question] {Category A}

Question Pattern: The question implies that   **Question Keywords:** in line 1 ("what did...1492?")

Step 1	Step 2	Step 3
Keywords from the Passage	Keywords from Answer	Tone & Concept
you would have but one answer.	C) enjoy privileges	Logical Conclusion

Incorrect Choices & Common Patterns		
Evidence	Incorrect keywords	Tone & Concept
If you were asked, "What did Columbus discover in 1492?" you would have but one answer.	A) intentionally ignored	opposite
	B) less profound	opposite
	D) only one answer	D), E) please do not choose
	E) revolutionary	too extreme word usage

1> Option D) is merely repeating the sentence instead of answering the question.

2> Inference question—if the same phrase is used—always considers it as an incorrect choice.

Q26. Pattern 5: Word-In-Context Question

Question Pattern: most nearly means   **Question Keywords:** In line 4, "blind"

Step 1	Step 2	Step 3
Keywords from the Passage	Keywords from Answer	Tone & Concept
He was looking for gold	B) uninterested	Similar Conception

Incorrect Choices & Common Patterns		
Evidence	Incorrect keywords	Tone & Concept
He was looking for gold when he landed on the island of Hayti on that second trip. So his eyes were blind to the importance of a simple game	A) unable to see clearly	Too literal Implication
	C) disinterested	means unbiased
	D) physically impaired	Too literal Implication
	E) obsessively entertained	Opposite

Q27. Pattern 3: Summary Question

Question Pattern: Which of the following was particularly important
Question Keywords: for "the men" In line 11?

Step 1	Step 2	Step 3
Keywords from the Passage	Keywords from Answer	Tone & Concept
no value. Since Columbus brought back no gold,	C) valuable minerals	Synonym
Incorrect Choices & Common Patterns		
Evidence	Incorrect keywords	Tone & Concept
men who sent out this second expedition gave the balls little thought and certainly <u>no value. Since Columbus brought back no gold,</u>	A) conquering	Not stated issues
	B) finding a new route	
	D) please their children	
	E) Spanish heritage	

Q28. Pattern 4: Relationship Question

Question Pattern: the author describes in order to
Question Keywords: In lines 9-10, "the little boys and girls of Spain"

Step 1	Step 2	Step 3
Keywords from the Passage	Keywords from Answer	Tone & Concept
so you may imagine how these bouncing balls	D) zealotry, bouncing ball	Similar Concept, Positive
Incorrect Choices & Common Patterns		
Evidence	Incorrect keywords	Tone & Concept
The little boys and girls of Spain were used to playing with balls made of rags or wool, <u>so you may imagine how these bouncing balls of the Indians must have pleased them.</u>	A) frustration, Columbus	Negative
	B) disparage	Negative
	C) parody the play	Negative
	E) modern soccer game	Unrelated word usage

1> The question phrase "in order to" is a typical cause-effect question that shows only the cause and asks the
   effect or vice versa.

2> Please look for a meaningful transitional words such as "so" in this sentence.

UNAUTHORIZED COPYING OR REUSE OF ANY PART OF THIS PAGE IS ILLEGAL

Q29. Type 2: Inference Question [Pattern 1: Local Question] {Category A}

Question Pattern: The author implies that

Question Keywords: Columbus would have never imagined that

Step 1	Step 2	Step 3
Keywords from the Passage	Keywords from Answer	Tone & Concept
gummy tree juice into more gold than	D) he brought popular activity	Logical Conclusion
Incorrect Choices & Common Patterns		
Evidence	Incorrect keywords	Tone & Concept
and he never imagined that, four hundred years later, men would turn that strange, <u>gummy tree juice into more gold than</u>	A) thrown into a prison	Unrelated word usage
	B) immediate popularity	Minor issue
	C) more valuable than gold	Inconsistent with the question
	E) better than rags	minor issue

Q30. Pattern 4: Relationship Question

Question Pattern: were alike in that they both

Question Keywords: "Indian boys" in line 5 and "The little boys and girls" in line 9

Step 1	Step 2	Step 3
Keywords from the Passage	Keywords from Answer	Tone & Concept
playing with balls	B) indulged in the similar	synonyms
Incorrect Choices & Common Patterns		
Evidence	Incorrect keywords	Tone & Concept
which he saw being <u>played with a ball</u> that bounced by some half-naked Indian boys The little boys and girls of Spain were used to <u>playing with balls</u> made of rags	A) were the ancestors	A), B),C), are all true statements but consistent with the question E) Not Logical Sequence
	C) significant influence	
	D) a popular	
	E) tree ball was better	

Q31. Pattern 2: Main Idea Question

Question Pattern: The primary purpose of the passage is to

Step 1	Step 2	Step 3
Keywords from the Passage	Keywords from Answer	Tone & Concept
In shape Egypt	C) shape of a country	Synonym

Incorrect Choices & Common Patterns		
Evidence	Incorrect keywords	Tone & Concept
In shape Egypt is like a lily with a crooked stem.	A) Egyptians' belief.	Minor Issue
	B) debunk the false	Negative
	D) understand ancient Egypt	Too Broad Concept
	E) impressive landscape	Not Supported by the passage

Q32. Type 2: Inference Question [Pattern 1: Local Question] {Category A}

Question Pattern: The phrase, refers to
Question Keywords: "The kings were called "chiefs of the Two Lands" (lines 13)

Step 1	Step 2	Step 3
Keywords from the Passage	Keywords from Answer	Tone & Concept
At the first glance, the country **seems to** divide	C) misconception	Similar Conception

Incorrect Choices & Common Patterns		
Evidence	Incorrect keywords	Tone & Concept
At the first glance, the country **seems to** divide itself into two strongly contrasted regions;	A) controlled by two kings	Opposite
	B) the symbol of power	Unrelated word usage
	D) tendency to boast	Not stated
	E) one of the many theories	Not stated

Q33. Pattern 5: Word-In-Context Question

Question Pattern: The primary literary device used in the passage is

Step 1	Step 2	Step 3
Keywords from the Passage	Keywords from Answer	Tone & Concept
Egypt is like a lily	D) Simile	Similar Conception
Incorrect Choices & Common Patterns		
Evidence	Incorrect keywords	Tone & Concept
In shape Egypt is like a lily with a crooked stem	A) Metaphor	Throughout the passage the author compares Egypt to lily. That is simile.
	B) Allusion	
	C) Personification	
	E) Oxymoron	

Literary device and terminology question asks only a handful of selected vocabularies. They are as follow:

Metaphor: a figure of speech that compares two subjects without using "like" or "as."
(e.g., It will rain cats and dogs next week.)

Allusion: a figure of speech when a person or author makes an indirect reference from literary sources
(e.g., Your garden is a Garden of Eden)

Personification: a figure of speech that gives human characteristics to abstract ideas.
(e.g., The sky is angry)

A figure of speech in which apparently contradictory terms appear in conjunction
(e.g., *faith unfaithful kept him falsely true*).

A figure of speech involving the comparison of one thing with another thing
(e.g., *crazy like a dog*).

Q34. Pattern 7: Understanding Attitude / Tone

Question Pattern: The author's references to, underscored by **Question Keywords: geographical, Egypt is**

Step 1	Step 2	Step 3
Keywords from the Passage	Keywords from Answer	Tone & Concept
hard to govern from a single centre.	E) difficulty to govern	Logical Conclusion
Incorrect Choices & Common Patterns		
Evidence	Incorrect keywords	Tone & Concept
so long compared to its width, so straggling, so hard to govern from a single centre.	A) barren landscape	Minor Issue
	B) exquisite	Opposite
	C) hieroglyph	Unrelated word usage
	D) two lands	Opposite

Q35. Pattern 7: Understanding Attitude / Tone

Question Pattern: The central tone of the author in the last paragraph is best described in which term?

Step 1	Step 2	Step 3
Keywords from the Passage	Keywords from Answer	Tone & Concept
At the first glance, the country **seems to**	B) Speculation	Similar Conception

Incorrect Choices & Common Patterns		
Evidence	Incorrect keywords	Tone & Concept
At the first glance, the country **seems to** divide itself into two strongly contrasted regions	A) Idealism	Not Supported by the passage
	C) Disappointment	
	D) Anticipation	
	E) Fascination	

Q36. Pattern 4: Relationship Question

Question Pattern: The statement functions primarily to

Question Keywords: The statement in lines 6-7 (a person...forty,)

Step 1	Step 2	Step 3
Keywords from the Passage	Keywords from Answer	Tone & Concept
desired to be taken for not more than forty,	C) reason, conflicting view	Physical Concept, Cause

Incorrect Choices & Common Patterns		
Evidence	Incorrect keywords	Tone & Concept
(EFFECT) doubtful whether it were not artificial so little did its jetty glossiness assimilate with the deep wrinkles stamped on his features (CAUSE) – a person, in a word, who, desired to be taken for not more than forty,	A) vivid imagery	Too broad concept
	B) character's mood	Mental Concept
	D) humorous outfit	Unrelated word usage
	E) anxious to be young	Too extreme word usage

1> The previous portion "doubtful whether ...on his features" is the effect of incongruity.

2> The following portion describes the reason of the incongruous view.

Q37. Type 2: Inference Question [Pattern 1: Local Question] {Category A}

Question Pattern: author views that

Question Keywords: As used in line 9 "glossiness,"   Dangles attempts to

Step 1	Step 2	Step 3
Keywords from the Passage	Keywords from Answer	Tone & Concept
artificial so little did its jetty glossiness assimilate	B) cover up incongruity	Similar Conception, Negative

Incorrect Choices & Common Patterns		
Evidence	Incorrect keywords	Tone & Concept
doubtful whether it were not artificial <u>so little did its jetty glossiness assimilate</u> with the deep wrinkles stamped on his features – "so little assimilate" means incongruity.	A) shiny feature	The remaining choices are all positive.
	C) form gesture	
	D) unaffected manner	
	E) preferred hairstyle	

Q38. Type 3: Analogy Question [Pattern 1: Local Question] {Category A}

Question Pattern: Which of the following situations is analogous

Question Keywords: to the image on lines 4-6 (black hair....on his features)

Step 1	Step 2	Step 3
Keywords from the Passage	Keywords from Answer	Tone & Concept
doubtful whether,,, artificial, assimilate	D) A criminal pretends	Similar Logic

Incorrect Choices & Common Patterns		
Evidence	Incorrect keywords	Tone & Concept
The logic should contain	A) police, restrains	Unrelated logic
(1) the negative value	B) teacher experiment	Unrelated logic
(2) an attempt to the concealment.	C) woman hides, donations	Positive
D) satisfies both premises.	E) A gentleman, hairstyle	Unrelated word usage

Q39. Pattern 5: Word-In-Context Question

Question Pattern: means

Question Keywords: In line 5, "assimilate"

Step 1	Step 2	Step 3
Keywords from the Passage	Keywords from Answer	Tone & Concept
not artificial so little, glossiness assimilate	C) resemble	synonym

Incorrect Choices & Common Patterns		
Evidence	Incorrect keywords	Tone & Concept
doubtful whether it were not artificial so little did its jetty glossiness assimilate with the deep wrinkles stamped on his features –	A) introduce	Unrelated word usage
	B) associate	
	D) make familiar to	
	E) make shiny	

Q40. Pattern 4: Relationship Question

Question Pattern: order to reveal

Question Keywords: In lines 10-14, the narrator illustrates the physical characteristic of a person

Step 1	Step 2	Step 3
Keywords from the Passage	Keywords from Answer	Tone & Concept
showed cunning, rather than intelligence	A) cunning character	Similar Conception

Incorrect Choices & Common Patterns		
Evidence	Incorrect keywords	Tone & Concept
showed cunning, rather than intelligence; his lips were straight, think that, drawn in over the teeth his cheek-bones , a never failing proof of audacity and craftiness: flatness of his forehead	B) social status	B),C),D) are all Repeating the Question because they are all parts of the sentence that asks for the reason. E) Opposite
	C) stylish attire	
	D) age, desire to be seen	
	E) truthful	

UNAUTHORIZED COPYING OR REUSE OF ANY PART OF THIS PAGE IS ILLEGAL

Test 1 ABSOLUTE PATTERNS for the Analogy Section

Q31. Absolute Pattern 2: Part-Whole Pattern

B is the best answer

Cattle (Whole) is to cow (Part); star (part) is to constellation (whole)

Although the order is flipped over, there is no other selection available except B.

*Constellation = a group of stars

Q32. Absolute Pattern 7: Association (Characteristic) Pattern

A is the best answer

1> Doctors give pills; baseball coaches give signs.

2> Both doctors and baseball coaches use (give) pills and signs respectively to operate their works.

3> Pills and signs, underpinning such a characteristic, are similar and provide the similar function in their unique purpose or existence.

4> They are both human concept

Q33. Absolute Pattern 7: Association (Characteristic) Pattern

D is the best answer

Both motel and stadium reserve guests and crowd respectively.

1> Choice A is wrong because coffee is a non-human concept although cups reserve coffee.

2> Choice E is wrong

3> Although (E) police station reserve police, its characteristic is different from that of the question and (D)

4> Guest and crowd are visitor-concept, while police is the host concept.

5> Therefore, (E) is less associated with the question

Q34. Absolute Pattern 2: Part-Whole Pattern + 7: Association (Characteristic) Pattern

C is the best answer.

Stanza is a group of lines in a poem; Paragraph is a group of sentences in writing.

In that sense, both Stanza and paragraph are whole, while both lines and sentences are parts.

They have the same characteristics and close associations than any other choices.

Q35. Absolute Pattern 5: Degree Pattern + 13: Mental-Physical Pattern

C is the best answer

1> Anguish is the greater degree of mentality than sadness.

2> Exultation is the greater degree of mentality than joy.

3> (A), (B), (D), (E) are all incorrect because they are all physical concept

4> That is, all the options are true statements underpinning the degree patterns

5> However, the subcategorization split the choices between the mental and physical concept.

Q.36 Absolute Pattern 4: Synonym Pattern

B is the best answer

Lunar is synonym to the moon; solar is synonym to the sun

Both choices A and C are part and whole patterns.

Q37. Absolute Pattern 4: Synonym Pattern

A is the best answer

The adherent is a synonym to a follower; Demagogue is a synonym to boss.

(D) is a true statement in synonym, but is a nonhuman concept, therefore, less associated with the question.

Q38. Absolute Pattern 1: Production (Cause-Effect) Pattern

E is the best answer.

Ambition produces achieve (achievement); lazy, fail.

Although each choice has a little bit of cause-effect relation, the conceptual similarity is not as clear as (E)

Q39. Absolute Pattern 7: Association (Characteristic) Pattern

D is the best answer

The characteristics of a desert are arid as the characteristic of a swamp is humid. Choice A and B are incorrect because they are human concept, while the question is a nonhuman concept.

Choice E is incorrect because the characteristics associated with the climate in the question and (D) are not evident

Q40. Absolute Pattern 1: Production (Cause-Effect) Pattern

E is the best answer

Celebrity creates (produces) awe; cow produces milk.

Choice A) is incorrect because the order has to be 'cry is to calf,' instead of 'calf is to cry' to maintain the same order as the question.

Q41. Absolute Pattern 6:Purpose (Job/Tool) Pattern

B is the best answer.

The purpose of healing is to treat wounds, the purpose of repair is to treat malfunction

Q42. Absolute Pattern 6:Purpose (Job/Tool) Pattern

E is the best answer

Handcuff is used as a tool to arrest; lamp is used as a tool for light.

Q43. Absolute Pattern 3: Antonym (Positive-Negative) Pattern

E is the best answer

Arrogant is the antonym to humble as forget is the antonym to remember.

Q44. Absolute Pattern 7: Association (Characteristic) Pattern

E is the best answer
Association Relations: WATCH! IT GOES LIKE THIS.
Legible is to articulate

(E) speak is to write

Articulate: speak clearly. Legible: write clearly

Q45. Absolute Pattern 7: Association (Characteristic) Pattern

E is the best answer.

Newspaper has a typo (a negative characteristic) as personality has a flaw (a negative characteristic)

A) is too extreme. (B), (C) are the parts of personal characteristics, but do not have the clear negative value.

Q46. Absolute Pattern 4: Synonym Pattern

D is the best answer

Discrepancy is a synonym to difference as equivalent is a synonym to equal.

Choice C is wrong because same and similar is different in degree.

Q47. Absolute Pattern 4: Synonym Pattern

D is the best answer

Equivocal is a synonym to unclear as equal society is a synonym to egalitarian

Equivocal = unclear, equal society = egalitarian

Q48. Absolute Pattern 1: Production (Cause-Effect) Pattern

E is the best answer

Volcano produces eruption; well produces spring.

Q49. Absolute Pattern 3: Antonym (Positive-Negative) Pattern

A is the best answer

Faction is antonym to union as cold is antonym to hot.

*Faction is a small, organized, dissenting group within a larger one

Q50. Absolute Pattern 7: Association (Characteristic) Pattern

D is the best answer

Futile is to arid as harvest is to plantation.

Arid is negative or unproductive just as Futile, while plantation is positive or productive just as harvest.

Q51. Absolute Pattern 1: Production (Cause-Effect) Pattern

E is the best answer.

Factory produces goods as fire produces heat.

Choice A: art center does not produce paintings; it displays it.

Choice C and D are flipped over

Q52. Absolute Pattern 3: Antonym (Positive-Negative) Pattern

A is the best answer

Habit is an antonym to innate as practice is an antonym to talent.

Choice D is wrong because, although the true statement in antonym pattern, it doesn't contain human values.

Q53. Absolute Pattern 2: Part-Whole Pattern

B is the best answer

Part-whole Relations

Romance is a part of the literary Genre. Cell is a part of an organism.

Q54. Absolute Pattern 1: Production (Cause-Effect) Pattern

D is the best answer

Being gentle produces praise; diligent produces success.

Q55. Absolute Pattern 1: Production (Cause-Effect) Pattern

D is the best answer

Abrasion (rubbing) produces ignition (ignite); Mistakes produces failure.

Choice B is vague in relation.

Choice C is flipped over

Q56. Absolute Pattern 2: Part-Whole Pattern

B is the best answer.

Ink cartridge belongs to (a part of) a printer; seat belongs to (a part of) a theater.

Choice A is wrong because candle is not part of a cake .

Choice C is wrong because employee and staff are the synonym.

Choice D is wrong because tomato and banana are within the same level of food category.

Choice E is wrong because the word order is flipped over.

Q57. Absolute Pattern 3: Antonym (Positive-Negative) Pattern

C is the best answer

Immense is opposite to narrow; sad movie is opposite to parody.

Q58. Absolute Pattern 3: Antonym (Positive-Negative) Pattern

B is the best answer

Improvisation is antonym to preparation; hostility is antonym to sympathy.

Improvisation means something done without preparation.

Hostility (dislike) sympathy (like)

Q59. Absolute Pattern 4: Synonym Pattern

E is the best answer

Synonym + Positive Relations

Unique is synonym to original as elegant is to attract.

A, B are synonyms but still incorrect because they have the negative value, while the question and (E) are positive.

Q60. Absolute Pattern 7: Association (Characteristic) Pattern

A is the best answer

The myth is filled with marvel just as history is filled with fact. The same characteristics

Choice B is wrong because biography is not defined by a true story, but a personal story.

Test 1 Recap

Word-in-Context Questions

Word-in-context (WIC) in the reading passage can be either literal or figurative. For instance, the word "fire" has several definitions: it could be fire with heat and flame, or it could be "love" between lovers.

WIC question despises options inhabit too literally. What is very normal in literal meaning does not fit in the psychology of WIC. That's why those who are desperately seeking the correct answer while struggling with the inner voice: *"why it should be so unusual for picking literal"* often choose an awful option.

The quintessential point is to understand the psychology of WIC.

To get to the right point, we should categorize WIC first:

Interpretation of Word

As seen in the Test 1, question 1 "mixed up"—relies on the qualification of emotion rather than literal meaning of the word.

While the answer (C) presents the qualification of emotion, options (A), (B) ,and (D) adopt the degree of literal meaning "mixed up"

Active vs. Passive Mental Concept

Imagine your loved one is dying in bed in front of you, you may feel terribly sad. That's the (pro) active mental concept".

The same degree of active emotional involvement goes with the feeling of rage or humiliation.

On the contrary, if you see an actor dying in bed while you are watching a movie that you have no idea why this actor is dying, your sad feeling is transformed to mere sympathy or passive mental concept.

Rhetoric Underpinning the Tone, Style and Meaning.

The tone often accompanies with negative-positive tone.

SSAT
Reading & Verbal Practice
Test 2

ALL THE LOGIC AND RULES

BEHIND THE EVERY SINGLE

SSAT QUESTION

Test 2 Reading Section
Time: 40 Minutes, 40 Questions

Directions: Each reading passage is followed by questions about it. Answer the questions that follow a passage on the basis of what is stated or implied in that passage.

Questions 1-6 are based on the following passage.

Line

Anyone familiar with the scope of biological enquiry, and the methods of biological instruction, will not need to be reminded that it is only by the most rigorous employment of precise directions for observation, that any good results are to be looked for at the hand of the elementary student.

5   In the case of two among the few students who passed through my hands, the result far exceeded my most sanguine anticipations. The notes sent in by one of them-- a man working at a distance, alone and unaided-- far excelled those wrung from many a student placed under the most favorable surroundings; and their promise for the future has been fulfilled to the utmost, the individual in question being now a recognized investigator. It thus became clear

10 that, not-with-standing the complex conditions of work in the biological field, tuition by correspondence would suffice to awaken the latent abilities of a naturally qualified enquirer.

Mr. Wells' little book is avowedly written for examination purposes, and in conformity with the requirements of the now familiar "type system" of teaching. Recent attempts have been made to depreciate this among a quarter of critics. No method of studying-- more especially

15 when the objects of study are tangible things-- can rival that prosecuted under the direction and in the constant presence of a teacher who has also a living and vivid knowledge of the matter which he handles with the student.

1

The word "rigorous" in line 2 most nearly means

A) diligent

B) extremely careful

C) convenient

D) repeating continuously

E) interesting

2

Which of the following analogy would resemble "the method of studying" mentioned in line 14?

A) A school sets out on a spring field trip

B) An instructor teaches alphabet to boys

C) Children attempt to learn magic by themselves

D) A math teacher teaches some theory to his students

E) A well-known former football player regularly plays with the youth in a community

CONTINUE

3

By referring to "the hand of the elementary student" (line 4), the author conveys the importance of

A) clarity
B) affordability
C) age limit
D) simplicity
E) legality

4

The author claims that the scope of biological enquiry should be the one with

A) an individualized attempt
B) the creativity
C) the utmost enjoyment
D) a unique method
E) a painstaking process

5

The primary function of the second paragraph (lines 5-11) is to

A) make a comparison
B) dispute a hypothesis
C) settle a controversy
D) justify a limitation
E) highlight an opinion

6

In lines 12-17, the author's descriptions of Mr. Wells' little book present the book

A) aroused some criticism
B) was unable to depict the familiar type of teaching
C) misled the purposes of examination
D) received a unanimous approval
E) was mediocre

Questions 7-12 are based on the following passage.

Line

For thousands of years before men had any accurate and exact knowledge of the changes of material things, they had thought about these changes, regarded them as revelations of spiritual truths, built on them theories of things in heaven and earth (and a good many things in neither), and used them in manufactures, arts, and handicrafts, especially in one very

5　curious manufacture wherein not the thousandth fragment of a grain of the finished article was ever produced.

　　The accurate and systematic study of the changes which material things undergo is called chemistry; we may, perhaps, describe alchemy as the superficial, and what may be called subjective, examination of these changes, and the speculative systems, and imaginary arts and

10　manufactures, founded on that examination.

　　We are assured by many old writers that Adam was the first alchemist. Certainly alchemy had a long life, for chemistry did not begin until about the middle of the 18th century.

　　No branch of science has had so long a period of incubation as chemistry. There must be some extraordinary difficulty in the way of disentangling the steps of those changes wherein

15　substances of one kind are produced from substances totally unlike them.

CONTINUE

7

The paragraph 1 implies that people

A) today rely less on spiritual truth than on science

B) lived without any knowledge for thousands of years

C) today do not realize how valuable the spiritual truth is

D) found pleasure in manufactures, arts, and handcrafts for thousands of years

E) today still apply theories of things in heaven and earth

8

The author's statement "the thousandth…article" in line 5 represents

A) a singularly valuable article

B) a particularly spiritual article

C) embarrassingly poor quality

D) an exceedingly infinitesimal article

E) a considerably old article

9

The author regards alchemists with

A) cynicism

B) bafflement

C) appreciation

D) nostalgia

E) resentment

10

The author's statement "the thousandth…article" in line 5 mostly like refers to

A) chemistry

B) spiritual truths

C) atoms

D) seeds

E) tangible things

11

The tone of author's remark in line 13 ("No branch of science…as chemistry.) is

A) great conviction

B) guarded concern

C) playful irony

D) religious veneration

E) cynicism

12

In line 13 (No branch of science…as chemistry.) the author emphasizes

A) the way alchemy hampered the scientific progress

B) the duration the modern chemistry contributed to the world

C) the extraordinarily difficult period chemistry had to undergone

D) the period people misunderstood between alchemy and chemistry

E) the extent to which alchemy contributed to modern chemistry

CONTINUE

Questions 13-18 are based on the following passage.

Line

In the examination of a sick horse it is important to have a method or system. If a definite plan of examination is followed one may feel reasonably sure, when the examination is finished, that no important point has been overlooked and that the examiner is in a position to arrive at an opinion that is as accurate as is possible for him.

5 Of course, an experienced eye can see, and a trained hand can feel, slight alterations or variations from the normal that are not perceptible to the unskilled observer. A thorough knowledge of the conditions that exist in health is of the highest importance, because it is only by a knowledge of what is right that one can surely detect a wrong condition.

A knowledge of anatomy, or of the structure of the body, and of physiology, or the functions

10 and activities of the body, lie at the bottom of accuracy of diagnosis. It is important to remember that animals of different races or families deport themselves differently under the influence of the same disease or pathological process. The sensitive and highly organized thoroughbred resists cerebral depression more than does the lymphatic draft horse.

Hence a degree of fever that does not produce marked dullness in a thoroughbred may cause

15 the most abject dejection in a coarsely bred, heavy draft horse.

13

The primary purpose of the passage is to

A) inform the guidelines to the new veterinarians

B) train ranchers to treat the sick animal well

C) discuss why horses of different breed react differently to the same disease

D) explain important principles of raising animals

E) survey the contribution made by veterinarians

14

The statement in lines 1-4 suggests that

A) the effective examination of a sick horse is more a method than plan

B) veterinarian's works require identifiable steps with scrutiny

C) veterinarian often forget the important method

D) the excellent veterinarian cannot be made without having a thorough method or system

E) people need to be more attuned to a sick animal

CONTINUE

15

According to the author, the knowledge of anatomy is based on the

A) experienced eye

B) trained hand

C) accuracy of diagnosis.

D) knowledge about pet

E) knowledge to cure any disease

16

The passage implies that if a coarsely bred, heavy draft horse experiences a minor dullness to a fever, a thoroughbred will experience

A) a typical symptom that only thoroughbred can experience

B) worse symptom than coarsely bred's

C) an unpredictable symptom

D) the same degree as the coarsely bred horse does

E) a very little, if no symptom at all

17

According to the passage, "the sensitive and highly organized thoroughbred"

A) demands more attention

B) is intrinsically valuable

C) does not work together with veterinarian

D) rarely gets sick

E) is robust

18

In line 15, "abject" most nearly means

A) total

B) significant

C) a little

D) sporadic

E) prolonged

CONTINUE

Questions 19-24 are based on the following passage.

Line

One day in spring four men were riding on horseback along a country road. These men were lawyers, and they were going to the next town to attend court. There had been a rain, and the ground was very soft like mashed potato. The four lawyers rode along, one behind another; for the pathway was narrow, and the mud on each side of it was deep. As they were passing

5 through a grove of small trees, they heard "Cheep! cheep! cheep!" came from the wet grass.

"What is the matter here?" asked the first lawyer, whose name was Speed. "Oh, it's only some old robins!" said the second lawyer, whose name was Hardin. "The storm has blown two of the little ones out of the nest. They are too young to fly, and the mother bird is making a great fuss about it." "What a pity! They'll die down there in the grass," said the third lawyer, whose

10 name I forget. "Oh, well! They're nothing but birds," said Mr. Hardin. "We ain't gonna bother" "Yes, why should we?" said Mr. Speed. The three men, as they passed, looked down and saw the little birds fluttering in the cold, wet grass. But the fourth lawyer, whose name was Abraham Lincoln, stopped. He got down from his horse and very gently took the little ones up in his big warm hands. They did not seem frightened, but chirped softly, as if they knew they

15 were safe like their mother. "Never mind, my little fellows." he said.

19

The three lawyers in the passage would most likely view the action of Mr. Lincoln with the

A) mild disapproval

B) considerable surprise

C) cynical mistrust

D) cautious optimism

E) complete appreciation

20

The narrator would most likely characterize the lawyer named Hardin as

A) insightful

B) atypical

C) simplistic

D) aloof

E) absurd

CONTINUE

21

The literary device used in 5 "Cheep!" is

A) Onomatopoeia

B) Euphemism

C) Consonance

D) Cacophony

E) Assonance

22

Throughout the passage, the narrator applies all of the following literary devices EXCEPT

A) personification

B) simile

C) cliché

D) slang

E) onomatopoeia

23

The narrator of the passage uses the quotation " never mind, my little fellows," primarily as a

A) vivid expression of how the person views the nature

B) powerful example of how a heroic person should act in a major crisis

C) credible historical citation from the government archives

D) comical introduction to a problem

E) pragmatic assessment of one person's action

CONTINUE

Questions 24-29 are based on the following passage.

Line   I have just buried my boy, my poor handsome boy of whom I was so proud, and my heart is
broken. It is very hard having only one son to lose him thus, but God's will be done. Who am I
that I should complain? The great wheel of Fate rolls on like a Juggernaut, and crushes us all
in turn, some soon, some late--it does not matter when, in the end, it crushes us all.

5   We do not prostrate ourselves before it like the poor Indians; we fly hither and thither--we cry
for mercy; but it is of no use, the black fate thunders on and in its season reduces us to
powder.

    Poor Harry to go so soon! just when his life was opening to him. He was doing so well at the
hospital, he had passed his last examination with honors, and I was proud of them, much

10 prouder than he was, I think. And then he must needs go to that smallpox hospital. He wrote to
me that he was not afraid of smallpox and wanted to gain the experience; and now the
disease has killed him, and I, old and grey and withered, am left to mourn over him, without a
chick or child to comfort me. I might have saved him, too--I have money enough for both of
us, and much more than enough--King Solomon's Mines provided me with that; but I said,

15 "No, let the boy earn his living, let him labor that he may enjoy rest." But the rest has come to
him before the labor. Oh, my boy, my boy! 'I am like the man in the Bible who laid up much
goods and builded barns--goods for my boy and barns for him to store them in.

24

In line 7, "prostate" most nearly means

A) sitting down

B) postpone

C) dying

D) fight

E) being quiet

25

"he wrote...comfort me." in lines 10-13 conveys the narrator's

A) justification of the situation

B) enthusiasm in spite of the circumstance

C) ambivalent feeling toward his son's death

D) regret to the significant outcome

E) advice to the reader about the dangers of smallpox

CONTINUE

26

The word used in line 5, "hither and thither" can be defined in literary form as

A) classic

B) assonance

C) consonance

D) jargon

E) metaphor

27

The narrator's explanation in the first paragraph (lines 1-7) suggests that

A) our lives will be fulfilled through God

B) our fate is independent from God's will

C) God feels the full range of human emotion

D) there's nothing we can do

E) we can create our own fate

28

Throughout the passage, the narrator's tone is best described as

A) measured frustration

B) concerned

C) ambivalent

D) encouragement

E) lamentation

29

The phrase "enjoy rest. But the rest " used in lines 15 can be best understood respectively as

A) love and fate

B) dignity and moral

C) respite and dying

D) play and rest

E) old and young

CONTINUE

Questions 30-35 are based on the following passage.

Line   Virtual Reality (VR) systems are relatively new visual display interaction methods that
enable the user to experience virtual environments (VEs) by letting the user to immerse into
the synthetic and artificial environment.

VR's capability that allows the user to interact with VEs in a strikingly different and complex
5   pattern has excited various industries to cope with its technological progress. According to
Deloitte Global, VR hardware and software are expected to be the major consumer market
drivers garnering $120 billion by 2020. Such a forecast gets the momentum and validation as
consumers are becoming more and more comfortable with "good enough" smartphones, which
will look for a new market replacement and driver.

10   However, like all new modes of developments such as TV, Internet, and smartphone
experienced in their initial stages, VR systems could not escape from the harsh criticisms
within both academia and the concerned public. Their major concerns are as extensive as VR
get attention from consumers, to name a few from Physical, Psychological, physiological, and
educational, etc.

15   With all due respect, criticism from those who blame the dangers of VR to the kids is
grossly misguided and trivial compared to the benefits that VR can bring to the kids.
The purpose of this report is to identify the scope of potential harmful effects when using VR
that are discussed widely, and will eventually put such a misconception into the correct
perspectives.

30

The primary purpose of the passage is to

A) invalidate the effectiveness of the gadget

B) examine closely the impact of the new gadget

C) compare VR with other mode of the development

D) forecast VR's overall sales figure in 2020

E) raise concern to the kids using VR

31

The quotation in "good enough" (line 8)
represents the smartphone industry's?

A) concern

B) enthusiasm

C) optimism

D) anger

E) beneficial in the long-term

CONTINUE

32

Which best describes the consumer's reaction to the smartphone these days

A) They are reluctant to better technology

B) They are attentive to new technology

C) They grossly ignore smartphone

D) They try to stop using smartphone

E) They prefer cheaper smartphone

33

In lines 10-12 ("like all new …public."), the author mainly suggests that VR's initial criticism

A) is historically parallel

B) is an outmoded warning

C) fails to recognize the major contribution to society

D) severely damaged its growth from the initial stage

E) successfully transformed VR as the valuable gadget

34

The author's reaction toward critics who blame the dangers of VR can be summarized as

A) anxious defiance

B) genuine hostility

C) spirited agreement

D) measured disagreement

E) mild consent

35

This passage can be mainly found in the

A) smartphone company advertisement

B) VR system manual

C) consumer watchdog guidelines for kids

D) report prepared by a student researching VR

E) smartphone industry annual report

CONTINUE

Questions 36-40 are based on the following passage.

Line   On an exceptionally hot evening early in July a young man came out of the garret in which
he lodged in S. Place and walked slowly, as though in hesitation, towards K. bridge.
He had successfully avoided meeting his landlady on the staircase.

    His garret was under the roof of a high, five-storied house and was more like a cupboard
5   than a room. The landlady who provided him with garret, dinners, and attendance, lived on the
floor below, and every time he went out he was obliged to pass her kitchen, the door of which
invariably stood open. And each time he passed, the young man had a sick, frightened feeling,
which made him scowl and feel ashamed. He was hopelessly in debt to his landlady, and was
afraid of meeting her.

10   This was not because he was cowardly and abject, quite the contrary; but for some time past
he had been in an overstrained irritable condition, verging on hypochondria. He had become
so completely absorbed in himself, and isolated from his fellows that he dreaded meeting, not
only his landlady, but anyone at all. He was crushed by poverty, but the anxieties of his
position had of late ceased to weigh upon him. He had given up attending to matters of
15   practical importance; he had lost all desire to do so. Nothing that any landlady could do had a
real terror for him. But to be stopped on the stairs, to be forced to listen to her trivial,
irrelevant gossip, to pestering demands for payment, threats and complaints, and to rack his
brains for excuses, to prevaricate, to lie--no, rather than that, he would creep down the stairs
like a cat and slip out unseen.

36

Which of the following old sayings is best applied
to the narrator's situation?
A) The grass is always greener on the other side of
   the fence
B) Time heals all wounds
C) Absence makes the heart grow fonder
D) There's no time like the present
E) Leave well enough alone

37

In the second paragraph (lines 4-9) the narrator
describes that the house
A) offers views of the surrounding countryside
B) serves meals like a local restaurant
C) converted a cupboard into a rental room
D) is well maintained by a charm landlady
E) has only one entrance

CONTINUE

38

The third paragraph (lines 10-19) suggests that the conversation between the narrator and the landlady has been

A) overshadowed by an unspoken resentment

B) carried out for the benefit of the narrator

C) always joyful

D) a part of a ritual which he wishes to avoid

E) baffling to those who may overhear it

39

In line 17, "trivial" means

A) considerable

B) important

C) insignificant

D) heartfelt

E) resentment

40

In lines 15-19 (nothing that any…slip out unseen.) depicts the landlady as

A) an ignorant person

B) a wealthy and attentive person

C) a person living in a confinement

D) a person enjoying a social distinction

E) a harmless person

Test 2 Verbal Section   30 MINUTES, 60 QUESTIONS

Directions: the synonym questions ask you to find the most appropriate synonym to the question.

The analogy questions ask you to find the most appropriate analogy to the question.
Select the answer that best matches to the question.

Synonym Sample Question:

Q: SUPERIOR

A higher rank

B inferior

C considerable

D supermarket

E supper

A) is the best answer because the synonym for superior is higher rank.

B) is incorrect because it applies the 'opposite concept.

C) and E) are irrelevant words.

D) is incorrect because it applies physical concept to mental concept

Test 2 Synonym questions 1 to 30

1. EERIE

(A) ear

(B) check

(C) correction

(D) error

(E) frightening

2. ELUDE

(A) lure

(B) luminary

(C) evade

(D) exit

(E) meeting

3. EFFICIENT

(A) efficacious

(B) evolve

(C) expansive

(D) fuse

(E) unusual

4. ESTEEM

(A) heat

(B) respect

(C) standing out

(D) clear

(E) stymie

5. EXPLOIT

(A) use

(B) moving

(C) explosion

(D) reach out

(E) late

CONTINUE

6. EXTRACT

(A) removal

(B) traction

(C) factor

(D) extrapolation

(E) exterminate

7. INGENIOUS

(A) engender

(B) genuine

(C) innocent

(D) generations

(E) gentle

8. INNOVATION

(A) novel

(B) noble

(C) cultivation

(D) trust

(E) notorious

9. LIBERATE

(A) leverage

(B) life

(C) free

(D) vibrate

(E) shackle

10. INTIMIDATION

(A) hostility

(B) intimacy

(C) precision

(D) combination

(E) round

11. JOVIAL

(A) promise

(B) cheerful

(C) capitalization

(D) mood

(E) relation

12. INCIDENTAL

(A) dependent

(B) minor

(C) untrue

(D) stylish

(E) loaded

13. REPLICA

(A) item

(B) motion

(C) worry

(D) function

(E) copy

14. INTERSECT

(A) recognize

(B) obtain

(C) predict

(D) converge

(E) dilute

15. FRETFUL

(A) provoked

(B) occupied

(C) worried

(D) masked

(E) ruined

CONTINUE

16. MAYHEM

(A) reform

 (B) hustle

(C) disorder

(D) notion

(E) preference

17. MAR

(A) attach

(B) decide

(C) hustle

(D) broaden

(E) spoil

18. DISCREET

(A) pleasing

(B) tactful

(C) uneasy

(D) guarded

(E) vigilant

19. TEMPERANCE

(A) logic

(B) irritation

(C) hospitality

(D) restraint

(E) protection

20. LIBERATE

(A) release

(B) bond

(C) transfer

(D) conceive

(E) answer

21. EXQUISITE

(A) generous

(B) precise

(C) elegant

(D) noteworthy

(E) justifying

22. PIGMENT

(A) farm feed

(B) color source

(C) blunt object

(D) animal skin

(E) busy schedule

23. PROLOGUE

(A) extension

(B) nonessential part

(C) humorous play

(D) introduction

(E) sequel

24. PLAUSIBLE

(A) reasonable

(B) inventive

(C) momentary

(D) discourteous

(E) overconfident

25. SUBSEQUENT

(A) understanding

(B) following

(C) danger

(D) discrepancy

(E) overwhelming

CONTINUE

26. SUPPLEMENT

(A) extra

(B) join

(C) teacher

(D) complement

(E) end

27. SWARM

(A) flock

(B) swimming

(C) warm

(D) individual

(E) boss

28. TANGIBLE

(A) touchable

(B) intangible

(C) attainable

(D) audible

(E) admissible

29. TERMINATE

(A) discontinue

(B) criticize

(C) gather

(D) build

(E) replace

30. TERRAIN

(A) body

(B) track

(C) land

(D) rainforest

(E) piece

Analogy Sample Question:

Q: River is to Ocean as:

A better is to good

B rain is to cloud

C father is to mother

D city is to country

E fork is to spoon

D is the correct answer. Just as the river is smaller than the Ocean, the city is smaller than the country. The pattern applied in this question is the Degree Pattern (small to big)

A) is incorrect because the word order is flipped over.

B) is incorrect because it applies the production pattern (cloud produces rain)

C), E) are incorrect because they apply the Antonym patterns.

Test 2 Analogy questions 31 to 60

31. Seat is to sit as

(A) car is to drive

(B) horn is to deer

(C) tire is to car

(D) foot is to human

(E) branch is to tree

CONTINUE

32. Sweet is sugar as

(A) legend is to book

(B) leaves is to grass

(C) ice is to winter

(D) water is to snow

(E) salt is to ocean

33. Believe is to real as tired is to

(A) sleep

(B) dream

(C) fatigue

(D) thirsty

(E) invest

34. Invest is to save as prodigal is to

(A) money

(B) conserve

(C) wisdom

(D) interview

(E) consume

35. Legends is to map as

(A) Menu is to restaurant

(B) excerpt is to noble

(C) close-up is to movie

(D) dance is to choreography

(E) election is to politics

36. Poem is to novel

(A) Backyard is to meadow

(B) kingdom is to king

(C) urban is to city

(D) bus is to car

(E) autumn is to September

37. Old is to die as

(A) born is to baby

(B) senior is to hospital

(C) best friend is to acquaintance

(D) battle is to war

(E) save is to prodigal

38. Training center is to practice as

(A) Court is to judgement

(B) hospital is to nurse

(C) polar is to bear

(D) police station is to police

(E) train station is to train

39. Poetry is to rhythm as

(A) woman is to weak

(B) man is to strong

(C) criminal is to guilty

(D) bus is to large

(E) comedy is to satire

40. Cup is to coffee as

(A) Milk is to glass

(B) cola is to bottle

(C) jug is to beer

(D) van is to tire

(E) ticket is to bus

41. Keyboard is to computer as

(A) lunch is to kitchen

(B) chemicals is to drug

(C) Earth is to moon

(D) finger is to hand

(E) attempt is to failure

CONTINUE

UNAUTHORIZED COPYING OR REUSE OF ANY PART OF THIS PAGE IS ILLEGAL

42. Women is to skirt as

(A) kindergarten girl is to nametag

(B) event is to interesting

(C) dog is to puppy

(D) hockey stick is to hockey

(E) belt is to man

43. Brawl is to war as

(A) sympathy is to friendship

(B) cancer is sick

(C) dark is to dawn

(D) shoplifting is to murder

(E) worm is to snake

44. Bridge is to cross as

(A) gun is to shoot

(B) smoke is to cancer

(C) fortune is to luck

(D) satellite is to orbit

(E) man is to work

45. Work is to cash as

(A) deportation is to smuggle

(B) afternoon is to dark

(C) exam is to study

(D) person is to name

(E) cow is to milk

46. Beautiful is to sublime as

(A) socks is to Jeans

(B) Ugly is to cosmetic surgery

(C) design is to creation

(D) intimacy is to romantic

(E) egg is to sandwich

47. Ancient is to modern as archaic is to

(A) experience

(B) history

(C) new age

(D) date

(E) church

48. Respect is to veneration as

(A) harmony is to marriage

(B) hate is to abomination

(C) lion is to lioness

(D) poor is to hunger

(E) river is to ocean

49. Introvert is to extrovert as convex is to

(A) depressed

(B) emotional

(C) figurative

(D) literal

(E) conspicuous

50. Mathematic is to pure logic as

(A) diamond is to stone

(B) God is to evil

(C) trunk is to wood

(D) religion is church

(E) art is to creation

51. Frequently is to never as seldom is to

(A) always

(B) little

(C) few

(D) periodic

(E) routine

CONTINUE ➤

52. Soldier is to weapon as

(A) gun is to ripple

(B) battle is to war

(C) dictator is to autocracy

(D) cosmologist is to telescope

(E) fortune teller is to money

53. City is to village as country is to

(A) continent

(B) people

(C) government

(D) democracy

(E) politics

54. Infinite is to limitless as

(A) warm is to hot

(B) big is to small

(C) beginning is to end

(D) bank is to money

(E) bland is to boring

55. Animal is to nature as baby is to

(A) child

(B) milk

(C) courage

(D) nurture

(E) human rights

56. Eye glasses is to tire as

(A) monitor is to chopping board

(B) computer is to program

(C) cup is tall

(D) bus is to seat

(E) triangle is to pyramid

57. Chef is to knife as

(A) banker is to money

(B) police is to criminal

(C) computer is to mouse

(D) architect is to blueprint

(E) architect is to hammer

58. Security guard is to building as

(A) vault is to bank

(B) artifact is to museum

(C) fish in the market

(D) maid is to hotel

(E) keeper is to lighthouse

59. Democracy is to parliament as monarch is to

(A) autocrat

(B) president

(C) congressman

(D) governor

(E) compass

60. Cow is to pig as

(A) meadow is to house

(B) bacon is to milk

(C) fire is to water

(D) switch is to darkness

(E) newspaper is to news

STOP

If you finish before time is called,
you may check your work on this section.

Do not turn to the next section.

Test 2

ABSOLUTE PATTERNS

For your Score Interpretation Resources, please use the official SSAT Guidebook or visit:
https://ssat.org/scores/read-score-report/score-interpretation-resources

UNAUTHORIZED COPYING OR REUSE OF ANY PART OF THIS PAGE IS ILLEGAL

TEST 2
READING SECTION

Please refer to the Reading Section Absolute Pattern Analysis next page

THE SYNONYM QUESTIONS THE ANALOGY QUESTIONS
TEST 2 NO.1 ~ 30.   TEST 2 NO. 31 ~ 60

1	E	16	C
2	C	17	E
3	A	18	D
4	B	19	D
5	A	20	A
6	A	21	C
7	C	22	B
8	A	23	D
9	C	24	A
10	A	25	B
11	B	26	A
12	B	27	A
13	E	28	A
14	D	29	A
15	C	30	C

Please refer to the Analogy Section Absolute Pattern Analysis in page 144

Test 2

ABSOLUTE PATTERNS for the Reading Section

Q1. Pattern 5: Word-In-Context Question

Question Pattern: most nearly means

Question Keywords: : The word "rigorous" in line 2

Step 1	Step 2	Step 3
Keywords from the Passage	Keywords from Answer	Tone & Concept
precise directions for observation	B) extremely careful	synonym

Incorrect Choices & Common Patterns		
Evidence	Incorrect keywords	Tone & Concept
that it is only by the most rigorous employment of precise directions for observation	A) diligent	Too weak implication
	C) convenient	Unrelated Word Usage
	D) repeating	
precise + observation = rigorous (careful)	E) interesting	

Q2. Type 3: Analogy Question [Pattern 1: Local Question] {Category A}

Question Pattern: Which of the following analogy would resemble

Question Keywords: "the method of studying" mentioned in line 14?

Step 1	Step 2	Step 3
Keywords from the Passage	Keywords from Answer	Tone & Concept
tangible things, constant presence of a teacher	A) school, spring field trip	Similar Conception

Incorrect Choices & Common Patterns		
Evidence	Incorrect keywords	Tone & Concept
No method of studying-- more especially when the objects of study are **tangible things**-- can rival that prosecuted under the direction and in the constant presence of a teacher	B) teaches alphabet	Intangible
	C) learn magic, themselves	teacher is absent
	D) A math teacher, theory	Intangible
	E) football player plays	teaching is absent

UNAUTHORIZED COPYING OR REUSE OF ANY PART OF THIS PAGE IS ILLEGAL

Q3. Type 2: Inference Question [Pattern 1: Local Question] {Category A}

Question Pattern: By referring to, the author conveys the importance of
Question Keywords: "the hand of the elementary student"

Step 1	Step 2	Step 3
Keywords from the Passage	Keywords from Answer	Tone & Concept
precise directions for observation	A) clarity	Similar Conception
Incorrect Choices & Common Patterns		
Evidence	Incorrect keywords	Tone & Concept
precise directions for observation, that any good results are to be looked for at the hand of the elementary student.	B) affordability	Unrelated word usage
	C) age limit	
	D) simplicity	
	E) legality	

Q4. Pattern 3: Summary Question

Question Pattern: The author claims that
Question Keywords: the scope of biological enquiry should be the one with

Step 1	Step 2	Step 3
Keywords from the Passage	Keywords from Answer	Tone & Concept
precise directions for observation	E) painstaking process	Similar Concept
Incorrect Choices & Common Patterns		
Evidence	Incorrect keywords	Tone & Concept
precise directions for observation, that any good results are to be looked for at the hand of the elementary student.	A) individualized attempt	A) is Opposite
	B) creativity	B) is Minor Issue
	C) utmost enjoyment	C), D) are Not stated in the passage
	D) unique method	

Q5. Pattern 6: Understanding Structure of the Passage

Question Pattern: The primary function of   **Question Keywords:** the second paragraph (lines 5-11) is to

Step 1	Step 2	Step 3
Keywords from the Passage	Keywords from Answer	Tone & Concept
case of two, few students, through my hands,	E) highlight an opinion	the example is highlighted

Incorrect Choices & Common Patterns		
Evidence	Incorrect keywords	Tone & Concept
In the case of two among the few students who passed through my hands,	A) make a comparison	Not stated issue
	B) dispute a hypothesis	Negative
	C) settle a controversy	Negative
	D) justify a limitation	Negative

Q6. Pattern 7: Understanding Attitude / Tone

Question Pattern: the author's descriptions
Question Keywords: Wells' little book present the book, In lines 12-17,

Step 1	Step 2	Step 3
Keywords from the Passage	Keywords from Answer	Tone & Concept
Recent attempts have been made to depreciate	A) **some** criticism	Synonym, Positive by the author

Incorrect Choices & Common Patterns		
Evidence	Incorrect keywords	Tone & Concept
Recent attempts have been made to depreciate this among a quarter of critics.	B) was unable	Negative
	C) misled the purposes	
*For this question (A) "some" is the keyword, not the criticism, which implies some people criticized what the author praises.	D) unanimous approval	Too extreme word usage
	E) was mediocre	Negative

A) criticism is not the author's, but some quarter of critics. The author is positive on books.

Q7. Type 2: Inference Question [Pattern 1: Local Question] {Category A}

Question Pattern: The paragraph 1 implies that people

Step 1	Step 2	Step 3
Keywords from the Passage	Keywords from Answer	Tone & Concept
before men had any accurate, knowledge	A) rely less on spiritual	Similar Conception

Incorrect Choices & Common Patterns		
Evidence	Incorrect keywords	Tone & Concept
For thousands of years <u>before men had any accurate and exact knowledge</u> of the changes of material things, they had thought about these changes, <u>regarded them as revelations of spiritual truths,</u>	B) without any knowledge	Too extreme word usage
	C) today do not realize	Too extreme and opposite
	D) pleasure, manufactures,	Unrelated word usage
	E) today still, heaven	Inconsistent with the question

1> "before men had any accurate knowledge" means people today have more accurate knowledge.

2> Therefore, A) people today rely less on spiritual because they rely more on science

Q8. Type 2: Inference Question [Pattern 1: Local Question] {Category A}

Question Pattern: The author's statement,
Question Keywords: "the thousandth…article" in line 5 represents

Step 1	Step 2	Step 3
Keywords from the Passage	Keywords from Answer	Tone & Concept
the thousandth fragment of a grain	D) infinitesimal	Similar Conception

Incorrect Choices & Common Patterns		
Evidence	Incorrect keywords	Tone & Concept
especially in one very curious manufacture wherein not the thousandth fragment of a grain of the finished article was ever produced. *infinitesimal = extremely small	A) valuable	"thousandth fragment of a grain" may refer to atom that they didn't know its existence.
	B) spiritual	
	C) poor quality	
	E) a considerably old	

Q9. Pattern 7: Understanding Attitude / Tone

Question Pattern: The author regards   **Question Keywords:** alchemists with

Step 1	Step 2	Step 3
Keywords from the Passage	Keywords from Answer	Tone & Concept
results, inquiry must surely be instructive	C) appreciation	Similar Conception

Incorrect Choices & Common Patterns		
Evidence	Incorrect keywords	Tone & Concept
Adam was the first alchemist	A) cynicism	Negative
results of that inquiry must **surely be**	B) bafflement	Negative
instructive.	D) nostalgia	Unrelated word usage
	E) resentment	Negative

Alchemists may view author's statement with appreciation.
Please review the following sentence:

> The author uses a concessional tone; therefore, he does not believe alchemy is superficial.

we may, perhaps, describe alchemy as the superficial, and what may be called subjective, examination of these changes, and the speculative systems, and imaginary arts and manufactures, founded on that examination.

> The author compares Adam and alchemist. (positive)

We are assured by many old writers that Adam was the first alchemist, and we are told by one of the initiated that Adam was created on the sixth day, being the 15th of March, of the first year of the world; certainly alchemy had a long life, for chemistry did not begin until about the middle of the 18th century.

To inquire how those of acute intellects and much learning regarded such occurrences in the times when man's outlook on the world was very different from what it is now, ought to be interesting, and the results of that inquiry must surely be instructive.   The author shows his respect to alchemy

Q10. Type 2: Inference Question [Pattern 1: Local Question] {Category A}

Question Pattern: The author's statement, mostly like refers to
Question Keywords: "the thousandth…article" in line 5

Step 1	Step 2	Step 3
Keywords from the Passage	Keywords from Answer	Tone & Concept
the thousandth fragment of a grain	C) atoms	Similar Conception

Incorrect Choices & Common Patterns		
Evidence	Incorrect keywords	Tone & Concept
especially in one very curious manufacture wherein not the thousandth fragment of a grain of the finished article was ever produced.	A) chemistry B) spiritual truths D) seeds E) tangible things	"thousandth fragment of a grain" may refer to atom that they didn't know its existence.

Q11. Pattern 7: Understanding Attitude / Tone

Question Pattern: The tone of author's remark
Question Keywords: in line 13 ("No branch of science…as chemistry.) is

Step 1	Step 2	Step 3
Keywords from the Passage	Keywords from Answer	Tone & Concept
No branch of science has had so long a period of	A) great conviction	Similar Concept, Positive

Incorrect Choices & Common Patterns		
Evidence	Incorrect keywords	Tone & Concept
No branch of science has had so long a period of incubation as chemistry. The author's statement is clear and emphatic. Therefore, it is made of a great conviction.	B) guarded concern	Negative
	C) playful irony	Negative
	D) religious veneration	Unrelated word usage
	E) cynicism	Negative

Q12. Pattern 3: Summary Question

Question Pattern: the author emphasizes

Question Keywords: In line 18 (No branch of science…as chemistry.)

Step 1	Step 2	Step 3
Keywords from the Passage	Keywords from Answer	Tone & Concept
No branch of science has had so long, as chemistry	E) alchemy contributed	Positive, Similar Conception
Incorrect Choices & Common Patterns		
Evidence	Incorrect keywords	Tone & Concept
had so long (the extent) incubation (contribution)	A) alchemy hampered	Negative
	B) chemistry contributed	modern chemistry is not the focus of the line
	C) chemistry	
	D) people misunderstood	Negative

Q13. Pattern76: Understanding Purpose Question

Question Pattern: The primary purpose of the passage is to

Step 1	Step 2	Step 3
Keywords from the Passage	Keywords from Answer	Tone & Concept
knowledge of anatomy, order of examination	A) guidelines, new veterinarians	Similar Conception

Evidence	Incorrect keywords	Tone & Concept
to treat sick animal well , differently to the same disease	B) train ranchers	Unrelated word usage
	C) why horses	Too specific example
	D) raising animals	Too broad
	E) contribution by veterinarians	Too broad

1> For the primary purpose question, always refer to the concluding paragraph.

2> The underlined portion of the sentence shows to whom this writing is written.

A knowledge of anatomy, or of the structure of the body, and of physiology, or the functions and activities of the body, lie at the bottom of accuracy of diagnosis. It is important to remember…The order of examination, as given hereafter, …

3> As seen in the above underlined portion of the text, the reader should be those who are knowledgeable in practicing medicine to animals. Therefore, the answer should be A)

UNAUTHORIZED COPYING OR REUSE OF ANY PART OF THIS PAGE IS ILLEGAL

Q14. Pattern 3: Summary Question

Question Pattern: The statement suggests that   **Question Keywords:** in lines 1-4

Step 1	Step 2	Step 3
Keywords from the Passage	Keywords from Answer	Tone & Concept
no, overlooked, accurate as possible	B) identifiable steps, scrutiny	synonym

Incorrect Choices & Common Patterns		
Evidence	Incorrect keywords	Tone & Concept
that no important point has been overlooked and that the examiner is in a position to arrive at an opinion that is as accurate as is possible for him.	A) method and a plan C) forget D) the excellent veterinarian E) people need	A) is ruled out because the author uses the method and the plan as synonyms. C) is Negative D) is Opposite E) is Not related issue.

Choice D is incorrect because, as mentioned in the question 13, the primary purpose is to educate the new veterinarian, not 'the excellent veterinarian'.

Choice E is wrong because the passage is not for general people.

Q15. Pattern 3: Summary Question

Question Pattern: According to the author,   **Question Keywords:** the knowledge of anatomy

Step 1	Step 2	Step 3
Keywords from the Passage	Keywords from Answer	Tone & Concept
A knowledge of anatomy, accuracy of diagnosis	C) accuracy of diagnosis.	Synonym

Incorrect Choices & Common Patterns		
Evidence	Incorrect keywords	Tone & Concept
A knowledge of anatomy, or of the structure of the body, and of physiology, or the functions and activities of the body, **lie at the bottom of accuracy of diagnosis**.	A) experienced eye B) trained hand D) knowledge about pet E) cure any disease	D) is Not stated issue E) the main point is not about cure, but about diagnose

Of course, an experienced eye can see, and a trained hand can feel,

Choices A) 'an experienced eye' and B) 'trained hand' are ruled out because the question seeks an answer related to teaching a new veterinarian, not "of course, ...experienced..."

Q16. Type 2: Inference Question [Pattern 1: Local Question] {Category A}

Question Pattern: The passage implies that
Question Keywords: if a coarsely horse experiences a minor dullness to a fever, a thoroughbred would

Step 1	Step 2	Step 3
Keywords from the Passage	Keywords from Answer	Tone & Concept
does not produce marked dullness, may cause ...	E) a very little	Logical Conclusion
Incorrect Choices & Common Patterns		
Evidence	Incorrect keywords	Tone & Concept
Hence a degree of fever that does not produce marked dullness in a thoroughbred may cause the most abject dejection in a coarsely bred, heavy draft horse.	A) a typical symptom	The question is seeking a reverse situation from the passage.
	B) worse symptom	
	C) an unpredictable	
	D) the same degree	

Q17. Pattern 3: Summary Question

Question Pattern: According to the passage,
Question Keywords: "the sensitive and highly organized thoroughbred"

Step 1	Step 2	Step 3
Keywords from the Passage	Keywords from Answer	Tone & Concept
does not produce marked dullness, may cause ...	E) robust	Similar Concept
Incorrect Choices & Common Patterns		
Evidence	Incorrect keywords	Tone & Concept
Hence a degree of fever that does not produce marked dullness in a thoroughbred may cause the most abject dejection in a coarsely bred, heavy draft horse.	A) more attention	As written on the previous question, it will (E) work better in similar symptoms or strong (robust)
	B) valuable	
	C) does not work	
	D) rarely get sick	

Q18. Pattern 5: Word-In-Context Question

Question Pattern: most nearly means **Question Keywords:** In line 15, "abject"

Step 1	Step 2	Step 3
Keywords from the Passage	Keywords from Answer	Tone & Concept
the most abject dejection	A) total	Synonym

Incorrect Choices & Common Patterns		
Evidence	Incorrect keywords	Tone & Concept
the most abject dejection in a coarsely bred, heavy draft horse. Only options B) and A) have the synonyms for "most" in the sentence.	B) significant	abject means total.
	C) a little	
	D) sporadic	
	E) prolonged	

Q19. Pattern 7: Understanding Attitude / Tone

Question Pattern: The three lawyers in the passage would most likely view
Question Keywords: the portrait of Mr. Lincoln with

Step 1	Step 2	Step 3
Keywords from the Passage	Keywords from Answer	Tone & Concept
But the fourth lawyer, Abraham Lincoln, stopped	A) mild disapproval	Logical Conclusion

Incorrect Choices & Common Patterns		
Evidence	Incorrect keywords	Tone & Concept
But the fourth lawyer, whose name was Abraham Lincoln, stopped. He got down from his horse and very gently took the little ones up. A) People usually justify their behaviors first. Therefore, mild disapproval of opposite action.	B) considerable surprise	Not Supported by the passage. E) They might appreciate, but should have justified their behavior first.
	C) cynical mistrust	
	D) cautious optimism	
	E) complete appreciation	

Q20. Pattern 7: Understanding Attitude / Tone

Question Pattern: The narrator would most likely characterize
Question Keywords: the lawyer named Hardin as

Step 1	Step 2	Step 3
Keywords from the Passage	Keywords from Answer	Tone & Concept
Oh, well! They're nothing but birds	D) aloof	aloof means standing off

Incorrect Choices & Common Patterns		
Evidence	Incorrect keywords	Tone & Concept
Oh, well! They're nothing but birds," said Mr. Hardin. "We ain't gonna bother"	A) insightful	Unrelated word usage
	B) atypical	
	C) simplistic	
	E) absurd	

Q21. Pattern 5: Word-In-Context Question

Question Pattern: The literary device used   **Question Keywords:** in 5 "Cheep!" is

Step 1	Step 2	Step 3
Keywords from the Passage	Keywords from Answer	Tone & Concept
"Cheep! cheep! cheep!"	A) Onomatopoeia	Similar Concept

Incorrect Choices & Common Patterns		
Evidence	Incorrect keywords	Tone & Concept
they heard "Cheep! cheep! cheep!" came from the wet grass.	B) Euphemism	'onomatopoeia' refers to words whose very sound is very close to the pronunciation to the actual sound they represent.
	C) Consonance	
	D) Cacophony	
	E) Assonance	

B) Euphemism: a mild expression for a harsh word

C) Consonance: the recurrence of similar sounds

D) Cacophony: a harsh, discordant sounds.

E) Assonance: The repetition of the sound of a vowel

Q22. Pattern 5: Word-In-Context Question

Question Pattern: Throughout the passage, the narrator applies all, literary devices EXCEPT

Step 1	Step 2	Step 3
Keywords from the Passage	Keywords from Answer	Tone & Concept
cliché means overused word like a proverb	C) cliché	Logical Conclusion

Incorrect Choices & Common Patterns		
Evidence	Incorrect keywords	Tone & Concept
Never mind, my little fellows (personification)	A) personification	There is no cliché, the overused word like proverb
they were safe like their mother. (simile)	B) simile	
"We ain't gonna bother" (slang)	D) slang	
"Stith! stith! stith!" (onomatopoeia)	E) onomatopoeia	

Q23. Pattern 7: Understanding Attitude / Tone

Question Pattern: The narrator of the passage uses the quotation
Question Keywords: "never mind, my little fellows," primarily as a

Step 1	Step 2	Step 3
Keywords from the Passage	Keywords from Answer	Tone & Concept
"Never mind, my little fellows." he said.	A) vivid expression	Similar Concept

Incorrect Choices & Common Patterns		
Evidence	Incorrect keywords	Tone & Concept
But the fourth lawyer, whose name was Abraham Lincoln, stopped. "Never mind, my little fellows." he said.	B) powerful example	Too extreme word usage
	C) government archives	Not stated
	D) comical	Opposite
	E) pragmatic assessment	Too extreme word usage

Q24. Pattern 5: Word-In-Context Question

Question Pattern: most nearly means	Question Keywords: In line 7, "prostate"	
Step 1	Step 2	Step 3
Keywords from the Passage	Keywords from Answer	Tone & Concept
prostrate ourselves, like the poor Indians; we fly	A) sitting down	Similar Concept
Incorrect Choices & Common Patterns		
Evidence	Incorrect keywords	Tone & Concept
We do not prostrate ourselves before it like the poor Indians; we fly hither and thither--we cry for mercy; but it	B) postpone	Unrelated word usage
	C) dying	
	D) fight	
	E) being quiet	

1> The sentence around the word "prostate" is passive tone such as "poor Indians"

2> This is the stark contrast to the following active tone like "we fly..."

3> The two underlined portions of the sentences shows opposite situation.

4> Prostrate vs. fly. Therefore, the answer is A.

Q25. Pattern 7: Understanding Attitude / Tone

Question Pattern: conveys the narrator's	Question Keywords: "he wrote...comfort me." in lines 10-13	
Step 1	Step 2	Step 3
Keywords from the Passage	Keywords from Answer	Tone & Concept
He wrote to me that he was not afraid of smallpox	D) regret	Logical Conclusion
Incorrect Choices & Common Patterns		
Evidence	Incorrect keywords	Tone & Concept
He wrote to me that he was not afraid of smallpox and wanted to gain the experience; and now the disease has killed him, ···.and now the disease has killed him.	A) Justification	We can see that the narrator didn't know the significance of the smallpox, which killed him,
	B) enthusiasm	
	C) ambivalent	
	E) advice	

Q26. Pattern 5: Word-In-Context Question

Question Pattern: The word used, can be defined in literary form as
Question Keywords: in line 5, "hither and thither"

Step 1	Step 2	Step 3
Keywords from the Passage	Keywords from Answer	Tone & Concept
We fly hither and thither	A) classic	Synonym

Incorrect Choices & Common Patterns		
Evidence	Incorrect keywords	Tone & Concept
B) assonance: resemblance of vowel sound C) consonance: a repetition of harmonious sound D) Jargon: a technical language E) metaphor: a figure of speech	B) assonance C) consonance D) jargon E) metaphor	We fly hither and thither is a classic language meaning from one place to another.

Q27. Pattern 3: Summary Question

Question Pattern: The narrator's explanation in the first paragraph
Question Keywords: (lines 1-7) suggests that

Step 1	Step 2	Step 3
Keywords from the Passage	Keywords from Answer	Tone & Concept
Who am I that I should complain?	D) there's nothing we can do	Similar Concept

Incorrect Choices & Common Patterns		
Evidence	Incorrect keywords	Tone & Concept
It is very hard having only one son to lose him thus, but God's will be done. Who am I that I should complain?	A) fulfilled through God B) independent from God's C) God feels E) we can create	The overall tone is negative, passive, and the pervasive depression. He is helplessly calling God's will. A),B),C), E) are all positive

Q28. Pattern 5: Word-In-Context Question

Question Pattern: Throughout the passage, the narrator's tone is best described as

Step 1	Step 2	Step 3
Keywords from the Passage	Keywords from Answer	Tone & Concept
my heart is broken.	E) lamentation	Similar Concept

Incorrect Choices & Common Patterns		
Evidence	Incorrect keywords	Tone & Concept
I have just buried my boy, my poor handsome boy of whom I was so proud, and my heart is broken. *lamentation = extremely sad	A) measured frustration	The author's tone is extremely sad because his son's life was taken away.
	B) concerned	
	C) ambivalent	
	D) encouragement	

Q29. Pattern 5: Word-In-Context Question

Question Pattern: The phrase can be best understood respectively as
Question Keywords: "enjoy rest. But the rest " used in lines 15

Step 1	Step 2	Step 3
Keywords from the Passage	Keywords from Answer	Tone & Concept
enjoy rest." But the rest has come to him	C) respite and dying	Logical Conclusion

Incorrect Choices & Common Patterns		
Evidence	Incorrect keywords	Tone & Concept
"No, let the boy earn his living, let him labor that he may enjoy rest." But the rest has come to him before the labor.	A) love and fate	Euphemism is employed to mollify the death of his young son. rest (play) v. Rest (dying)
	B) dignity and moral	
	D) play and rest	
	E) old and young	

Q30. Pattern 2: Main Idea Question

Question Pattern: The primary purpose of the passage is to

Step 1	Step 2	Step 3
Keywords from the Passage	Keywords from Answer	Tone & Concept
The purpose of this report is...correct misconception	B) impact of new gadget	Positive
Incorrect Choices & Common Patterns		
Evidence	Incorrect keywords	Tone & Concept
The purpose of this report is to identify the scope of potential harmful effects when using VR that are discussed widely, <u>and will eventually put such a</u> **misconception** into the **correct perspectives.**	A) invalidate	Negative
	C) other, development	Not stated
	D) VR's overall sales	Minor Issue
	E) raise concern	Negative

"correct misconception" into the "correct perspectives" implies that the author supports VR system

Q31. Pattern 7: Understanding Attitude / Tone

Question Pattern: The quotations in, represents
Question Keywords: "good enough" (line 8) the smartphone industry's?

Step 1	Step 2	Step 3
Keywords from the Passage	Keywords from Answer	Tone & Concept
comfortable with "good enough", market replacement	A) concern	Negative
Incorrect Choices & Common Patterns		
Evidence	Incorrect keywords	Tone & Concept
Such a forecast gets the momentum and validation as consumers are becoming more and more <u>comfortable with</u> <u>"good enough" smartphones, which will look for a new</u> <u>market replacement</u> and driver.	B) enthusiasm	Positive
	C) optimism	Positive
	D) anger	Too extreme
	E) beneficial	Positive

...consumers are becoming more and more <u>comfortable with "good enough" smartphones</u> means consumers won't buy newer and better smartphone, which will concern the smartphone industry.

Q32. Pattern 7: Understanding Attitude / Tone

Question Pattern: Which best describes
Question Keywords: the consumer's reaction to the smartphone these days

Step 1	Step 2	Step 3
Keywords from the Passage	Keywords from Answer	Tone & Concept
comfortable with "good enough",	A) reluctant	Logical Conclusion, negative

Incorrect Choices & Common Patterns		
Evidence	Incorrect keywords	Tone & Concept
Such a forecast gets the momentum and validation as consumers are becoming more and more comfortable with "good enough" smartphones, which will look for a new market	B) attentive	Positive
	C) ignore smartphone	Too extreme word usage
	D) stop using smartphone	Too extreme word usage
	E) cheaper smartphone	Not stated in the passage

1> The underlined portions display the consumers' view on smartphone.

2> They do not mind using a good enough smartphone. In other word, A) they are reluctant to more enhanced technology.

3> good enough does not necessarily mean cheap. It rather insinuates the okay quality. Therefore, (E) is incorrect.

Q33. Pattern 4: Relationship Question

Question Pattern: the author mainly suggests that
Question Keywords: In lines 10-12 ("like all new …public."), VR's initial criticism

Step 1	Step 2	Step 3
Keywords from the Passage	Keywords from Answer	Tone & Concept
like all new, developments, VR could not escape	A) historically parallel	Similar Concept, Negative

Incorrect Choices & Common Patterns		
Evidence	Incorrect keywords	Tone & Concept
However, like all new modes of developments such as TV, Internet, and smartphone experienced in their initial stages, VR systems could not escape from the harsh criticisms	B) outmoded warning	Opposite
	C) fails, contribution	Too extreme word usage
	D) severely damaged	Too extreme word usage
	E) successfully	Positive

1> The author brings up T.V, Internet, etc. that have been around for awhile in modern society.

2> By presenting these antecedents, the author forecasts the similar reaction from the critics.

3> Therefore, the sentence refers to the historical parallel about the view of the consumers.

UNAUTHORIZED COPYING OR REUSE OF ANY PART OF THIS PAGE IS ILLEGAL

Q34. Pattern 7: Understanding Attitude / Tone

Question Pattern: The author's reaction toward
Question Keywords: critics who blame the dangers of VR can be summarized as

Step 1	Step 2	Step 3
Keywords from the Passage	Keywords from Answer	Tone & Concept
such a misconception into the correct	D) measured disagreement	Negative
Incorrect Choices & Common Patterns		
Evidence	Incorrect keywords	Tone & Concept
The purpose of this report is to identify the scope of _potential harmful effects of VR and then_ eventually put such a misconception into the correct perspectives.	A) anxious defiance	The underlined portions indirectly mention about the critics of VR.
	B) hostility	
	C) agreement	
	E) mild consent	The author supports VR.

Q35. Pattern 2: Main Idea Question

Question Pattern: This passage can be mainly found in the

Step 1	Step 2	Step 3
Keywords from the Passage	Keywords from Answer	Tone & Concept
The purpose of this report is to identify VR	D) student researching VR	Synonym Keywords
Incorrect Choices & Common Patterns		
Evidence	Incorrect keywords	Tone & Concept
The whole passage is about VR systems in positive tone. The remaining choices are all veered from the main theme of the passage	A) smartphone	Minor example
	B) VR system manual	Not related issue
	C) consumer watchdog	Not stated
	E) smartphone	Minor example

Q36. Type 3: Analogy Question [Pattern 1: Local Question] {Category A}

Question Pattern: Which of the following old sayings is best applied to the narrator's situation?

Step 1	Step 2	Step 3
Keywords from the Passage	Keywords from Answer	Tone & Concept
dreaded meeting, but anyone at all	E) Leave, alone	Similar Concept

Incorrect Choices & Common Patterns		
Evidence	Incorrect keywords	Tone & Concept
He had become so completely absorbed in himself, and isolated from his fellows that he dreaded meeting, not only his landlady, but anyone at all	A) The grass is always	they are all Unrelated word usage
	B) Time heals	
	C) Absence makes	
	D) There's no time	

Q37. Type 2: Inference Question [Pattern 1: Local Question] {Category A}

Question Pattern: In the second paragraph (lines 4-9) the narrator, describes that
Question Keywords: the house

Step 1	Step 2	Step 3
Keywords from the Passage	Keywords from Answer	Tone & Concept
obliged to pass her kitchen."	E) has only one entrance	Similar Concept

Incorrect Choices & Common Patterns		
Evidence	Incorrect keywords	Tone & Concept
L6: every time he went out he was obliged to pass her kitchen." Therefore, we can infer that there is no other entrance in the house.	A) offers views	Not stated in the passage
	B) serves meals	
	C) converted a cupboard	
	D) well maintained	

Q38. Pattern 4: Relationship Question

Question Pattern: The third paragraph (lines 10-19) suggests that the
Question Keywords: conversation between the narrator and the landlady has been

Step 1	Step 2	Step 3
Keywords from the Passage	Keywords from Answer	Tone & Concept
to be stopped on the stairs,	D) a ritual, wishes, avoid	Negative, Logical Conclusion

Incorrect Choices & Common Patterns		
Evidence	Incorrect keywords	Tone & Concept
But to be stopped on the stairs, to be forced to listen to her trivial, irrelevant gossip, to pestering demands for payment, ...”	A) resentment	Too extreme word usage
	B) benefit of the narrator	Positive
	C) joyful	Positive
	E) overhear it	Not stated

Q39. Pattern 5: Word-In-Context Question

Question Pattern: means   **Question Keywords:** In line 17, "trivial"

Step 1	Step 2	Step 3
Keywords from the Passage	Keywords from Answer	Tone & Concept
trivial, irrelevant gossip....”	C) insignificant	Synonym

Incorrect Choices & Common Patterns		
Evidence	Incorrect keywords	Tone & Concept
But to be stopped on the stairs, to be forced to listen to her trivial, irrelevant gossip....”	A) considerable	Trivial = insignificant
	B) important	
	D) heartfelt	
	E) resentment	

Q40. Pattern 7: Understanding Attitude / Tone

Question Keywords: In lines 15-19 (nothing that any…slip out unseen.) depicts the landlady as

Step 1	Step 2	Step 3
Keywords from the Passage	Keywords from Answer	Tone & Concept
Nothing that any landlady could do had a real terror	E) a harmless person	Similar Concept

Incorrect Choices & Common Patterns		
Evidence	Incorrect keywords	Tone & Concept
Nothing that any landlady could do had a real terror for him. <u>But to be stopped on the stairs, to be</u> <u>forced to listen to her trivial, irrelevant gossip….</u>	A) an ignorant	Not stated in the passage
	B) a wealthy	
	C) confinement	
	D) a person enjoying	

Test 2 ABSOLUTE PATTERNS for the Analogy Section

Q31. Absolute Pattern 6: Purpose (Job/Tool) Pattern

A is the best answer

The purpose of a seat is to sit as the purpose of a car is to drive.

Q32. Absolute Pattern 13: Mental-Physical Pattern

A is the best answer

Sweet is a mental concept, while sugar is physical.

Legend is a mental concept, while a book is physical.

Q33. Absolute Pattern 1: Production (Cause-Effect) Pattern + 5: Degree Pattern

A is the best answer.

Believing becomes a real (Degree); Feeling tired causes sleep (Degree)

Choice C is a synonym.

Q34. Absolute Pattern 4: Synonym Pattern

E is the best answer

Invest is synonym to save as prodigal is synonym to consume

Q35. Absolute Pattern 6:Purpose (Job/Tool) Pattern

A is the best answer

Legends on the map are used as a tool to symbolize the geographical characteristics;

A menu in a restaurant is used as a tool to symbolize meals.

Q36. Absolute Pattern 5: Degree Pattern

A is the best answer

Poem is shorter than novels as backyard is smaller than meadows.

Choice C is a a synonym.   Choice D is Part-Whole Pattern.

Choice E is flipped over

Q37. Absolute Pattern 5: Degree Pattern

D is the best answer

Degree Relations: Gradual increment

When something gets old, it eventually dies; continuing battle will lead to wars.

Q38. Absolute Pattern 6:Purpose (Job/Tool) Pattern

A is the best answer

The purpose of going to a training centre is to practice as the purpose of going to the court is for the judgement.

Q39. Absolute Pattern 7: Association (Characteristic) Pattern

E is the best answer.

Poetry has a rhythmic characteristic, while comedy has a satiric characteristic.

Choice A, B, C are human concepts and don't belong to the question category (Art).

Q40. Absolute Pattern 6:Purpose (Job/Tool) Pattern

C is the best answer

We drink coffee in a cup as we drink beer in a jug.

Choices A and B are wrong because the word orders are flipped over.

Choice D is close to the part-whole pattern.

Q41. Absolute Pattern 2: Part-Whole Pattern

D is the best answer

A keyboard is a part of a computer as fingers are parts of the hand.

Q42. Absolute Pattern 6:Purpose (Job/Tool) Pattern

A is the best answer

As women wear skirts so do kindergarten girls wear nametags.

(E) is wrong because the word orders are flipped over

For (D), although a hockey stick is used as a tool for hockey, it doesn't have the same category as the question and (A) have: the human concept.

Q43. Absolute Pattern 5: Degree Pattern

D is the best answer (small to big)

Brawl becomes wars as shoplifting becomes murder.

Choice A is wrong because both the question and (D) share the same negative tone, while (A) is positive.

Choice B is flipped over in degree.

Q44. Absolute Pattern 6:Purpose (Job/Tool) Pattern

A is the best answer

A bridge is used as a tool to cross a river; A gun is used as a tool to shoot

Q45. Absolute Pattern 6:Purpose (Job/Tool) Pattern

C is the best answer.

The purpose of work is to earn cash; the purpose of the study is to take an exam.

Q46. Absolute Pattern 5: Degree Pattern

D is the best answer

Sublime is the greater degree of beautiful.

Romance is the greater degree of intimacy.

Q47. Absolute Pattern 4: Synonym Pattern

C is the best answer

Ancient is a synonym to archaic; modern is a synonym to a new age.

Q48. Absolute Pattern 5: Degree Pattern

B is the best answer

Degree Relations + Positive vs. negative Relations

Veneration is a greater degree of respect; abomination is a greater degree of hate.

Choice A) has no degree.

D) is Association Pattern.

E) is Degree Pattern, but does not contain the same mental concept as in the question and (B)

Q49. Absolute Pattern 3: Antonym (Positive-Negative) Pattern

A is the best answer

Introvert and extrovert are antonym, referring to a human's personality.

Convex and depressed are antonym, referring to lens.

Q50. Absolute Pattern 7: Association (Characteristic) Pattern

E is the best answer

Pure logic is the main characteristics of Mathematics, so is creation to art.

Q51. Absolute Pattern 5: Degree Pattern

A is the best answer.

Degree Relations + shuffled word order

Frequently is less often than always (Positive); seldom is less than never (Negative).

Q52. Absolute Pattern 6:Purpose (Job/Tool) Pattern

D is the best answer

A soldier uses a weapon as a tool; cosmologist uses a telescope as a tool.

Q53. Absolute Pattern 5: Degree Pattern

A is the best answer (big to small)

City is bigger than village as continent is bigger than country.

Q54. Absolute Pattern 4: Synonym Pattern

E is the best answer

Infinite is limitless; bland is boring

Q55. Absolute Pattern 7: Association (Characteristic) Pattern

D is the best answer

Animals are associated with nature, as baby is associated with a nurture.

Q56. Absolute Pattern 8: Shape Pattern

A is the best answer

Both eyeglasses and tire have the same round shape; both monitor and chopping board have the same square shape.

Q57. Absolute Pattern 6:Purpose (Job/Tool) Pattern

D is the best answer.

A chef uses a knife as an architect uses a blueprint

Choice C is the Part-Whole Pattern.

Choice E is wrong because architect does not use a hammer, but a carpenter does.

Q58. Absolute Pattern 6:Purpose (Job/Tool) Pattern

E is the best answer.

The job of a security guard is to keep a building; the job of a keeper is to keep a lighthouse.

Q59. Absolute Pattern 7: Association (Characteristic) Pattern

A is the best answer

Parliament is the characteristic of the democracy so is of monarch to autocrat

Q60. Absolute Pattern 1: Production (Cause-Effect) Pattern

B is the best answer

A cow produces milk and a pig produces bacon.

Test 2 Recap

Universal Type Questions start with the phrase such as

-The main purpose of the passage is...

-The overall tone of the passage is...

-The author's attitude in the passage is...

-The author's argument throughout the passage is...

-The ideas relate to the first and the second paragraph are...

-Unlike Passage 1, the Passage 2 mainly discusses....

When the universal type questions appear, you should leave the questions until all the local type questions are solved. Keep in mind that the answer to the universal type questions is mainly found

The local type question gives you the exact line reference (e.g., according to line 2, In lines 19-22). The most critical concept in this type of question is to localize the information. You do not have to—should not—find the answer far way from the line reference.

The line reference itself stands for the question. Therefore, it seldom provides the answer in the exactly same line.

If the question asks you to read lines 10-12 (e.g., the example sentence for instance), you should find the answer from the topic sentence or the concluding sentence that embraces the example sentence.

Therefore, it is logical to think that the answer should generally be located right above or below the line reference.

Please do not apply this concept to the universal type question.

SSAT

Reading & Verbal Practice

Test 3

ALL THE LOGIC AND RULES

BEHIND THE EVERY SINGLE

SSAT QUESTION

Test 3 Reading Section
Time: 40 Minutes, 40 Questions

Directions: Each reading passage is followed by questions about it. Answer the questions that follow a passage on the basis of what is stated or implied in that passage.

Questions 1-6 are based on the following passage.

Line

About a year ago, my brother, who is a very sagacious physician, advised me to take the fresh liver of a mountain sheep for certain nervous symptoms which were troublesome. None of the local druggists could fill the prescription, and so it was decided that I should seek the materials in person. With me went my friend J. B., the pearl of companions, and we began the
5 campaign by outfitting at San Diego, with a view to exploring the resources of the sister republic in the peninsula of Lower California. Lower California is very different from Southern California. The latter is--well, a paradise, or something of that kind, if you believe the inhabitants, of whom I am an humble fraction. The former is what you may please to think.

10 At San Diego we got a man, a wagon, four mules and the needed provisions and kitchen-- all hired at reasonable rates, except the provisions and kitchen, which we bought. Then we tried to get a decent map, but were foiled.

The Mexican explorer will find the maps of that country a source of curious interest. Many of them are large and elaborately mounted on cloth, spreading to a great distance when
15 unfolded. The political divisions are marked with a tropical profusion of bright colors, which is very fit. A similar sense of fitness and beauty leads the designer to insert mountain ranges, rivers and towns where they best please the eye.

1

The narrator views his brother physician as a

A) confidante

B) swindler

C) maverick

D) dilettante

E) prophet

2

In line 9, the term "fraction" refers to

A) a digit

B) a particle

C) an atom

D) a person

E) a modest person

CONTINUE

3

The purpose of the narrator's traveling is to

A) realize his ambition in California

B) find a medicine

C) discover a mountain sheep

D) live in San Diego

E) settle the dispute with the inhabitants

4

In line 5, "the pearl of companions" emphasizes the

A) imagery that fits his friend's figure

B) scope of knowledge his friend has

C) background of his friend's occupation

D) nature of their relations

E) close tie with his friend

5

In describing the map, the author is mainly delighted with its

A) sensory stimulants

B) auditory functions

C) historical speculation

D) physical contrast

E) theoretical elaboration

6

It can be inferred from the passage that when designing the map, the cartographer mainly focused on

A) Physical accuracy

B) literary quality

C) conventional wisdom

D) visual intuition

E) first-hand information

CONTINUE

Questions 7-12 are based on the following passage.

Line   As life broadens with advancing culture, and people are able to appropriate to themselves more of the various forms of art, the artist himself attains to greater power, his abilities increase in direct ratio with the progress in culture made by the people and their ability to comprehend him. When one side or phase of an art comes to be received, new and more
5   difficult problems are invariably presented, the elucidation of which can only be effected by a higher development of the faculties. There is never an approach to equilibrium between the artist and his public. As it advances in knowledge of his art, he maintains the want of balance, the disproportion that always exists between the genius and the ordinary man, by rising ever to greater heights.

10   If Bach is the mathematician of music, as has been asserted, Beethoven is its philosopher. In his work the philosophic spirit comes to the fore. To the genius of the musician is added in Beethoven a wide mental grasp, an altruistic spirit, that seeks to help humanity on the upward path. He addresses the intellect of mankind.

        Up to Beethoven's time musicians in general (Bach is always an exception) performed their
15   work without the aid of an intellect for the most part; they worked by intuition. In everything outside their art they were like children. Beethoven was the first one having the independence to think for himself--the first to have ideas on subjects unconnected with his art. It was he who established the dignity of the artist over that of the simply well-born.

7

In line 7, the word "want" means

A) desire

B) lack

C) wish

D) independence

E) luck

8

The transition of music after Beethoven can be defined as the period of

A) dependence on tradition

B) self-awareness

C) Christianity

D) enhanced art

E) intuition

9

The author characterizes the relations between the artist and culture as they are

A) insightfully coherent

B) artistically exclusive

C) equally responsive to old art

D) different in their view of future art

E) generally agreeable with trends

10

In the second paragraph (lines 10-13), the author analogously compares Bach and Beethoven as a pair of

A) science and tradition

B) modern and tradition

C) accuracy and cerebral

D) locality and foreign

E) religious and secular

11

In line 13 the author depicts Beethoven's quality as

A) the love of mankind

B) the highly skilled in artistic expression

C) the noble mind

D) opportunistic

E) insightful

12

The parenthesis (Bach…exception) in line 14 mainly functions as a

A) qualification to the previous portion of the sentence

B) speculation to the previous portion of the sentence

C) confirmation to the previous portion of the sentence

D) contradiction to the following sentence

E) yield to a different opinion

CONTINUE

Questions 13-18 are based on the following passage.

Line

The ancient fable of two antagonistic spirits imprisoned in one body, equally powerful and having the complete mastery by turns-of one man, that is to say, inhabited by both a devil and an angel seems to have been realized, if all we hear is true, in the character of the extraordinary man whose name we have written above. Our own impression of the nature of Edgar A. Poe, differs in

5 some important degree, however, from that which has been generally conveyed in the notices of his death. Let us, before telling what we personally know of him, copy a graphic and highly finished portraiture, from the pen of Dr. Rufus W. Griswold, which appeared in a recent number of the "Tribune":"Edgar Allen Poe is dead. He died in Baltimore on Sunday, October 7th.This announcement will startle many, but few will be grieved by it. The poet was known, personally

10 or by reputation, in all this country; he had readers in England and in several of the states of Continental Europe; but he had few or no friends; and the regrets for his death will be suggested principally by the consideration that in him literary art has lost one of its most brilliant but erratic stars." His conversation was at times almost supramortal in its eloquence. His voice was modulated with astonishing skill and variably expressive eyes.

15

13

In line 1, "two antagonistic spirits" implies

A) the devil spirits. angel spirit

B) the erratic nature of Edgar Allen Poe

C) Edgar Allen Poe's works

D) the reputation of Edgar Allen Poe among critics

E) Dr. Rufus W. Griswold

14

The quote from Dr. Rufus W. Griswold most strongly supports which of the following statement?

A) The long-term popularity of an artist is lying upon charm and personality.

B) It is only after the death that we know the quality of brilliant stars

C) Poe chose to live in confinement without friends

D) Even brilliant stars should concern about their social status and reputation

E) Poe's death debunks a different viewpoint

CONTINUE

15

The author describes Edgar Allen Poe's literary skills as

A) mysterious and unknowable

B) mildly oppressive

C) orderly and appealing

D) drab and boring

E) menacing yet alluring

16

In line 13, "eloquence" most nearly means

A) contradiction

B) persuasive speech

C) evil sprit

D) deceptive nature

E) ethics

17

In lines 14 (His voice...eyes), the author addresses that Edgar Allen Poe's works

A) broadly expressed with visual and auditory senses

B) combined supramotal with mortal

C) led his reader with powerful expression

D) alluded his reader carelessly

E) revealed his personality into his writing

18

The tone of the passage is more

A) anecdotal

B) tentative

C) analytical

D) flippant

E) humorous

Questions 19-24 are based on the following passage.

Line There is no subject so deeply interesting and important to rational beings as the knowledge of language, or one which presents a more direct and powerful claim upon all classes in the community; for there is no other so closely interwoven with all the affairs of human life, social, moral, political and religious.

5 Great difficulty has been experienced in the common method of explaining language, and grammar has long been considered a dry, by nearly all the teachers in the land. But it is to be presumed that the fault in this case is to be sought for in the manner of teaching, rather than in the science itself; for it would be unreasonable to suppose that a subject which occupies the earliest attention of the parent, which is acquired at great expense of money and thought, can

10 possibly be dull or unimportant, if rightly explained. Children have been required to learn verbal forms, to look at the mere signs of ideas, instead of the things represented by them. The consequence has been that the whole subject has become uninteresting to all who do not possess a retentive verbal memory. The philosophy of language has not been sufficiently regarded to render it delightful and profitable.

15

CONTINUE

19

The first paragraph defines language mainly as

A) a restrictive subject

B) a pervasive identity in all humankind

C) different rules and system applied in
   different countries

D) an unavoidable challenge

E) an opportunity for the philanthropist

20

Which of the following situations is most analogous
to the statement in lines 10-11(Children…by them.)

A) A music teacher teaches the history of violin
   instead of teaching how to play violin

B) The police tries to find a clue to a crime

C) A church minister works for the poor people
   instead of preaching at the church

D) A businessman learns a foreign language by
   himself instead of buying a grammar book

E) A school organize a field trip to a museum instead
   of teaching the art theory in class

21

The parent in line 9 is used to

A) cast aspersions of people who focus on grammar

B) convey deep concern about teaching language
   to their children

C) alarm the acceptance of teaching language
   indiscriminately

D) explain further about the impact of the weak
   manner of teaching

E) rail against those focus on the science of
   language

22

The author's attitude to the verbal forms in line
11 is best described as

A) a puzzling form

B) an unscientific method

C) an undeveloped form

D) appreciation

E) an obstacle

23

The second paragraph suggests that the difficulty
of language is mainly due to the

A) grammar

B) manner of teaching

C) science of language

D) parent's education to their child

E) method of explaining language

24

The last paragraph (lines 5-13) conveys the general
tone of

A) gratitude

B) detachment

C) admonishment

D) hostility

E) indignation

CONTINUE

Questions 25-30 are based on the following passage.

Line   The remains of pueblo architecture are found scattered over thousands of square miles of the arid region of the southwestern plateaus. This vast area includes the drainage of the Rio Pecos on the east and that of the Colorado on the west, and extends from central Utah on the north beyond the limits of the United States southward, in which direction its boundaries are still
5   undefined.

    The descendants of those who at various times built these stone villages are few in number and inhabit about thirty pueblos distributed irregularly over parts of the region formerly occupied. The province has been often visited by whites, but the remoteness of Tusayan and the arid and forbidding character of its surroundings have caused its more complete isolation.
10   The architecture of this district exhibits a close adherence to aboriginal practices, still bears the marked impress of its development under the exacting conditions of an arid environment, and is but slowly yielding to the influence of foreign ideas.

    The present study of the architecture of Tusayan and Cibola embraces all of the inhabited pueblos of those provinces, and includes a number of the ruins traditionally connected with
15   them.

25

In the first paragraph, the author describes the remains of pueblo architecture is

A) impressive

B) puzzling

C) intriguing

D) immense

E) undeveloped

26

In line 10, "adherence" most nearly means

A) inheritance

B) following

C) addition

D) kinship

E) technique

CONTINUE →

27

Which of the following factors prevented whites from their visiting to the pueblos villages?

I. Few numbers of stone villages

II. Proximity

III. Aridity

IV. Uninviting nature of its surrounding

A) I only

B) I and II only

C) I, II, III only

D) I, II, III, IV

E) II, III, IV

28

The author views Pueblos

A) are constantly evolving

B) successfully protected themselves from the foreign intrusion

C) were inevitably divisive

D) tried to maintain their tradition

E) could not advance due to the exacting condition

29

The passage demonstrates the characteristics of pueblos village EXCEPT?

A) The materials used for the construction of the village was stone

B) Distribution was more sporadic in the region

C) Due to its uninviting surroundings, it received some white visitors, but no white settlers

D) The village remained intact from outside influence

E) Aboriginal practice can be found in their architecture

30

In the last paragraph (lines 13-15), the author mainly focuses on Pueblos'

A) regional language

B) size

C) population

D) origin

E) vestige

CONTINUE

UNAUTHORIZED COPYING OR REUSE OF ANY PART OF THIS PAGE IS ILLEGAL

Questions 31-35 are based on the following passage.

Line   Amongst the vestiges of antiquity which abound in this country, are the visible memorials
of those nations which have succeeded one another in the occupancy of this island. To the age
of our Celtic ancestors, the Cromlechs and Stone Circles which lie scattered over the land;
and these are conceived to have been derived from the Phoenicians, whose merchants first
5 introduced amongst the aboriginal Britons the arts of incipient civilization.

    Of these most ancient relics the prototypes appear, as described in Holy Writ in the altars
erected by the Patriarchs, and in the circles of stone set up by Moses at the foot of Mount
Sinai. Many of these structures, perhaps from their very rudeness, have survived the
vicissitudes of time, whilst there scarce remains a vestige of the temples erected in this island
10 by the Romans; yet it is from Roman edifices that we derive, and can trace by a gradual
transition, the progress of that peculiar kind of architecture called GOTHIC. The Romans
having conquered almost the whole of Britain in the first century and during their
occupancy they not only instructed the natives in the arts of civilization, but also with their
aid, as we learn from Tacitus, began at an early period to erect temples and public edifices,
15 though doubtless much inferior to those at Romies.

31

The Romans transferred all of the followings to the Britain EXCEPT

A) civilization

B) knowledge to build edifices

C) more advanced skills to build temples

D) religion

E) GOTHIC styled architecture

32

In line 6, "the prototypes" primarily serves to

A) lament the complete destructions of the vestige

B) condemn those who ruined the structures

C) enumerate the origins of the structures

D) specify the material of the structure

E) indicate the cooperation from several nations

33

In line 5, "conceived" is primarily used to

A) underscore the importance of the statement

B) educate the reader who the Phoenicians are

C) effectively confirm the author's statement

D) acknowledge the limited knowledge

E) support a flawed hypothesis

34

Which choice best describes the function of the statement in lines 15 ("though…at Romies")

A) It summarizes the points made in the previous portion of the sentence

B) It provides support for the argument made in the previous paragraph

C) It introduces a new view of the information

D) It challenges the findings made in the previous paragraph

E) It qualifies the previous portion of the sentence

CONTINUE ➡

35

It can be inferred from the passage that the island had

A) a commercial interest with foreign state

B) was the under-control from foreigners

C) had a plenty of warfare

D) had no civilization

E) had no meaningful temples

Questions 36-40 are based on the following passage.

Line

On 1st May, arriving at Vienna early next morning; should have arrived at 6:46, but train was an hour late. Buda-Pesth seems a wonderful place, from the glimpse which I got of it from the train and the little I could walk through the streets. I feared to go very far from the station, as we had arrived late and would start as near the correct time as possible. The impression I

5 had was that we were leaving the West and entering the East; the most western of splendid bridges over the Danube, which is here of noble width and depth, took us among the traditions of Turkish rule.

We left in pretty good time, and came after nightfall to Klausenburgh. Here I stopped for the night at the Hotel Royale. I had for dinner, or rather supper, a chicken done up some way with

10 red pepper, which was very good but thirsty. I asked the waiter, and he said it was called "paprika hendl," and that, as it was a national dish, I should be able to get it anywhere along the Carpathians. I found my smattering of German very useful here; indeed, I don't know how I should be able to get on without it.

Having had some time at my disposal when in London, I had visited the British Museum,

15 and made search among the books and maps in the library regarding Transylvania; it had struck me that trivial foreknowledge of the country could hardly fail to have some importance in dealing with a nobleman of that country. I was not able to light on any map or work giving the exact locality of the Castle Dracula, as there are no maps of this country as yet to compare with our own Ordnance Survey maps; but I found that Bistritz, the post town named by Count Dracula, is a fairly well-known place.

CONTINUE

36

In the first paragraph, the narrator feels

A) unrestrained joy

B) sentimental reminiscence

C) bitter disappointment

D) cautious curiosity

E) dark foreboding

37

The narrator feared most in the first paragraph for

A) being new to the place

B) the lack of German language skills

C) adjusting to local time

D) entering from west to east

E) following the Turkish traditions

38

The narrator believes speaking German would be

A) an excitement

B) a mark of social distinction

C) an identification of the ethnic origin

D) an annoyance

E) not an option

39

Which choice resembles most the situation mentioned in line 15-17 (It had struck…country)?

A) A Walmart employee shops at the Target

B) The Target C.E.O. got caught by stealing a pack of gum

C) A rookie starts his position as a benchwarmer

D) An unknown classmate was the son of Saudi King

E) The Walmart C.E.O. decided to step down

40

In line 16, "trivial" means

A) considerable

B) important

C) insignificant

D) heartfelt

E) resentment

Test 3 Verbal Section   30 MINUTES, 60 QUESTIONS

Directions: the synonym questions ask you to find the most appropriate synonym to the question.

The analogy questions ask you to find the most appropriate analogy to the question.
Select the answer that best matches to the question.

Synonym Sample Question:

Q: SUPERIOR

A higher rank

B inferior

C considerable

D supermarket

E supper

A) is the best answer because the synonym for superior is higher rank.

B) is incorrect because it applies the 'opposite concept.

C) and E) are irrelevant words.

D) is incorrect because it applies physical concept to mental concept

Test 3 Synonym questions 1 to 30

1. MANUFACTURE

(A) make

(B) copy

(C) print

(D) fabricate

(E) elect

2. WHOLEHEARTEDLY

(A) entirely

(B) duplicity

(C) sincerely

(D) deadly

(E) gladly

3. REVEAL

(A) abate

(B) giving

(C) clandestine

(D) divulge

(E) generate

4. RECKLESSLY

(A) rashly

(B) subside

(C) reduce

(D) lackey

(E) embarrassingly

5. PUSH

(A) impoverish

(B) step

(C) throb

(D) abdicate

(E) propel

CONTINUE

6. ABERRATION

(A) attentive

(B) abhorrence

(C) typical

(D) deviation

(E) power

7. ERRATIC

(A) error

(B) standard

(C) inconsistent

(D) rhythmic

(E) habitual

8. SPECIFY

(A) end

(B) rescue

(C) special

(D) state

(E) pacify

9. ABJECT

(A) hopeless

(B) poverty

(C) reject

(D) unimportant

(E) disbelief

10. AGILE

(A) transparent

(B) quick

(C) slow

(D) agree

(E) again

11. NAIVE

(A) complex

(B) kind

(C) kid

(D) generous

(E) unsophisticated

12. ABNEGATE

(A) begin

(B) reject

(C) remove

(D) negate

(E) abnormal

13. TRIVIAL

(A) valuable

(B) fast

(C) trifle

(D) serious

(E) triumvirate

14. ABORTIVE

(A) deliver baby

(B) unsuccessful

(C) aboard

(D) boating

(E) abridge

15. MOTIVE

(A) force

(B) happy

(C) moving

(D) reason

(E) motor

CONTINUE

16. BEWILDERED

(A) wild

(B) confused

(C) forested

(D) vegetated

(E) natural

17. SPECULATION

(A) speed

(B) stall

(C) think

(D) see

(E) spectacle

18. ABSOLVE

(A) forgive

(B) solve

(C) regret

(D) add

(E) know

19. OBSESSED

(A) seeded

(B) grown

(C) natural

(D) oversized

(E) overly concerned

20. ABSTINENT

(A) standing low

(B) abysmal

(C) approving

(D) useful

(E) avoiding

21. VARY

(A) slow

(B) change

(C) full

(D) extremely

(E) very

22. DIGNITY

(A) honor

(B) degree

(C) design

(D) notice

(E) advice

23. PASSIVE

(A) slow

(B) submissive

(C) hiding

(D) passionate

(E) artificial

24. ABSTRACT

(A) theoretical

(B) track

(C) straight

(D) abysmal

(E) abound

25. OPPORTUNITY

(A) luck

(B) fortune

(C) basic

(D) turn

(E) a good chance

CONTINUE

UNAUTHORIZED COPYING OR REUSE OF ANY PART OF THIS PAGE IS ILLEGAL

26. ABSTRUSE

(A) difficult to understand

(B) bottom

(C) structure

(D) baseless

(E) transitional

27. PERPLEXITY

(A) laxity

(B) clear

(C) elegance

(D) confusion

(E) purple

28. DRAB

(A) easy

(B) dull

(C) clear

(D) puzzle

(E) drain

29. VERSATILE

(A) argumentative

(B) changing

(C) colorful

(D) verisimilitude

(E) satellite

? inverse ?
, verse !

30. HARDY

(A) tough

(B) unchanging

(C) complex

(D) ossified

(E) dangerous

Analogy Sample Question:

Q: River is to Ocean as:

A better is to good

B rain is to cloud

C father is to mother

D city is to country

E fork is to spoon

D is the correct answer. Just as the river is smaller than the Ocean, the city is smaller than the country. The pattern applied in this question is the Degree Pattern (small to big)

A) is incorrect because the word order is flipped over.

B) is incorrect because it applies the production pattern (cloud produces rain)

C), E) are incorrect because they apply the Antonym patterns.

Test 3 Analogy questions 31 to 60

31. beautiful is to Miss. World Universe 2018 as

(A) drive is to driver

(B) sector is to district

(C) supermarket is to mall

(D) compartment is to part

(E) useless is to penny

CONTINUE

32. Goalie is to Missile as spend is to

(A) climax

(B) save

(C) character

(D) setting

(E) price

33. Museum is to quiet as open market is to

(A) shopping

(B) low value

(C) noisy

(D) busy

(E) cheap

34. Brick is to wall as

(A) heart is to mind

(B) sand is to the ocean

(C) gold is to king

(D) ink is to painting

(E) wood is to church

35. Egg yolk is to egg as

(A) apple is to core

(B) pencil lead is to pencil

(C) lens is to telescope

(D) nut is to peanut

(E) patty is to hamburger

36. Coffee is to bean

(A) gasoline is to crude oil

(B) gas is to gasoline

(C) water is to fire

(D) battery is to car

(E) boat is to propeller

37. Mechanic is to car as editor is to

(A) writer

(B) book

(C) publishing

(D) money

(E) company

38. Pen is to marker as student is to

(A) professor

(B) dancer

(C) father

(D) salesman

(E) worker

39. Geese is to migrate as frog is to

(A) ugly

(B) jumpy

(C) hibernate

(D) amphibian

(E) wet

40. Student is to report card as

(A) taxi driver is to money

(B) school is to test

(C) print is to printer

(D) phone bill is to telephone

(E) wedding is to invitation

41. Window is to wall as

(A) mirror is to car

(B) principal is to school

(C) crab is to ocean

(D) telescope is to sky

(E) business card is to company

CONTINUE

UNAUTHORIZED COPYING OR REUSE OF ANY PART OF THIS PAGE IS ILLEGAL

42. Winning is to lottery as

(A) work is to contribution

(B) championship is to hockey league

(C) money is to luck

(D) chance is to risk

(E) peak is to mountain

43. Sweat suit is to uniform as address is to

(A) house

(B) chat

(C) announce

(D) party

(E) company

44. Half time is to soccer as

(A) five centuries is to millennium

(B) middleman is to sports

(C) fifty cents is to dollar

(D) medium is to steak

(E) recess at school

45. Mechanic is to surgeon as drill to

(A) doctor

(B) patient

(C) hospital

(D) scalpel

(E) car

46. Hot is to warm as tepid is to

(A) clouds

(B) movie

(C) spicy

(D) boring

(E) ice

47. Alibi is to criminal as investigation is to

(A) guilty

(B) jail

(C) police

(D) evidence

(E) clue

48. December is to year as

(A) November is to Thanksgiving

(B) moonlit is to night

(C) sports is to game

(D) sunrise is to morning

(E) deadlock is to negotiation

49. Frog is to amphibian as

(A) sprint is to marathon

(B) whale is to fish

(C) human is to mammal

(D) orchestra is to violin

(E) cat is to lion

50. Busy is to play as

(A) study is to exam

(B) bride is to pretty

(C) twisted is to straight

(D) police is to thief

(E) bee is to ant

51. Lullaby is to calm as cacophony is to

(A) music

(B) singing

(C) text

(D) speech

(E) noise

CONTINUE

52. Seminar is to concert as

(A) music is to speech

(B) meeting is to people

(C) orchestra is to composer

(D) speaker is to address

(E) ticket is to movie

53. Bread is to bakery as

(A) medicine is to painkiller

(B) coffee is to juice

(C) bar is to beer

(D) student is to school

(E) jail is to criminals

54. Humorous is to hilarious as

(A) warm is to parched

(B) sad is to gloomy

(C) tell is to chat

(D) sunrise is to sunset

(E) friend is to lover

55. Milk is to refrigerator as

(A) fish is to river

(B) bread is to mold

(C) employee is to office

(D) game is to match

(E) book is to library

56. Remote control is to T.V. as

(A) music is to sound

(B) drama is to series

(C) trigger is to gun

(D) rhythm is to melody

(E) dryer is to washer

57. Military is to draft notice as car is to

(A) fight

(B) gun

(C) insurance

(D) gas

(E) accident

58. Referring is to implying as

(A) racing is to accident

(B) touching is to guessing

(C) critical is to praising

(D) praying is to moving

(E) believing is to worshiping

59. House is to elevator as building is to

(A) stairs

(B) janitor

(C) drawing

(D) window

(E) officers

60. Apprentice is to maestro as guess

(A) work

(B) cooperation

(C) steadfast

(D) thinking

(E) forgiveness

STOP

If you finish before time is called,
you may check your work on this section.

Do not turn to the next section.

Test 3

ABSOLUTE PATTERNS

TEST 3
READING SECTION

Please refer to the Reading Section Absolute Pattern Analysis next page

THE SYNONYM QUESTIONS
NO.1 ~ 30

THE ANALOGY QUESTIONS
NO.31 ~ 60.

Please refer to the Analogy Section Absolute Pattern Analysis in page 193

1	A	16	B
2	C	17	C
3	D	18	A
4	A	19	E
5	E	20	E
6	D	21	B
7	C	22	A
8	D	23	B
9	A	24	A
10	B	25	E
11	E	26	A
12	B	27	D
13	C	28	B
14	B	29	B
15	A	30	A

Test 3

ABSOLUTE PATTERNS for the Reading Section

Q1. Pattern 5: Word-In-Context Question

Question Pattern: The narrator views　　　　　**Question Keywords:** his brother physician as a

Step 1	Step 2	Step 3
Keywords from the Passage	Keywords from Answer	Tone & Concept
sagacious *physician, advised*	A) confidante	Similar Concept

Incorrect Choices & Common Patterns		
Evidence	Incorrect keywords	Tone & Concept
About a year ago, my brother, who is a very sagacious *physician, advised* me to take the fresh liver of a mountain sheep for certain nervous symptoms which were troublesome.	B) swindler C) maverick D) dilettante E) prophet	The words like "physician" and "advised" are positive. B), C), D) are negative concept E) is Unrelated word usage

Q2. Pattern 5: Word-In-Context Question

Question Pattern: the term, refers to　　　　**Question Keywords:** In line 9, the term "fraction" refers to

Step 1	Step 2	Step 3
Keywords from the Passage	Keywords from Answer	Tone & Concept
I am an **humble** fraction	D) person	Synonym

Incorrect Choices & Common Patterns		
Evidence	Incorrect keywords	Tone & Concept
if you believe the inhabitants, of whom I am an humble fraction. The "humble fraction" refers to the narrator himself.	A) digit B) particle C) atom E) modest person	E) is incorrect because of the Inconsistency error. The question asks "fraction", not "humble fraction"

E) The sort of trick applied in E) often appears in the actual test.

Q3. Pattern 3: Summary Question

Question Pattern: The purpose of the narrator's **Question Keywords:** traveling is to

Step 1	Step 2	Step 3
Keywords from the Passage	Keywords from Answer	Tone & Concept
seek the materials in person.	B) medicine	Logical Conclusion

Incorrect Choices & Common Patterns		
Evidence	Incorrect keywords	Tone & Concept
None of the local druggists could fill the prescription, and so it was decided that I should seek the materials in person.	A) ambition	The narrator took the advice from his brother and decided to travel to South, looking for medicine
	C) mountain sheep	
	D) live	
	E) dispute	

Choice C is wrong because discovering mountain sheep is not the final purpose. He indeed needs the liver and takes it as a medicine

Q4. Type 2: Inference Question [Pattern 1: Local Question] {Category A}

Question Pattern: emphasizes **Question Keywords:** In line 5, "the pearl of companions"

Step 1	Step 2	Step 3
Keywords from the Passage	Keywords from Answer	Tone & Concept
the pearl of companions,	E) close tie	Similar Concept

Incorrect Choices & Common Patterns		
Evidence	Incorrect keywords	Tone & Concept
With me went my friend J. B., the pearl of companions,	A) imagery	By referring his companion as a pearl (precious jewelry), the narrator expresses how close their relationship is.
	B) knowledge	
	C) occupation	
	D) nature	

Q5.   Pattern 3: Summary Question

Question Pattern: In describing, the author is mainly   **Question Keywords:** the map, delighted with its

Step 1	Step 2	Step 3
Keywords from the Passage	Keywords from Answer	Tone & Concept
tropical profusion of bright colors, please the eye	A) sensory stimulants	Similar Concept

Incorrect Choices & Common Patterns		
Evidence	Incorrect keywords	Tone & Concept
The political divisions are marked with a tropical profusion of bright colors, which is very fit. A similar sense of fitness and beauty leads the designer to insert mountain ranges, rivers and towns where they best please the eye	B) auditory C) historical D) physical E) theoretical	The narrator uses sensory stimulants. D) is wrong because it is not about physical California, but about the map.

Q6. Type 2: Inference Question [Pattern 1: Local Question] {Category A}

Question Pattern: It can be inferred from the passage that
Question Keywords: when designing the map, the cartographer mainly focused on

Step 1	Step 2	Step 3
Keywords from the Passage	Keywords from Answer	Tone & Concept
where they best please the eye.	D) visual intuition	Similar Concept

Incorrect Choices & Common Patterns		
Evidence	Incorrect keywords	Tone & Concept
"A similar sense of fitness and beauty leads the designer to insert mountain ranges, rivers and towns where they best please the eye. "	A) Physical B) literary C) conventional E) first-hand	The designers were drawn by visual intuition.

Q7. Pattern 5: Word-In-Context Question

Question Pattern: the word, means   **Question Keywords:** In line 7, "want"

Step 1	Step 2	Step 3
Keywords from the Passage	Keywords from Answer	Tone & Concept
the want (lack) of balance, disproportion	B) lack	Synonym

Incorrect Choices & Common Patterns		
Evidence	Incorrect keywords	Tone & Concept
As it advances in knowledge of his art, he maintains the want (lack) of balance, the disproportion that always exists between the genius and the ordinary man, by rising ever to greater heights. "want" means "lack"	A) desire C) wish D) independence E) luck	**As it advances / want / balance / disproportion,** indicate negative value. Therefore, choices A, C, D, E are all incorrect.

Q8. Pattern 4: Relationship Question

Question Pattern: can be defined

Question Keywords: The transition of music after Beethoven, as the period of

Step 1	Step 2	Step 3
Keywords from the Passage	Keywords from Answer	Tone & Concept
Up to Beethoven's, without, intellect, intuition.	B) self-awareness	Similar Concept

Incorrect Choices & Common Patterns		
Evidence	Incorrect keywords	Tone & Concept
Up to Beethoven's time musicians in general performed their work without the aid of an intellect for the most part; they worked by intuition.	A) tradition C) Christianity D) enhanced art E) intuition	A), C), E) are opposite and came before Beethoven's era.

Q9. Pattern 3: Summary Question

Question Pattern: The author characterizes the relations
Question Keywords: between the artist and culture as they are

Step 1	Step 2	Step 3
Keywords from the Passage	Keywords from Answer	Tone & Concept
his abilities increase, direct ratio, in culture	E) agreeable with trends	Similar Concept

Incorrect Choices & Common Patterns		
Evidence	Incorrect keywords	Tone & Concept
<u>his abilities increase in direct ratio with the progress in culture made by the people and their ability to comprehend him</u> * the sentence states that the artist responds and progresses based on culture	A) insightful B) exclusive C) old art D) different	B), D) are opposite C) old art is not stated A) is wrong because of the word "insightful." is Too extreme word usage

A) The author's tone of voice was more cling to the necessity under desperation. In that regards, "insightful" is a too extreme word.

Q10. Pattern 4: Relationship Question

Question Pattern: In the second paragraph, the author analogously compares
Question Keywords: Bach and Beethoven as a pair of

Step 1	Step 2	Step 3
Keywords from the Passage	Keywords from Answer	Tone & Concept
Bach, mathematician, Beethoven, philosopher	C) accuracy and cerebral	Similar Concept

Incorrect Choices & Common Patterns		
Evidence	Incorrect keywords	Tone & Concept
If Bach is the mathematician of music, as has been asserted, Beethoven is a philosopher	A) science and tradition B) modern and tradition D) locality and foreign E) religious and secular	Bach as the mathematician refers to his accuracy in music. Beethoven in cerebral or brainy.

Q11. Pattern 3: Summary Question

Question Pattern: the author depicts, quality as
Question Keywords: In line 13 Beethoven's in artistic expression

Step 1	Step 2	Step 3
Keywords from the Passage	Keywords from Answer	Tone & Concept
altruistic spirit	A) love of mankind	Synonym
Incorrect Choices & Common Patterns		
Evidence	Incorrect keywords	Tone & Concept
Beethoven a wide mental grasp, an altruistic spirit, that seeks to help humanity on the upward path.	B) highly skilled	D) is Negative C), E) are Too broad
	C) noble mind	
	D) opportunistic	
	E) insightful	

Q12. Type 4: Structural Characteristics [Pattern 7: Understanding Structure of the Passage]

Question Pattern: The parenthesis mainly functions as a
Question Keywords: line 14 (Bach...exception) in

Step 1	Step 2	Step 3
Keywords from the Passage	Keywords from Answer	Tone & Concept
(Bach is always an <u>exception</u>)	A) qualification	Synonym
Incorrect Choices & Common Patterns		
Evidence	Incorrect keywords	Tone & Concept
Up to Beethoven's time musicians in general (Bach is always an <u>exception</u>) performed their work without the aid of an intellect for the most part	B) speculation	When the author says "Bach is always an exception," he is giving a qualification to Bach.
	C) confirmation	
	D) contradiction	
	E) different opinion	

Q13. Type 2: Inference Question [Pattern 1: Local Question] {Category A}

Question Pattern: implies   **Question Keywords:** In line 1, "two antagonistic spirits"

Step 1	Step 2	Step 3
Keywords from the Passage	Keywords from Answer	Tone & Concept
devil and an angel, realized, character of the man	B) erratic nature	Similar Concept

Incorrect Choices & Common Patterns

Evidence	Incorrect keywords	Tone & Concept
Lines 1-5: The ancient fable of two antagonistic spirits **imprisoned in one body**, equally powerful and having the complete mastery by turns-of one man, that is to say, inhabited by both a devil and an angel seems to have been realized **in the character of the extraordinary man**	A) devil, angel spirit C) Allen Poe's works D) reputation of Edgar E) Dr. Rufus W. Griswold	A) Too literal implication

Q14. Pattern 7: Understanding Attitude / Tone

Question Pattern: The quote from, most strongly support which of the following statement?
Question Keywords: Dr. Rufus W. Griswold

Step 1	Step 2	Step 3
Keywords from the Passage	Keywords from Answer	Tone & Concept
startle many, but few will be grieved	E) debunks, viewpoint	Similar Concept

Incorrect Choices & Common Patterns

Evidence	Incorrect keywords	Tone & Concept
This announcement will startle many, but few will be grieved by it. The poet was known, personally or by reputation, in all this country; ...but he had few or no friends; and the regrets for his death will be suggested principally, literary art has lost	A) Long-term popularity B) brilliant stars C) Poe chose to live D) Even brilliant stars	The author alludes "by his death, many people startled, but few will be grieved by it." or E) debunk a different view

UNAUTHORIZED COPYING OR REUSE OF ANY PART OF THIS PAGE IS ILLEGAL

Q15. Pattern 3: Summary Question

Question Pattern: The author describes		Question Keywords: Edgar Allen Poe's literary skills as
Step 1	Step 2	Step 3
Keywords from the Passage	Keywords from Answer	Tone & Concept
eloquence (alluring)..., pallor (menacing)	E) menacing yet alluring	Synonym

Incorrect Choices & Common Patterns		
Evidence	Incorrect keywords	Tone & Concept
Line 18-20: His conversation was at times almost supramortal in its eloquence (alluring)... changeless in pallor (menacing), as his imagination quickened his blood or drew it back frozen to his heart.	A) mysterious, unknowable B) mildly oppressive C) orderly and appealing D) drab and boring	The text surrounding the word, 'eloquent' is positive. the remaining choices are all negative.

Q16. Pattern 5: Word-In-Context Question

Question Pattern: means		Question Keywords: In line 13, "eloquence"
Step 1	Step 2	Step 3
Keywords from the Passage	Keywords from Answer	Tone & Concept
voice, astonishing skill, expressive eyes, listened	B) persuasive speech	Similar Concept

Incorrect Choices & Common Patterns		
Evidence	Incorrect keywords	Tone & Concept
His voice was modulated with astonishing skill, and his large and variably expressive eyes ... shot fiery tumult into theirs who listened, while his own face glowed, or was changeless in pallor, as his	A) contradiction C) evil spirit D) deceptive nature E) ethics	e/loq/uence (e=happy); (loq=speech) = persuasive speech

Q17. Pattern 3: Summary Question

Question Pattern: the author addresses
Question Keywords: In lines 14 (His voice...eyes), Edgar Allen Poe's works

Step 1	Step 2	Step 3
Keywords from the Passage	Keywords from Answer	Tone & Concept
eloquence, voice, expressive eyes.	C) powerful expression	Similar Concept

Incorrect Choices & Common Patterns

Evidence	Incorrect keywords	Tone & Concept
His conversation was at times almost supramortal in its eloquence. His voice was modulated with astonishing skill and variably expressive eyes.	A) visual and auditory	E) is wrong because his works and life are mentioned in the first paragraph.
	B) supramotal with mortal	
	D) carelessly	
	E) personality	

Q18. Pattern 7: Understanding Attitude / Tone

Question Pattern: The tone of the passage is more

Step 1	Step 2	Step 3
Keywords from the Passage	Keywords from Answer	Tone & Concept
Poe is dead. Baltimore, Sunday, October 7th.	C) analytical	Similar Concept

Incorrect Choices & Common Patterns

Evidence	Incorrect keywords	Tone & Concept
The author analyzes between Poe's works and his posthumous reputation. Therefore, the tone is analytical by giving the exact date of his demise.	A) anecdotal	A) means personal. It's not personal.
	B) tentative	B) means not certain. The author's analysis is clear and certain.
	D) flippant	D) means insignificant. The tone is grave.
	E) humorous	

Q19. Pattern 3: Summary Question

Question Pattern: The first paragraph defines   **Question Keywords:** language mainly as

Step 1	Step 2	Step 3
Keywords from the Passage	Keywords from Answer	Tone & Concept
interwoven with all the affairs of human life	B) pervasive, all human	Similar Concept

Incorrect Choices & Common Patterns		
Evidence	Incorrect keywords	Tone & Concept
Lines 1-7: There is no subject so deeply interesting and important to ... upon all classes in the community; for there is no other so closely interwoven with all the affairs of human life	A) a restrictive C) different countries D) challenge E) an opportunity	the author characterizes language as a pervasive identity in all humankind. Choices A, C, D are negative. The passage is positive.

Q20. Type 3: Analogy Question [Pattern 1: Local Question] {Category A}

Question Pattern: Which of the following situations is most analogous to the statement
Question Keywords: in lines 10-11(Children...by them.)

Step 1	Step 2	Step 3
Keywords from the Passage	Keywords from Answer	Tone & Concept
Children, required, mere signs	E) school, fieldtrip	Similar Concept

Incorrect Choices & Common Patterns		
Evidence	Incorrect keywords	Tone & Concept
Children have been required to learn verbal forms, to look at the mere signs of ideas, instead of the things represented by them.	A) teaches history of violin B) The police, find a clue C) A church minister, works D) businessman learns	A) is opposite B), C) are Unrelated issue D) is one person action. the passage discusses two: school, children.

Q21. Type 1: Example Question [Pattern 1: Local Question] {Category A}

Question Keywords: The parent in line 9 is used to

Step 1	Step 2	Step 3
Keywords from the Passage	Keywords from Answer	Tone & Concept
the fault...be sought for in the manner of teaching,	D) manner of teaching	Similar Concept

Incorrect Choices & Common Patterns		
Evidence	Incorrect keywords	Tone & Concept
But it is to be presumed that the fault...be sought for in the manner of teaching, rather than in the science itself; earliest attention of the parent,	A) grammar	Minor Issue
	B) teaching language	Too broad
	C) indiscriminately	Not mentioned
	E) rail against	Too extreme word usage

1> As shown above, the fault is the manner of teaching, and the parents are used as an example.

2> The purpose of the example sentence is to emphasize its topic or main concern in the passage,

Q22. Pattern 7: Understanding Attitude / Tone

Question Pattern: The author's attitude toward is best described as

Question Keywords: the verbal forms in line 11

Step 1	Step 2	Step 3
Keywords from the Passage	Keywords from Answer	Tone & Concept
Children, required to learn, mere signs	E) obstacle	Similar Concept

Incorrect Choices & Common Patterns		
Evidence	Incorrect keywords	Tone & Concept
Lines 24-26:Children have been required to learn verbal forms and changes, to look at the mere signs of ideas, instead of the things represented by them. The consequence has been that the whole subject has become uninteresting to all	A) puzzling	The phrase 'the verbal forms' is surrounded by words such as 'required to learn' 'mere signs', which is an obstacle.
	B) unscientific	
	C) undeveloped	
	D) appreciative	

Q23. Pattern 2: Main Idea Question

Question Pattern: The second paragraph suggests that, mainly due to
Question Keywords: the difficulty of language is

Step 1	Step 2	Step 3
Keywords from the Passage	Keywords from Answer	Tone & Concept
But ...be <u>sought for in the manner of teaching</u>,	B) manner of teaching	Similar Concept
Incorrect Choices & Common Patterns		
Evidence	Incorrect keywords	Tone & Concept
Lines 10-13: <u>Great difficulty</u> has been experienced in the common <u>method of explaining language</u>, and grammar has long been considered a dry, But it is to be presumed that the fault in this case, if there is any, is to be <u>sought for in the manner of teaching</u>,	A) grammar C) science of language D) parent E) explaining language	A) "grammar" and E) "explaining language" are the parts of elements that make the manner of teaching difficult.

Q24. Pattern 7: Understanding Attitude / Tone

Question Pattern: The last paragraph (lines 5-13) conveys the general tone of

Step 1	Step 2	Step 3
Keywords from the Passage	Keywords from Answer	Tone & Concept
Great difficulty, Children have been required	C) admonishment	Similar Concept, Negative
Incorrect Choices & Common Patterns		
Evidence	Incorrect keywords	Tone & Concept
But it is to be presumed that <u>the fault in this case</u> is to be sought for in the manner of teaching, ...<u>Children have been required to learn verbal forms</u>,	A) gratitude	Positive
	B) detachment	means indifference
	D) hostility	Too extreme word usage
	E) indignation	Too extreme word usage

Q25. Pattern 2: Main Idea Question

Question Pattern: In the first paragraph, the author describes
Question Keywords: the remains of pueblo architecture is

Step 1	Step 2	Step 3
Keywords from the Passage	Keywords from Answer	Tone & Concept
This vast area, boundaries are still undefined.	D) immense	Quantity Measurement
Incorrect Choices & Common Patterns		
Evidence	Incorrect keywords	Tone & Concept
Lines 3-6: This vast area (immense) includes the and extends from central Utah on the north beyond the limits of the United States southward, in which direction its boundaries are still undefined.	A) impressive	A), C) are true statement but focuses on quality concept. The passage focuses on vastness (quantity measurement)
	B) puzzling	
	C) intriguing	
	E) undeveloped	

Q26. Pattern 5: Word-In-Context Question

Question Pattern: most nearly means   **Question Keywords:** In line 10, "adherence"

Step 1	Step 2	Step 3
Keywords from the Passage	Keywords from Answer	Tone & Concept
a close adherence...still bears	B) following	Synonym
Incorrect Choices & Common Patterns		
Evidence	Incorrect keywords	Tone & Concept
The architecture of this district exhibits a close adherence to aboriginal practices, still bears the …	A) inheritance	Adherence (ad: addition, here: to stick to) = following
	C) addition	
	D) kinship	
	E) technique	

Q27. Pattern 3: Summary Question

Question Pattern: Which of the following factors
Question Keywords: prevented whites from their visiting to the pueblos villages?

Step 1	Step 2	Step 3
Keywords from the Passage	Keywords from Answer	Tone & Concept
remoteness (II), arid (III), surroundings (IV)	E) II, III, IV	Similar Concept
Incorrect Choices & Common Patterns		
Evidence	keywords	Tone & Concept
Lines 10-12: The province has been often visited by whites, but the remoteness (II) of Tusayan and the arid (III) and forbidding character of its surroundings (IV) have caused its more complete isolation.	I. Few villages II. Proximity III. Aridity IV. Uninviting nature	I. "Few number of stone villages" is not found as a reason.

Q28. Pattern 7: Understanding Attitude / Tone

Question Pattern: The author views   **Question Keywords:** Pueblos

Step 1	Step 2	Step 3
Keywords from the Passage	Keywords from Answer	Tone & Concept
exhibits a close adherence to aboriginal practices,	D) tradition	Similar Concept
Incorrect Choices & Common Patterns		
Evidence	Incorrect keywords	Tone & Concept
The architecture of this district (C), (D) exhibits a close adherence to aboriginal practices, (E) under the exacting conditions of an arid environment, (B) but slowly yielding to the influence of foreign Ideas.	A) evolving	is using the present tense
	B) foreign intrusion	is opposite
	C) divisive	is opposite
	E) due to condition	is opposite

Q29. Pattern 3: Summary Question

Question Pattern: The passage demonstrates EXCEPT?
Question Keywords: the characteristics of pueblos village

Step 1	Step 2	Step 3
Keywords from the Passage	Keywords from Answer	Tone & Concept
stone villages/visited by whites/<u>yielding influence</u>	D) outside influence	Logical Conclusion
Incorrect Choices & Common Patterns		
Evidence	Incorrect keywords	Tone & Concept
(A) The descendants ,,,built these stone villages (B) inhabit pueblos distributed irregularly . (C) The province has been often visited by whites, (E) present study of the architecture...traditionally connected with them. (E) <u>but slowly yielding to the influence of foreign ideas.</u>	A) materials	they slowly yielded to the influence of foreign ideas.
	B) Distribution	
	C) white visitors	
	E) Aboriginal practice	

Always look for "but" from the passage because that's where the answer is hiding.

Q30. Pattern 2: Main Idea Question

Question Pattern: In the last paragraph (lines 13-15), the author mainly focuses
Question Keywords: on Pueblos'

Step 1	Step 2	Step 3
Keywords from the Passage	Keywords from Answer	Tone & Concept
ruins .... pueblo culture once extended.	E) vestige	Logical Conclusion
Incorrect Choices & Common Patterns		
Evidence	Incorrect keywords	Tone & Concept
The present study of the architecture of Tusayan and Cibola embraces... includes a number of <u>the ruins traditionally connected with them</u>.... <u>pueblo culture once extended.</u>	A) regional language	The last paragraph mainly deals with the present study of the architecture and their vestige.
	B) size	
	C) population	
	D) origin	

Q31. Pattern 3: Summary Question

Question Pattern: all of the followings EXCEPT

Question Keywords: The Romans transferred to Britain

Step 1	Step 2	Step 3
Keywords from the Passage	Keywords from Answer	Tone & Concept
though doubtless much inferior to those at Romies.	C) advanced build	Similar Concept
Incorrect Choices & Common Patterns		
Evidence	Incorrect keywords	Tone & Concept
Line 26: but also with their aid, as we learn from Tacitus, began at an early period to erect temples and public edifices, though doubtless much inferior to those at Romies.	A) civilization B) knowledge to build D) religion E) GOTHIC	Romans built many inferior temples on the island.

Q32. Pattern 5: Word-In-Context Question

Question Pattern: primarily serves to   **Question Keywords:** In line 6, "the prototypes"

Step 1	Step 2	Step 3
Keywords from the Passage	Keywords from Answer	Tone & Concept
these most ancient relics the prototypes appear,	C) enumerate	Similar Concept
Incorrect Choices & Common Patterns		
Evidence	Incorrect keywords	Tone & Concept
Prototype = original model Of these most ancient relics the prototypes appear, as described in Holy Writ, in the pillar raised at Bethel by Jacob, …	A) lament	Negative
	B) condemn	Negative
	D) material	Not stated
	E) cooperation	Not stated

Q33. Pattern 7: Understanding Attitude / Tone

Question Pattern: is primarily used to   **Question Keywords:** In line 5, "conceived"

Step 1	Step 2	Step 3
Keywords from the Passage	Keywords from Answer	Tone & Concept
are conceived to have been derived from	D) limited knowledge	Similar Concept

Incorrect Choices & Common Patterns		
Evidence	Incorrect keywords	Tone & Concept
and these are conceived to have been derived from the Phoenicians,…	A) importance	The usage of a word "conceived to be" (imagined) acknowledge the author's limited conviction.
	B) educate the reader	
	C) effectively confirm	
	E) flawed hypothesis	

Q34. Pattern 6: Understanding Structure of the Passage

Question Pattern: Which choice best describes the function of the
Question Keywords: statement in lines 15 ("though…at Romies")

Step 1	Step 2	Step 3
Keywords from the Passage	Keywords from Answer	Tone & Concept
though doubtless much inferior to those at Romies.	E) It qualifies	Similar Concept

Incorrect Choices & Common Patterns		
Evidence	Incorrect keywords	Tone & Concept
they not only instructed the natives in the arts of civilization, but also with their aid, as we learn from Tacitus, began at an early period to erect temples and public edifices, though doubtless much inferior to those at Romies.	A) It summarizes	By referring "though" the author qualifies (limits) the previous portion of the statement
	B) It provides support	
	C) It introduces	
	D) It challenges	

UNAUTHORIZED COPYING OR REUSE OF ANY PART OF THIS PAGE IS ILLEGAL

Q35. Type 2: Inference Question [Pattern 1: Local Question] {Category A}

Question Pattern: It can be inferred from the passage
Question Keywords: that the island had

Step 1	Step 2	Step 3
Keywords from the Passage	Keywords from Answer	Tone & Concept
merchants first introduced, aboriginal Britons	A) a commercial	Similar Concept
Incorrect Choices & Common Patterns		
Evidence	Incorrect keywords	Tone & Concept
Lines 8-9: …the Phoenicians, whose <u>merchants</u> first introduced amongst the aboriginal Britons the arts of incipient civilization."	B) under-control	Not stated
	C) warfare	
	D) no civilization	Opposite
	E) no temples	

Q36. Pattern 7: Understanding Attitude / Tone

Question Pattern: In the first paragraph, the narrator feels

Step 1	Step 2	Step 3
Keywords from the Passage	Keywords from Answer	Tone & Concept
I feared to go very far... The impression I had	D) cautious curiosity	Similar Concept
Incorrect Choices & Common Patterns		
Evidence	Incorrect keywords	Tone & Concept
<u>I feared to go very far</u> from the station, as we had arrived late and would start as near the correct time as possible. <u>The impression I had was that we were leaving the West</u> and entering the East;	A) unrestrained joy	The mood, based on the underlined words, shows a curiosity, tinged with caution.
	B) reminiscence	
	C) disappointment	
	E) foreboding	

Q37. Pattern 7: Understanding Attitude / Tone

Question Keywords: The narrator feared most in the first paragraph for

Step 1	Step 2	Step 3
Keywords from the Passage	Keywords from Answer	Tone & Concept
I feared to go very far...correct time	C) local time	Similar Concept

Incorrect Choices & Common Patterns		
Evidence	Incorrect keywords	Tone & Concept
Line 5: I feared to go very far from the station, as we had arrived late and would start as near the correct time as possible	A) new to the place	opposite
	B) the lack of German	Opposite
	D) entering from west	opposite
	E) Turkish traditions	Not stated

Q38. Pattern 7: Understanding Attitude / Tone

Question Pattern: The narrator believes   **Question Keywords:** speaking German would be

Step 1	Step 2	Step 3
Keywords from the Passage	Keywords from Answer	Tone & Concept
I don't know how I should be able to, without it.	E) not an option	Similar Concept

Incorrect Choices & Common Patterns		
Evidence	Incorrect keywords	Tone & Concept
I found my smattering of German very useful here; indeed, I don't know how I should be able to get on without it.	A) an excitement	The narrator found the ability to speak German a relief. A) he found it a necessity, not excitement for using German.
	B) social distinction	
	C) ethnic origin	
	D) an annoyance	

UNAUTHORIZED COPYING OR REUSE OF ANY PART OF THIS PAGE IS ILLEGAL

Q39. Type 3: Analogy Question [Pattern 1: Local Question] {Category A}

Question Pattern: Which choice resembles most the situation mentioned
Question Keywords: in line 15-17 (It had struck...country)?

Step 1	Step 2	Step 3
Keywords from the Passage	Keywords from Answer	Tone & Concept
trivial foreknowledge of the country, nobleman	D) unknown, Saudi King	Similar Concept
Incorrect Choices & Common Patterns		
Evidence	Incorrect keywords	Tone & Concept
It had struck me that trivial foreknowledge of the country (**an unknown classmate**) could hardly fail to have some importance in dealing with a nobleman (Saudi King) of that country.	A) shops at the Target	All the other options have no logical relations to the question.
	B) C.E.O. got caught	
	C) A rookie starts	
	E) C.E.O. step down	

Q40. Pattern 5: Word-In-Context Question

Question Pattern: means   **Question Keywords:** In line 16, "trivial"

Step 1	Step 2	Step 3
Keywords from the Passage	Keywords from Answer	Tone & Concept
trivial foreknowledge, hardly fail, importance	C) insignificant	Similar Concept
Incorrect Choices & Common Patterns		
Evidence	Incorrect keywords	Tone & Concept
it had struck me that trivial foreknowledge of the country could hardly fail to have some importance in dealing with a nobleman of that country. *Trivial = insignificant	A) considerable	The narrator emphasizes the importance of a nobleman compared to the insignificant knowledge about the country.
	B) important	
	D) heartfelt	
	E) resentment	

The word in context question always hides a clue word in the same line of the question.

Test 3 ABSOLUTE PATTERNS for the Analogy Section

Q31. Absolute Pattern 10: Subjective-Objective Pattern

E is the best answer

Beautiful is the subjective concept because there is no way to measure beautiful.

Miss. World Universe 2018, however, is the objective concept because she meets all the standards that measure her beauty.   This same concept is applied to (E)

Q32. Absolute Pattern 12: Active-Passive Pattern

B is the best answer

The goalie is a passive concept, while Missile is an active concept; save is passive, while spend is active.

Q33. Absolute Pattern 7: Association (Characteristic) Pattern

C is the best answer.

Museum is a quiet place as open market is a noisy place.

Choice A,B,D, and E are all wrong because they are not corresponding to "quiet" in the question.

Q34. Absolute Pattern 7: Association (Characteristic) Pattern

D is the best answer.   (Materials)

Wall is made of brick (characteristics) as painting is made of ink (characteristics)

Q35. Absolute Pattern 2: Part-Whole Pattern

E is the best answer

Egg yolk is a part of an egg as patty is a part of a hamburger

Choice A is Opposite

Q36. Absolute Pattern 1: Production (Cause-Effect) Pattern

A is the best answer

Coffee is produced by bean as gasoline is produced by crude oil.

Q37. Absolute Pattern 6:Purpose (Job/Tool) Pattern

B is the best answer

A job of mechanics is to fix cars as a job of editors is to fix the content of books.

Q38. Absolute Pattern 6:Purpose (Job/Tool) Pattern

A is the best answer

Students use pens, as professors use markers

Q39. Absolute Pattern 7: Association (Characteristic) Pattern

C is the best answer.

Geese migrate; frogs hibernate. In that sense, they have the same characteristics in responding winter.

Q40. Absolute Pattern 6:Purpose (Job/Tool) Pattern

A is the best answer.

The purpose of study for students is to get good report cards; The purpose of taxi drivers is to earn money.

Choice C is the true purpose statement but (A) is closer because the question and (A) are both human concepts.

Q41. Absolute Pattern 6:Purpose (Job/Tool) Pattern

A is the best answer

Both windows and mirrors have the same purpose on the wall and on the car.

Choice D is incorrect because telescopes are not attached to the sky.

Q42. Absolute Pattern 6:Purpose (Job/Tool) Pattern

B is the best answer

The purpose of a lottery is to win as the purpose of hockey leagues is for the championship.

Q43. Absolute Pattern 7: Association (Characteristic) Pattern

B is the best answer

Both sweat suits and chat are casual; both uniform and address are official.

Q44. Absolute Pattern 6:Purpose (Job/Tool) Pattern

E is the best answer

The purpose of half time at a soccer game is for a break; the purpose of the recess at school is for a break.

Q45. Absolute Pattern 6:Purpose (Job/Tool) Pattern

D is the best answer

The mechanic uses a drill as the surgeon uses a scalpel.

Q46. Absolute Pattern 5: Degree Pattern

C is the best answer.   Degree (strong to weak)

Both hot and spicy are greater degree than warm and tepid (medium)

Q47. Absolute Pattern 7: Association (Characteristic) Pattern

C is the best answer

Alibi is associated with criminal as investigations are associated with the police.

Q48. Absolute Pattern 5: Degree Pattern

A is the best answer

December is a part of a year as Thanksgiving is a part of the day in November.

Choice (B) is Association Pattern; (C), (D) are Part-Whole Pattern

(E) is Production Pattern

Q49. Absolute Pattern 2: Part-Whole Pattern

C is the best answer

Frog belongs to amphibian, as human belongs to mammal

Choice B) whale is not fish

Choice D) is flipped over.

Q50. Absolute Pattern 3: Antonym (Positive-Negative) Pattern

C is the best answer

Busy is an antonym to play and twisted is an antonym to straight.

Choice D has no antonym relations.

Q51. Absolute Pattern 1: Production (Cause-Effect) Pattern

E is the best answer.

Lullaby produces clam, and cacophony produces noise.

Q52. Absolute Pattern 6:Purpose (Job/Tool) Pattern

A is the best answer.

The purpose of a seminar is to present speech; the purpose of a concert is to present music.

Q53. Absolute Pattern 2: Part-Whole Pattern

A is the best answer

Bread is a part of bakery as painkiller is a part of medicine

Q54. Absolute Pattern 5: Degree Pattern

A is the best answer

Both humorous and warm are milder degree compared to hilarious and parched.

Q55. Absolute Pattern 6:Purpose (Job/Tool) Pattern

E is the best answer

The purpose of a refrigerator is to store milk, as the purpose of a library is to store books.

Choice A and C do not have the storage concept.

Q56. Absolute Pattern 2: Part-Whole Pattern

C is the best answer

The remote control is the part of T.V. set, and its main function is to aim a specific channel.

The trigger is the part of a gun, and its main function is to aim a specific target

Q57. Absolute Pattern 6:Purpose (Job/Tool) Pattern

C is the best answer

The draft notice is a sort of certificate to serve in the military. The car insurance is a sort of certificate to allow the automobile operation.

Q58. Absolute Pattern 4: Synonym Pattern

B is the best answer.

Referring and implying are synonyms, so are touching and guessing.

Q59. Absolute Pattern 6:Purpose (Job/Tool) Pattern

A is the best answer.

Stairs in a house are used to climb upstairs. Elevators in a building are used to climb upstairs.

Q60. Absolute Pattern 5: Degree Pattern

C is the best answer

An apprentice is a trainee and a maestro is a master.

In terms of the degree, the relations between a guess and steadfast are the same.

Test 3 Recap

Analyzing Purpose of Example

The answer to this type of question can be found not in the example sentence, but in the topic or concluding sentence that hosts the example text.

Author (narrator/character) usually employs an example text to emphasizes his argument.

The example sentence assesses the significance of the main argument by merely illustrating the event, idea, or theory. Especially, it often uses historical figures or authorities' quotation, or analogy, etc. Please note that the example sentence is easier to understand than the main argument.

That is why students try to find the answer by focusing on the example.

The crux of the matter is that when a question asks example, it doesn't necessarily mean the answer should automatically be found in the example sentence. Instead, the answer should mostly be located in the topic or the concluding sentence.

SSAT

Reading & Verbal Practice

Test 4

ALL THE LOGIC AND RULES

BEHIND THE EVERY SINGLE

SSAT QUESTION

Test 4 Reading Section
Time: 40 Minutes, 40 Questions

Directions: Each reading passage is followed by questions about it. Answer the questions that follow a passage on the basis of what is stated or implied in that passage.

Questions 1-6 are based on the following passage.

Line

We hold these truths to be self-evident, that all men are created equal, that they are endowed by their Creator with certain unalienable Rights, that among these are Life, Liberty, and the pursuit of Happiness. That to secure these rights, Governments are instituted among Men, deriving their just powers from the consent of the governed, that whenever any Form of

5 Government becomes destructive of these ends, it is the Right of the People to alter or to abolish it, and to institute new Government, laying its foundation on such principles and organizing its powers in such form, as to them shall seem most likely to effect their Safety and Happiness. Prudence, indeed, will dictate that Governments long established should not be changed for light and transient causes; and accordingly all experience hath shown, that

10 mankind are more disposed to suffer, while evils are sufferable, than to right themselves by abolishing the forms to which they are accustomed. But when a long train of abuses and usurpations, pursuing invariably the same Object evinces a design to reduce them under absolute Despotism, it is their right, it is their duty, to throw off such Government, and to provide new Guards for their future security.

15 Such has been the patient sufferance of these Colonies; and such is now the necessity which constrains them to alter their former Systems of Government.

1

The phrase "self-evident" in line 1 can be understood as some truths are

A) beyond our judgment

B) morally perfect

C) beyond the political interpretation

D) open-ended debate

E) determined by staunch advocacy

2

The author defines the government is

A) the most suitable way to protect rights of the people

B) the binding contract that cannot be altered

C) the one that can be newly instituted if a form of government gets destructive

D) people's responsibility to divide the powers within the government

E) that it can do whatever to protect the lives of the citizens.

CONTINUE

3

According to the passage, the colonies to institute new government was driven by?

A) despotism

B) deprive of suffrage

C) deprive of slavery

D) deprive of loyalty

E) unequal treatment

4

In line 2, "Unalienable" most nearly means

A) insecure

B) cannot be taken away

C) familiar

D) not foreign

E) incompatible

5

The author's attitude to "Despotism" in line 13 is best described as

A) admiration

B) appreciation

C) enthusiasm

D) warning

E) necessity

6

The statement "such is now" (line 15) serves to indicate the

A) vitality

B) anger

C) excitement

D) forecast

E) urgency

CONTINUE

Questions 7-12 are based on the following passage.

Line   The natural position of woman is clearly, to a limited degree, a subordinate one. Such it has always been throughout the world, in all ages, and in many widely different conditions of society. There are three conclusive reasons why we should expect it to continue so for the future.

5   FIRST. Woman in natural physical strength is so greatly inferior to man that she is entirely in his power, quite incapable of self-defense, trusting to his generosity for protection. In savage life this great superiority of physical strength makes man the absolute master, woman the abject slave. This difference in physical strength must, in itself, always prevent such perfect equality, since woman is compelled every day of her life to appeal to man for

10   protection, and for support.

    Woman is also, though in a very much less degree, inferior to man in intellect. The difference in this particular may very probably be only a consequence of greater physical strength, giving greater power of endurance and increase of force to the intellectual faculty. connected with it. In many cases, as between the best individual minds of both sexes, the

15   difference is no doubt very slight.

7

The primary purpose of the passage is to

A) advance unilateral opinion

B) question a common belief

C) modify one's feeling

D) predict an outcome from the reader

E) advocate the generally accepted principle

8

The author believes that woman's subordinate position

A) will remain unchanged

B) is predicted to get worse in the future

C) is within geographic constraints

D) has been altered greatly recently

E) is limited to women's ages

CONTINUE

9

Male chauvinist would most likely disagree with which assertion from the passage?

A) Man's greater physical strength gives greater endurance

B) Woman's subordinate natural position can be found throughout the world

C) The difference is no doubt very slight among the best individual minds of both sexes

D) Woman is intellectually inferior to man

E) Woman is physically greatly inferior to man

10

In line 7 "abject" most nearly means

A) defiant

B) total

C) miserable

D) submissive

E) objective

11

The main difference between the second and third paragraph is that the second paragraph presents

A) the author's view; the third, public view

B) woman's intellectual inferiority; the third, the physical inferiority

C) woman's physical inferiority; the third, intellectual inferiority

D) widely accepted perspective; the third, the view of the author

E) woman's intellectual inferiority; the third, its exceptional case

12

From the male chauvinist's view, lines 14-15 ("the difference is no doubt very slight".) can be best understood as the

A) general pattern

B) interesting deviance

C) absolute fact

D) ambivalent hypothesis

E) atypical perspective

CONTINUE

Questions 13-18 are based on the following passage.

Line   The medical profession is justly conservative. Human life should not be considered as the proper material for wild experiments. Conservatism, however, is too often a welcome excuse for lazy minds, loath to adapt themselves to fast changing conditions. Remember the scornful reception which first was accorded to Freud's discoveries in the domain of the unconscious.

5   When after years of patient observations, he finally decided to appear before medical bodies to tell them modestly of some facts which always recurred in his dream and his patients' dreams, he was first laughed at and then avoided as a crank.

       Some of them, like Professor Boris Sidis, reach at times conclusions which are strangely similar to Freud's, but in their ignorance of psychoanalytic literature, they fail to credit Freud for

10   observations antedating theirs.

13

"The medical bodies " in line 5 viewed the research of Professor Boris Sidis in line 8 with

A) curiosity
B) acceptance
C) ambivalence
D) skepticism
E) respect

14

The author feels Professor Boris Sidis' research is

A) a valuable theory
B) a central example of his belief and theory
C) an example of unfair treatment to Freud's thesis
D) as equally problematic as Frud's thesis
E) a proof of Freud's thesis

15

The author characterizes the "conservatism" in line 2 as the

A) cult physicians should not attempt to follow
B) harmful tradition that are unlikely to yield any meaningful medical advancement
C) valuable perceptions but too rigid in its application
D) axiom that should always be venerated
E) value that has little relevance to medical profession

16

It can be inferred from the passage that unlike Freud's theories, Boris Sidis applied in his theories the

A) meaningful information
B) support from renown scientists
C) principles of conservatism
D) personal experience
E) scientific experiment

CONTINUE

17

"psychoanalytic literature" in line 24 is significant because it is

A) the major backbone of all of the Freud's theories

B) something similar to that of Professor Boris Sidis

C) practical theory in psychology

D) creative theory initiated by Freud

E) pseudoscience

18

According to the passage, Freud was primarily motivated by which of the following?

A) conservatism in the medical profession

B) human unconsciousness

C) Professor Boris Sidis,

D) psychoanalytic literature

E) the medical bodies of his era

Questions 19-24 are based on the following passage.

Line

There is a something in you, as in every one, that requires the tonic life of the wild. You may not know it, but there is a part of your nature that only the wild can reach. The much-housed, overheated, overdressed, and over-entertained life of most girls is artificial.

What is it about a true woodsman that instantly compels our respect, that sets him apart from
5 the men who might be of his class in village, though he may be exteriorly rough and have little or no book education? The real Adirondack or the North Woods guide, alert, clean-limbed, clear-eyed, hard-muscled, bearing his pack-basket or duffel-bag on his back, doing all the hard work of the camp, never loses his poise or the simple dignity which he shares with all the things of the wild. He is as conscious of his superior knowledge of the woods as an astronomer
10 is of his knowledge of the stars, and patiently tolerates the ignorance and awkwardness of the "tenderfoot" from the city. Only a keen sense of humor can make this toleration possible, for I have seen things done by a city-dweller at camp that would enrage a woodsman, unless the irresistibly funny side of it made him laugh his inward laugh that seldom reaches the surface. To live for a while in the wild strengthens the muscles of your mind as well as of your body.
15 Flabby thoughts and flabby muscles depart together and are replaced by enthusiasm and vigor of purpose. To *have* seems not so desirable as to *be*.

CONTINUE

19

The author is primarily concerned with

A) To have in the nature

B) To have in our lives

C) The creative life

D) To be in the nature

E) To have ethical life

20

From the author's perspective, "though he may be…

no book education?" (lines 5-6) can be considered as

A) lack of persistence

B) an ignorant person

C) the major defects in life

D) the inessential quality to earn respect

E) an uncultivated person

21

In lines 13-14 "inward laugh that seldom reaches

the surface" suggests that the woodsman

A) rarely reveals his true feelings

B) tends to be a reclusive person

C) is by nature inclined to be discontented

D) uncommunicative person

E) is most skillful deceiver

22

The passage as a whole suggests that the world of wild

is

A) the rarified region that should be protected

B) the unique place to see our deeper soul

C) the remote place that requires arduous life

D) an ideal but impractical place for city dwellers

E) where it dismisses village people

23

"To_have_…to_be." in line 16 serves to provide

an example of

A) a part of our nature that only the wild can provide

B) the tonic life

C) something that everyone has

D) skepticism towards city life and joy in the wilderness

E) particular references that impress city dwellers

24

The author's view on the true woodsman and the city

dwellers are a pair of, respectively

A) the poor and the abundant

B) the uneducated and the educated

C) to be and to have

D) the wise and the stupid

E) the respected and the inferior

CONTINUE

Questions 25-30 are based on the following passage.

Line It was on the way to Sandown Park that I met him first, on that horribly wet July afternoon. He sat opposite to me in the train going down, and my attention was first attracted to him by the marked contrast between his appearance and his attire: he had not thought fit to adopt the regulation costume for such occasions, and I think I never saw a man who had made himself

5 more aggressively horsey.

  The mark of the beast was sprinkled over his linen: he wore snaffle sleeve-links, a hard hunting-hat, a Newmarket coat, and extremely tight trousers. His expression was mild and inoffensive, and his watery pale eyes and receding chin gave one the idea that he was hardly to be trusted astride anything more spirited than a gold-headed cane. And yet, somehow, he

10 aroused compassion rather than any sense of the ludicrous: he had that look of shrinking self-effacement which comes of a recent humiliation, and, in spite of all extravagances, he was obviously a gentleman; while something in his manner indicated that his natural tendency would, once at all events, have been to avoid any kind of extremes.

  He puzzled me so much that I did my best to enter into conversation with him, only to be

15 baffled by the jerky embarrassment with which he met all advances.

25

The intended effect of the portrayal of a man (line 4) is to show

A) an inescapable fate

B) the person's peculiarity

C) the origin of the companionship

D) the resemblance of his face with an animal

E) the person's brutality

26

In the second paragraph (lines 6-15) , the author characterizes the man as one who EXCEPT

A) has a receding face

B) wears a humorous outfit

C) has a suspicious nature

D) has a certain way of his speech

E) enjoys occasional extremes

27

In the third paragraph, the narrator's feeling shifts from

A) fear to courage

B) curiosity to humiliation

C) regret to the determination

D) uncertainty to despair

E) anger to forgiveness

28

Throughout the passage the author reflects his observation from the perspective of

A) personal speculation

B) broad generalizations

C) familiar acquaintance

D) scholarly analysis

E) factual exposure

CONTINUE

29

The passage as a whole is written by the narrator who?

A) speculates about a man

B) became a friend to a man

C) reflects a man's younger days

D) wishes to improve their relationships

E) knows everything about the man

30

The man might have reacted to the narrator's advancement (lines 14-15) as

A) an unsophisticated plan

B) a generous invitation

C) a humorous attempt

D) a friendly invitation

E) an annoying intrusion

Questions 31-35 are based on the following passage.

Line

What is the peculiar charm of that mighty, snow-capped sea of mountains, whose stupendous waves tossed far into the heavens seem ever about to overwhelm the level wheat-fields of Western Canada? The lure of the mountains defies analysis, but it is surely there with its irresistible appeal to all in whom the spirit of romance is not quite dead. It stirs

5 the blood strangely when, far out on the plains of Alberta, you get your first glimpse of the Canadian Alps--a line of white, glittering peaks just above the horizon, infinitely remote and ethereal, something altogether apart from the prosaic world about you of grain and cattle, neat farm-house and unsightly elevator.

As you follow the course of the sun, the peaks loom gradually up into the sky and dominate

10 the scene, but still retain the atmosphere of another world. The rolling foothills in the foreground, like spent waves from the storm-tossed sea, seem tangible and comprehensible, but beyond and above the dark ramparts of the outer range, the towering outer wave of the mountains, float silvery outlines that seem to be the fabric of some other and purer world.

One who has seen this vision may not resist the insistent call to explore the mountain world,

15 to discover what lies beyond the frowning battlements that guard this other realm. The call has been working in the hearts of men for generations. They came alone in the early days, each man fighting his way up through some doorway that led into the heart of the Glittering Mountains.

CONTINUE

31

"The lure of the mountains defies analysis" (line 3)

A) emphasizes the importance of analysis

B) distinguishes what can be and cannot be
    analyzed

C) sets apart the entity that has no analytical concept

D) elevates the rarified position of the mountains

E) shows the author's analytical skills

32

The author's characterization to Canadian Alps
includes all of the followings EXCEPT

A) the romantic appeal

B) the heavenly appearance

C) the impressiveness

D) the earthly view

E) the immensity

33

The passage calls attention to which aspect of the
mountain?

A) Its sublimity

B) Its mysteriousness

C) Its influence to human

D) Its national identity

E) Its popular appeal

34

"The rolling foothills" (line 10) and "purer world"

(line 13) are used to refer to the distinction between

A) a short distance and a long distance

B) the everyday world and the fictional world

C) a safe place and a dangerous place

D) the earthly scene and the ethereal scene

E) our worldview and foreigners' worldview

35

Which of Alps' features does the author mainly
describes in paragraph 3?

A) skepticism to the climbers

B) stylistic features of the mountain

C) the historical importance

D) people's desire to approach

E) the symbolic meaning of the mountain

CONTINUE

Questions 36-40 are based on the following passage.

Line

First let us say how the question presents itself to us. The fact which we must take as there exists something which is "knowable." Not only science, but ordinary life and our everyday conversation, imply that there are things that we know. It is with regard to these things that we have to ask ourselves if some belong to what we call the mind and others to what we call

5 matter. Let us suppose, by way of hypothesis, the knowable to be entirety and absolute. In that case we should be obliged to set aside the question as one already decided because there is no distinction to be drawn. But this hypothesis is, as we all know, falsified by observation. The whole body of the knowable is formed from an agglomeration of extremely varied elements, amongst which it is easy to distinguish a large number of divisions. Things

10 may be classified according to their color, their shape, their weight, the pleasure they give us, their quality of being alive or dead, and so on; one much given to classification would only be troubled by the number of possible distinctions.

Since so many divisions are possible, at which shall we stop and say: this is the one which corresponds exactly to the opposition of mind and matter? The choice is not easy to make.

15 Since we propose to make ourselves judges of these distinctions, since, in fact, we shall reject most of them in order to suggest entirely new ones, it must be supposed that we shall do so by means of a criterion. Otherwise, we should only be acting fantastically.

36

"Let us…to be drawn." in lines 5-7 is best understood as everything is

A) homogeneous

B) beyond analytical

C) measured by data

D) tangible

E) intangible

37

The author suggests that the term "knowable" (line 2) is an entity that should be

A) applied better in the scientific boundary

B) limited to the ordinary life

C) Interdependent from all theories.

D) encompassed by our mind and matter

E) excluded from our mind and matter

CONTINUE

38

All of the following elements can be classified as a knowable entirety EXCEPT

A) color

B) mortality

C) the mood of a person watching a movie

D) the mood of a character in a movie

E) weight

39

In line 17, when the author says "acting fantastically", it can be interpreted as

A) theoretically

B) empirically

C) randomly

D) wonderfully

E) magically

40

In the last paragraph (lines 13-17), the author suggests which of the following?

A) offering a criterion for unknowable is impossible

B) offering a criterion for unknowable should start by adding knowable

C) there's no division to unknowable

D) the current distinctions between knowable and unknowable will only blur the lines

E) unknowable is not necessarily a new thing

Test 4 Verbal Section   30 MINUTES, 60 QUESTIONS

Directions: the synonym questions ask you to find the most appropriate synonym to the question.

The analogy questions ask you to find the most appropriate analogy to the question.
Select the answer that best matches to the question.

Synonym Sample Question:

Q: SUPERIOR

A higher rank

B inferior

C considerable

D supermarket

E supper

A) is the best answer because the synonym for superior is higher rank.

B) is incorrect because it applies the 'opposite concept.

C) and E) are irrelevant words.

D) is incorrect because it applies physical concept to mental concept

---

Test 4 Synonym questions 1 to 30

1. ACQUIESCE
(A) accept
(B) acquire
(C) quiet
(D) account
(E) acquisition

2. VIGOR
(A) victory
(B) strength
(C) model
(D) gorgeous
(E) great

3. PINNACLE
(A) fruit
(B) paint
(C) clever
(D) peak
(E) sharp

4. CITADEL
(A) tired
(B) delegate
(C) fortress
(D) city
(E) town

5. OMINOUS
(A) onion
(B) forbidding
(C) vocabulary
(D) agree
(E) manner

CONTINUE

6. FRENZY

(A) easy

(B) fire

(C) fury

(D) freelance

(E) friend

7. ACRID

(A) harsh

(B) arcane

(C) agree

(D) accept

(E) accordance

8. VITAL

(A) vibration

(B) talent

(C) energetic

(D) state

(E) vision

9. TRANQUIL

(A) noise

(B) peace

(C) train

(D) automobile

(E) people

10. SYMBOL

(A) representation

(B) simple

(C) abnormal

(D) signature

(E) similarity

11. SHUN

(A) sun

(B) avoid

(C) wait

(D) sign

(E) copy

12. RESTORE

(A) fix

(B) shop

(C) make

(D) produce

(E) repeat

13. ADAMANT

(A) stubborn

(B) flexible

(C) address

(D) mantle

(E) adage

14. ADHERENT

(A) follower

(B) place

(C) inflexible

(D) advice

(E) addition

15. MOCK

(A) make fun of

(B) test

(C) modify

(D) mode

(E) pain

CONTINUE

16. COLLABORATE

(A) university

(B) labor

(C) work together

(D) union

(E) toothpaste

17. FALTER

(A) pause

(B) palpitate

(C) parent

(D) continue

(E) fable

18. ADMONISH

(A) chastise

(B) teach

(C) add

(D) demonstrate

(E) monster

19. SOBER

(A) wet

(B) not drunk

(C) animal

(D) accept

(E) base

20. SURGE

(A) supplement

(B) surrogate

(C) upwelling

(D) doctor

(E) certificate

21. DRASTIC

(A) easy going

(B) draconian

(C) extreme

(D) design

(E) down

22. DISPLACE

(A) habitat

(B) get rid of

(C) relocation

(D) dance

(E) fix

23. SOMBER

(A) sad

(B) joy

(C) hate

(D) argue

(E) someday

24. ADROIT

(A) dexterous

(B) unskillful

(C) difficult

(D) add

(E) itinerary

25. ADULATION

(A) reintroduction

(B) praise

(C) deny

(D) boring

(E) refrain

CONTINUE

26. STUBBORN

(A) obstinate

(B) yielding

(C) idea

(D) state

(E) strategy

27. UNIFORM

(A) vary

(B) dress

(C) official

(D) even

(E) colorful

28. OFFENSIVE

(A) defensive

(B) propensity

(C) belligerent

(D) skillful

(E) protect

29. TOXIC

(A) poisonous

(B) alcoholic

(C) transported

(D) excite

(E) healing

30. PRECISE

(A) exact

(B) loosen

(C) deviant

(D) similar

(E) cut

Analogy Sample Question:

Q: River is to Ocean as:

A better is to good

B rain is to cloud

C father is to mother

D city is to country

E fork is to spoon

D is the correct answer. Just as the river is smaller than the Ocean, the city is smaller than the country. The pattern applied in this question is the Degree Pattern (small to big)

A) is incorrect because the word order is flipped over.

B) is incorrect because it applies the production pattern (cloud produces rain)

C), E) are incorrect because they apply the Antonym patterns.

Test 4 Analogy questions 31 to 60

31. Money is to counterfeit as genuine art is to

(A) resemblance

(B) match

(C) auction

(D) museum

(E) forgery

CONTINUE

32. Rat is to cat as

(A) zebra is to lion

(B) tiger is to chicken

(C) cow is to man

(D) food is to refrigerator

(E) word is to sentence

33. Music is to melody as cacophony is to

(A) phone

(B) noise

(C) conservation

(D) dialog

(E) conference

34. Arduous is to work as poignant is to

(A) heart

(B) sympathy

(C) friend

(D) competition

(E) argument

35. Midwife is to nurse as

(A) wife is to husband

(B) officer is to trainee

(C) cut is to trim

(D) gift is to souvenir

(E) tradition is to modern

36. Striker is to goal as

(A) police is to uniform

(B) soccer is to goalkeeper

(C) car is to gas

(D) money is to happiness

(E) sleep is to rest

37. Bathroom is to toilet bowl as

(A) tail is to lion

(B) speaker is to radio

(C) kitchen is to sink

(D) juice is to orange

(E) road is to passerby

38. Movie is to close-up as

(A) life is to happiness

(B) typing is to font

(C) work is to money

(D) book is to excerpt

(E) book is to editor

39. Cub is to bear as rookie is to

(A) captain player

(B) spectator

(C) baseball player

(D) trainee

(E) benchwarmers

\40. Bandage is to blood as

(A) dam is to flood

(B) fire is to extinguisher

(C) library is to book

(D) police is to crime

(E) fight is to conciliation

41. Fan is to circulate as wall is to

(A) brick

(B) insulate

(C) attack

(D) strong

(E) high

CONTINUE

42. Gaggle is to goose
(A) spectator is to crowd
(B) viewer is to audience
(C) school is to fish
(D) ram is ewe
(E) lender is to loaner

43. Wrap is to conceal as
(A) present is to heart
(B) preserve to store
(C) study is to succeed
(D) dignity is to king
(E) insult is to blame

44. Blade is to cut as
(A) florist is to flower
(B) pin is to grenade
(C) island is to ocean
(D) draw is to chalk
(E) needle is to stitch

45. Pound is to weight as
(A) liter is to volume
(B) centimeter is to inch
(C) square is to cubic square
(D) heavy is to ponderous
(E) radius is to half

46. Serial number is to item is
(A) carat (k) is to gold
(B) domain address is to website
(C) editor is to book
(D) cage is to animal
(E) calorie is to burn

47. Epoch is to era as
(A) stanza is to paragraph
(B) airplane is to fly
(C) teacher is to teach
(D) loan is to interest
(E) chronic is to history

48. Brawn is to intelligence as
(A) lemonade is to lemon
(B) present is to past
(C) ancient temple is to myth
(D) swamp is to alligator
(E) plastic is to house

49. Grace is to old lady as wizened is to
(A) boy
(B) girl
(C) queen
(D) army
(E) king

50. Coffee is to brew as
(A) fire is to extinguish
(B) fire is to boil
(C) bread is to bake
(D) orange is to juice
(E) crayon is to drawing

51. Food is to expiry date as airline ticket is to
(A) paper
(B) logo
(C) passenger name
(D) itinerary
(E) airline company name

CONTINUE

52. Gold is to silence as

(A) anarchist is to order

(B) rebel is to maverick

(C) money is to time

(D) king is to chief

(E) baseball fan is to enthusiastic

53. Painter is to brush as editor is to

(A) book

(B) pen

(C) newspaper

(D) publisher

(E) library

54. School is to knowledge as

(A) factory is to machine

(B) government office is to officer

(C) cross is to bridge

(D) animal is to zoo

(E) church is to prayer

55. Chandelier is to ceiling as

(A) root is to fungus

(B) bat is to cave

(C) tiger is to cage

(D) neck is to necklace

(E) tree is to apple

56. Swamp is to wet as

(A) sand is to beach

(B) fire is to boil

(C) desert is to arid

(D) orange is to citrus

(E) alcohol is to drink

57. Baseball is to diamond as

(A) pearl is to white

(B) sprint is to track

(C) jewelry is to mall

(D) stadium is to spectator

(E) defense is to offense

58. Happiness is to sadness as

(A) boy is to girl

(B) queen is to king

(C) amiable is to antagonism

(D) guilty is to not guilty

(E) politician is to voters

59. Secret is to exposure as intangible is to

(A) tangible

(B) spy

(C) floor

(D) discussion

(E) inspection

60. Lion is to brave as

(A) geese is to gaggle

(B) fish is to swim

(C) robot is to walk

(D) honey bee is to tremble dance

(E) bagger is to lazy

STOP

If you finish before time is called,
you may check your work on this section.

Do not turn to the next section.

UNAUTHORIZED COPYING OR REUSE OF ANY PART OF THIS PAGE IS ILLEGAL

Test 4

ABSOLUTE PATTERNS

TEST 4
READING SECTION

Please refer to the Reading Section Absolute Pattern Analysis next page

| THE SYNONYM QUESTIONS | | THE ANALOGY QUESTIONS |
| TEST 4 NO.1 ~ 30 | | TEST 4 NO. 31 ~ 60 |

Please refer to the Analogy Section Absolute Pattern Analysis in page 242

1	A	16	C
2	B	17	A
3	D	18	A
4	C	19	B
5	B	20	C
6	C	21	C
7	A	22	C
8	C	23	A
9	B	24	A
10	A	25	B
11	B	26	A
12	A	27	D
13	A	28	C
14	A	29	A
15	A	30	A

Test 4

ABSOLUTE PATTERNS for the Reading Section

Q1. Pattern 5: Word-In-Context Question

Question Pattern: The phrase can be understood as
Question Keywords: "self-evident" in line 1 some truths are

Step 1	Step 2	Step 3
Keywords from the Passage	Keywords from Answer	Tone & Concept
be self-evident, ... unalienable Rights,	A) beyond our judgment	Similar Concept
Incorrect Choices & Common Patterns		
Evidence	Incorrect keywords	Tone & Concept
We hold these truths to be self-evident, that all men are created equal, that they are endowed by their Creator with certain unalienable Rights, * unalienable Rights = Rights that is absolute and can't be taken away.	B) morally C) political D) open-ended debate E) advocacy	B) it's not about morality. C) it's not limited to "the political" D) is Opposite E) it's not about advocacy.

The phrase "self-evident" in line 1 can be understood as some truths are perfect and cannot be questioned.
Self-evident = beyond our judgment

Q2. Pattern 2: Main Idea Question

Question Pattern: The author's analysis   **Question Keywords:** of government is

Step 1	Step 2	Step 3
Keywords from the Passage	Keywords from Answer	Tone & Concept
the Right of the People to alter or to abolish it	C) can be newly instituted	Similar Concept
Incorrect Choices & Common Patterns		
Evidence	Incorrect keywords	Tone & Concept
Line 6: ...that whenever any Form of Government becomes destructive of these ends, it is the Right of the People to alter or to abolish it, and to institute new Government.	A) the most suitable	Too extreme word usage
	B) the binding contract	Opposite
	D) divide the power	not stated
	E) it can do whatever	Too extreme word usage

Q3. Pattern 3: Summary Question

Question Pattern: According to the passage,
Question Keywords: colonies to institute new government was driven by?

Step 1	Step 2	Step 3
Keywords from the Passage	Keywords from Answer	Tone & Concept
But abuses, to reduce absolute Despotism	A) despotism	Synonym

Incorrect Choices & Common Patterns		
Evidence	Incorrect keywords	Tone & Concept
But when a long train of abuses and usurpations, pursuing invariably the same Object evinces a design to reduce them under absolute Despotism, Despot = cruel ruler	B) deprive of suffrage C) deprive of slavery D) deprive of loyalty E) unequal treatment	B) is wrong because suffrage means the right to vote, and instituting the new colony government is not about the voting right

Q4. Pattern 5: Word-In-Context Question

Question Pattern: most nearly means	**Question Keywords:** In line 2, "Unalienable"	
Step 1	Step 2	Step 3
Keywords from the Passage	Keywords from Answer	Tone & Concept
L be self-evident, unalienable Rights,	B) cannot be taken away	Synonym

Incorrect Choices & Common Patterns		
Evidence	Incorrect keywords	Tone & Concept
We hold these truths to be self-evident, that all men are created equal, that they are endowed by their Creator with certain unalienable Rights,	A) insecure C) familiar D) not foreign E) incompatible	* unalienable Rights = Rights that is absolute and can't be taken away.

Q5. Pattern 7: Understanding Attitude / Tone

Question Pattern: The author's attitude is best described as
Question Keywords: toward "Despotism" in line 13

Step 1	Step 2	Step 3
Keywords from the Passage	Keywords from Answer	Tone & Concept
design to reduce them under absolute Despotism	D) warning	similar concept

Incorrect Choices & Common Patterns		
Evidence	Incorrect keywords	Tone & Concept
But when a long train of **abuses and usurpations**, pursuing invariably the same Object evinces a design to **reduce them under absolute Despotism**,	A) admiration B) appreciation C) enthusiasm E) necessity	The author's tone is grave and negative. Therefore, all the other choices are wrong Despot = cruel ruler

Q6. Type 2: Inference Question [Pattern 1: Local Question] {Category A}

Question Pattern: The statement, serves to indicate   **Question Keywords:** "such is now" (line 15)

Step 1	Step 2	Step 3
Keywords from the Passage	Keywords from Answer	Tone & Concept
Such has been the patient, and such is now	E) urgency	Similar Concept

Incorrect Choices & Common Patterns		
Evidence	Incorrect keywords	Tone & Concept
--Such has been the patient sufferance of these Colonies; and such is now the necessity which constrains them to alter their former Systems of Government.	A) vitality B) anger C) excitement D) forecast	"Such is now" refers to the urgency.

Q7. Pattern 2: Main Idea Question

Question Pattern: The primary purpose of the passage is to

Step 1	Step 2	Step 3
Keywords from the Passage	Keywords from Answer	Tone & Concept
The natural position of woman, subordinate	A) advance unilateral opinion	Similar Concept

Incorrect Choices & Common Patterns		
Evidence	Incorrect keywords	Tone & Concept
The natural position of woman is clearly, to a limited degree, a subordinate one.	B) question, common belief	Unilateral (one-sided opinion) The author does not compare others' view. Therefore, it is a unilateral
	C) modify one's feeling	
	D) predict an outcome	
	E) advocate principle	

Q8. Absolute Pattern 8: Understanding Primary Purpose

Question Pattern: The author believes that   **Question Keywords:** woman's subordinate position

Step 1	Step 2	Step 3
Keywords from the Passage	Keywords from Answer	Tone & Concept
we should expect it to continue so for the future.	A) remain unchanged	Similar Concept

Incorrect Choices & Common Patterns		
Evidence	Incorrect keywords	Tone & Concept
There are three conclusive reasons why <u>we should expect it to continue so for the future</u>.	B) get worse	Not stated
	C) geographic	Not stated
The author believes that woman's subordinate position will remain unchanged	D) altered	Opposite
	E) women's ages	Not stated

When the entire paragraph is in question, don't forget to focus on the last sentence of the previous paragraph or the topic sentence of the following paragraph. That's where you can find the answer

Q9. Type 3: Analogy Question [Pattern 1: Local Question] {Category A}

Question Keywords: Male chauvinist would most likely disagree with which assertion from the passage?

Step 1	Step 2	Step 3
Keywords from the Passage	Keywords from Answer	Tone & Concept
women of a very high order of genius	C) difference very slight	Similar Concept

Incorrect Choices & Common Patterns		
Evidence	Incorrect keywords	Tone & Concept
There have been women of a very high order of genius; there have been very many women of great talent	A) Man's strength	male chauvinist will disagree with the statement (C) "the difference is no doubt very slight."
	B) Woman's subordinate	
*male chauvinist =a person who is excessively prejudiced to male dominancy.	D) Woman inferior	
	E) Woman inferior	

Q10. Pattern 5: Word-In-Context Question

Question Pattern: most nearly means   **Question Keywords:** In line 7 "abject"

Step 1	Step 2	Step 3
Keywords from the Passage	Keywords from Answer	Tone & Concept
man the **absolute** master, *woman the abject slave*.	B) total	Similar Concept

Incorrect Choices & Common Patterns		
Evidence	Incorrect keywords	Tone & Concept
In savage life this great superiority of physical strength makes **man the absolute master**, *woman the abject slave*.	A) defiant	Abject = absolute (total)
	C) miserable	
	D) submissive	
	E) objective	

The hint for the Word-In-Context question lies in the same line with the question.

Q11. Pattern 6: Understanding Structure of the Passage

Question Pattern: The main difference between the second and third paragraph is that

Step 1	Step 2	Step 3
Keywords from the Passage	Keywords from Answer	Tone & Concept
physical, inferior intellect	C) physical, intellectual	Logical Conclusion

Incorrect Choices & Common Patterns		
Evidence	Incorrect keywords	Tone & Concept
The second paragraph presents a woman's physical inferiority, whereas the third one presents intellectual inferiority.	A) public view	There's no public view
	B) intellectual & physical inferiority	the order is switched
	D) widely accepted	There's no accepted view
	E) exceptional case	There's no exceptional case

1> When two paragraphs are being compared in a question, you should do two things

2> Read the topic sentence of each paragraph.

3> Read the conclusion of each paragraph, so that you can finalize the author's opinion.

Q12. Type 2: Inference Question [Pattern 1: Local Question] {Category A}

Question Pattern: can be best understood as

Question Keywords: From the male chauvinist's view, lines 14-15 ("the difference is no doubt very slight".)

Step 1	Step 2	Step 3
Keywords from the Passage	Keywords from Answer	Tone & Concept
There have been women, very high order of genius	E) atypical perspective	Not typical = atypical

Incorrect Choices & Common Patterns		
Evidence	Incorrect keywords	Tone & Concept
There have been women of a very high order of genius; there have been very many women of great talent a general quickness and clearness… *Male chauvinist = a believer male is superior to female.	A) general pattern	From the male chauvinist's view, the phrase "there is a slight difference between man and woman" must be unusual (atypical) concept.
	B) interesting deviance	
	C) absolute fact	
	D) ambivalent hypothesis	

UNAUTHORIZED COPYING OR REUSE OF ANY PART OF THIS PAGE IS ILLEGAL

Q13. Type 2: Inference Question [Pattern 1: Local Question] {Category A}

Question Keywords: "The medical profession" in line 5 viewed the research of Professor Boris Sidis

Step 1	Step 2	Step 3
Keywords from the Passage	Keywords from Answer	Tone & Concept
they fail to credit Freud , antedating theirs.	B) acceptance	Similar Concept
Incorrect Choices & Common Patterns		
Evidence	Incorrect keywords	Tone & Concept
Some of them, <u>like professor Boris Sidis</u>, reach at times conclusions which are strangely similar to Freud's, but in **their** <u>ignorance of psychoanalytic literature, they fail to credit Freud</u> for observations **antedating theirs.**	A) curiosity C) ambivalence D) skepticism E) respect	Not Supported by the passage C) ambivalence = undecided E) is Too extreme word usage

1> "antedating" means before, and "theirs" refers to "Some of them, like professor Boris Sidis,".

2> The underlined portions states that Freud, unlike Boris Sidis, was not well received even though their conclusions were similar to each other.

3> This proves that Boris sides earned creditable research title in his work.

Q14. Pattern 7: Understanding Attitude / Tone

Question Pattern: The author feels   **Question Keywords:** Professor Boris Sidis' research is

Step 1	Step 2	Step 3
Keywords from the Passage	Keywords from Answer	Tone & Concept
they fail to credit Freud , antedating theirs.	C) unfair treatment	Similar Concept, Negative
Incorrect Choices & Common Patterns		
Evidence	Incorrect keywords	Tone & Concept
E) is the true statement. But the author neither focuses on the professor Boris Sidis nor gives such importance to him. He is just an object of the unfair treatment to Freud.	A) a valuable theory	Not Supported
	B) his belief	Opposite
	D) equally problematic	Opposite
	E) a proof of Freud	Positive

Q15. Pattern 7: Understanding Attitude / Tone

Question Pattern: The author characterizes   **Question Keywords:** the "conservatism" in line 2 as the

Step 1	Step 2	Step 3
Keywords from the Passage	Keywords from Answer	Tone & Concept
Conservatism, however, excuse for lazy minds,"	C) too rigid	Similar Concept

Incorrect Choices & Common Patterns		
Evidence	Incorrect keywords	Tone & Concept
Conservatism, however, is too often a welcome excuse for lazy minds,"	A) should not follow	All the options are using Too extreme words in either negative or positive way
	B) harmful tradition	
	D) axiom	
	E) little relevance	

Q16. Type 2: Inference Question [Pattern 1: Local Question] {Category A}

Question Pattern: It can be inferred from the passage that unlike
Question Keywords: Freud's theories, Boris Sidis applied in his theories

Step 1	Step 2	Step 3
Keywords from the Passage	Keywords from Answer	Tone & Concept
Conservatism, however, excuse for lazy minds,"	C) principles of conservatism	Similar Concept

Incorrect Choices & Common Patterns		
Evidence	Incorrect keywords	Tone & Concept
professor Boris Sidis, reach at times conclusions which are strangely similar to Freud's, but in **their** ignorance of psychoanalytic literature, they fail to credit Freud for observations	A) meaningful	Not Supported by the passage
	B) renown scientists	
	D) personal experience	
	E) scientific experiment	

1> **"their** ignorance of psychoanalytic literature", implies that psychoanalytic literature is created by Freud

2> Conservatism, however, is too often a welcome excuse for lazy minds,

3> By combining the above two elements, we can reach to the conclusion that professor Boris Sidis was accepted because he followed the principle of conservatism.

Q17. Type 2: Inference Question [Pattern 1: Local Question] {Category A}

Question Keywords: "psychoanalytic literature" in line 24 is significant because it is

Step 1	Step 2	Step 3
Keywords from the Passage	Keywords from Answer	Tone & Concept
but ignorance of psychoanalytic literature, fail, credit	D) initiated by Freud	Similar Concept

Incorrect Choices & Common Patterns		
Evidence	Incorrect keywords	Tone & Concept
but in <u>their ignorance of psychoanalytic literature, they fail to credit Freud</u> for observations antedating theirs.	A) the major backbone	The underlined portion implies that it's a new thesis brought by Freud.
	B) similar to Boris	
	C) practical theory	
	E) pseudoscience	

"**their** ignorance of psychoanalytic literature", implies that psychoanalytic literature is created by Freud

Q18. Pattern 3: Summary Question

Question Pattern: According to the passage, which of the following?
Question Keywords: , Freud was primarily, motivated by

Step 1	Step 2	Step 3
Keywords from the Passage	Keywords from Answer	Tone & Concept
Freud's discoveries, unconscious.	B) unconsciousness	Similar Concept

Incorrect Choices & Common Patterns		
Evidence	Incorrect keywords	Tone & Concept
Freud's discoveries in the domain of the unconscious.	A) conservatism	D) is the result created by his motivation.
	C) Professor Boris Sidis	
	D) psychoanalytic literature	
	E) the medical bodies	

Q19. Pattern 2: Main Idea Question

Question Pattern: The author is primarily concerned with the

Step 1	Step 2	Step 3
Keywords from the Passage	Keywords from Answer	Tone & Concept
tonic life of the wild. To *have* not desirable, to *be*.	D) To be in nature	Similar Concept

Incorrect Choices & Common Patterns		
Evidence	Incorrect keywords	Tone & Concept
(TOPIC) There is a something in you, as in every one, that requires the tonic life of the wild. (CONLCUSION) To *have* seems not so desirable as to *be*.	A) To have	By combining the topic and the conclusion, we can reach the conclusion.
	B) To have	
	C) creative life	
	E) ethical life	

Q20. Pattern 6: Understanding Structure of the Passage

Question Pattern: From the author's perspective can be considered as
Question Keywords: , "though he may be…no book education?" (lines 5-6)

Step 1	Step 2	Step 3
Keywords from the Passage	Keywords from Answer	Tone & Concept
though	D) inessential quality	concessional tone

Incorrect Choices & Common Patterns		
Evidence	Incorrect keywords	Tone & Concept
The author mainly focuses on the true woodsman living in wildness or his persistence. Line 5 …though he may be exteriorly rough and have little or no book education.	A) lack of persistence	the concessional part of the sentence implies something is an inessential part, not the main part.
	B) ignorant person	
	C) major defects in life	
	E) uncultivated person	

Q21. Pattern 3: Summary Question

Question Keywords: In lines 13-14 "inward laugh that seldom reaches the surface", that the woodsman

Step 1	Step 2	Step 3
Keywords from the Passage	Keywords from Answer	Tone & Concept
his inward laugh that seldom reaches the surface	A) rarely reveals feelings	Similar Concept, Positive

Incorrect Choices & Common Patterns		
Evidence	Incorrect keywords	Tone & Concept
his inward laugh that seldom reaches the surface.	B) a reclusive person	Except for the choice A, the remaining choices are all negative.
	C) discontented	
	D) uncommunicative	
	E) deceiver	

Q22. Pattern 2: Main Idea Question

Question Pattern: The passage as a whole suggests that   **Question Keywords:** the world of wild is

Step 1	Step 2	Step 3
Keywords from the Passage	Keywords from Answer	Tone & Concept
the wild strengthens the muscles of your mind	B) a unique place, soul	wildness enriches our soul.

Incorrect Choices & Common Patterns		
Evidence	Incorrect keywords	Tone & Concept
To live for a while in the wild strengthens the **muscles of your mind** as well as of your body. A) It is opposite to say the wilderness as a place to be protected. The author says it is a place to live.	A) should be protected	C),D),E) are all negative. while the passage is positive about the wilderness.
	C) a remote place	
	D) impractical	
	E) dismisses	

Q23. Type 2: Inference Question [Pattern 1: Local Question] {Category A}

Question Pattern: serves to provide, an example of   **Question Keywords:** "To have...to be." in line 16

Step 1	Step 2	Step 3
Keywords from the Passage	Keywords from Answer	Tone & Concept
To have (our cultivated world) to be (heartfelt joy)	D) city life vs. wilderness	only the wild can provide

Incorrect Choices & Common Patterns		
Evidence	Incorrect keywords	Tone & Concept
The author's comparison is evident throughout the passage.	A) a part of our nature	C),D),E) are all Opposite from the author's view.
	B) the tonic life	
The author is skeptical towards the modern world and expresses heartfelt attachment to wilderness.	C) everyone has	
	E) city dwellers	

A), B) is insufficient because it describes the "to be" or the life in the wilderness only"

C) is insufficient because it describes the "to have" only

Q24. Pattern 4: Relationship Question

Question Pattern: The author's view on, are a pair of respectively
Question Keywords: a true woodsman and city dwellers

Step 1	Step 2	Step 3
Keywords from the Passage	Keywords from Answer	Tone & Concept
Woodsman (TO BE) vs. City dwellers (TO HAVE)	C) to be and to have	Similar Concept

Incorrect Choices & Common Patterns		
Evidence	Incorrect keywords	Tone & Concept
The much-housed, overheated, overdressed, and over-entertained life of most girls is artificial (TO HAVE), go through life not knowing the joy, the strength, the poise that real outdoor life can give. (TO BE)	A) the poor, abundant	Woodsman (TO BE) = Positive City dwellers (TO HAVE)= Negative.
	B) the uneducated	
	D) the wise, stupid	
	E) the respected	

Q25. Pattern 3: Summary Question

Question Pattern: The intended effect of , to show
Question Keywords: the portrayal of a man (line 4) is

Step 1	Step 2	Step 3
Keywords from the Passage	Keywords from Answer	Tone & Concept
I never saw a man, made himself horsey	B) peculiarity	peculiarity means weirdly unique

Incorrect Choices & Common Patterns		
Evidence	Incorrect keywords	Tone & Concept
...and I think I never saw a man who had made himself more aggressively horsey.	A) fate	the portrayal of a man focuses on his outfit and physicality.
	C) companionship	A), C), E) are all emotional concept.
	D) his face, an animal	D) is Too literal Implication
	E) brutality	

Q26. Pattern 3: Summary Question

Question Pattern: the author, characterizes EXCEPT
Question Keywords: In the second paragraph (lines 6-15) , the man as one who

Step 1	Step 2	Step 3
Keywords from the Passage	Keywords from Answer	Tone & Concept
avoid any kind of extremes.	E) enjoys extremes	Opposite

Incorrect Choices & Common Patterns		
Evidence	Incorrect keywords	Tone & Concept
His expression was mild and inoffensive (D), and his watery pale eyes and receding chin (A) gave one the idea that he was hardly to be trusted (C) have been to avoid any kind of extremes. (E)	A) receding face	a man who made himself more aggressively horsey (B)
	B) humorous outfit	
	C) suspicious	
	D) way of his speech	

Q27. Pattern 6: Understanding Structure of the Passage

Question Pattern: In the third paragraph, the narrator's feeling shifts from

Step 1	Step 2	Step 3
Keywords from the Passage	Keywords from Answer	Tone & Concept
interested me vs. embarrassment	B) curiosity to humiliation	Synonym

Incorrect Choices & Common Patterns		
Evidence	Incorrect keywords	Tone & Concept
He puzzled and interested me (CURIOSITY) so much that I did my best to enter into conversation with him, only to be baffled by the jerky embarrassment (HUMILIATION)	A) fear to courage	interested me (CURIOSITY)
	C) regret to determination	embarrassment (HUMILIATION)
	D) uncertainty to despair	
	E) anger to forgiveness	

Q28. Pattern 3: Summary Question

Question Pattern: Throughout the passage the author reflects his observation
Question Keywords: from the perspective of

Step 1	Step 2	Step 3
Keywords from the Passage	Keywords from Answer	Tone & Concept
He puzzled me so much	A) personal speculation	observation = speculation

Incorrect Choices & Common Patterns		
Evidence	Incorrect keywords	Tone & Concept
Throughout the passage, the narrator speculates and observes one character.	B) generalizations	B), C) are Opposite
	C) familiar acquaintance	D) is not scholarly
	D) scholarly	E) "is described only at the last sentence
	E) factual	

UNAUTHORIZED COPYING OR REUSE OF ANY PART OF THIS PAGE IS ILLEGAL

Q29. Pattern 2: Main Idea Question

Question Pattern: The passage as a whole is written by the narrator who?

Step 1	Step 2	Step 3
Keywords from the Passage	Keywords from Answer	Tone & Concept
I did my best to enter into conversation	A) speculates	The narrator wants to know him

Incorrect Choices & Common Patterns		
Evidence	Incorrect keywords	Tone & Concept
He puzzled me so much that I did my best to enter into conversation	B) became friend	Not Supported by the passage
	C) younger days	
The passage is written by a man who speculates about a man he saw in the train.	D) improve relationships	
	E) knows everything	E) is Opposite

Q30. Type 2: Inference Question [Pattern 1: Local Question] {Category A}

Question Keywords: The man might have reacted to the narrator's advancement (lines 14-15) as

Step 1	Step 2	Step 3
Keywords from the Passage	Keywords from Answer	Tone & Concept
only to be baffled by the jerky embarrassment	E) an annoying intrusion	reciprocal reaction

Incorrect Choices & Common Patterns		
Evidence	Incorrect keywords	Tone & Concept
He puzzled me so much that I did my best to enter into conversation with him, only to be baffled by the jerky embarrassment with which he met all advances.	A) unsophisticated plan	A) is Unrelated word usage
	B) generous	B),C).D) are positive
	C) humorous	
	D) friendly	

Q31. Type 2: Inference Question [Pattern 1: Local Question] {Category A}

Question Keywords: "The lure of the mountains defies analysis" (line 3)

Step 1	Step 2	Step 3
Keywords from the Passage	Keywords from Answer	Tone & Concept
The lure, defies analysis, irresistible	D) elevates the rarified	cannot be questioned = defies

Incorrect Choices & Common Patterns		
Evidence	Incorrect keywords	Tone & Concept
The lure of the mountains defies analysis, but it is surely there with its irresistible appeal to all	A) importance of analysis	Defies = refuses
	B) distinguishes what can be	Because the rarified status of the mountain is self-evident and can't be questioned, it defies the analysis.
	C) no analytical concept	
	E) author's analytical skills	

Q32. Pattern 2: Main Idea Question

Question Pattern: The author's characterization to EXCEPT

Question Keywords: Canadian Alps includes all of the followings

Step 1	Step 2	Step 3
Keywords from the Passage	Keywords from Answer	Tone & Concept
whom the spirit of romance ethereal (B)	D) earthly view	Opposite Concept

Incorrect Choices & Common Patterns		
Evidence	Incorrect keywords	Tone & Concept
whose stupendous (E) waves tossed far into the heavens seem ever about to overwhelm (C) the level whom the spirit of romance (A) ethereal (B)	A) romantic appeal	D) earthly view is the direct opposite to the statement in the passage that refers it as ethereal (heavenly) view.
	B) heavenly	
	C) impressiveness	
	E) immensity	

UNAUTHORIZED COPYING OR REUSE OF ANY PART OF THIS PAGE IS ILLEGAL

Q33. Pattern 2: Main Idea Question

Question Pattern: The passage calls attention to which aspect of
Question Keywords: the mountain?

Step 1	Step 2	Step 3
Keywords from the Passage	Keywords from Answer	Tone & Concept
its <u>irresistible appeal</u> to all	A) Its sublimity	Sublimity = impressive

Incorrect Choices & Common Patterns		
Evidence	Incorrect keywords	Tone & Concept
The <u>lure</u> of the mountains <u>defies analysis</u>, but it is surely there with its <u>irresistible appeal</u> to all	B) Its mysteriousness	These are all Minor Issues
	C) Its influence to human	
	D) Its national identity	
	E) Its popular appeal	

Q34. Pattern 4: Relationship Question

Question Pattern: are used to refer to the distinction between
Question Keywords: "The rolling foothills" (line 10) and "purer world" (line 13)

Step 1	Step 2	Step 3
Keywords from the Passage	Keywords from Answer	Tone & Concept
foothills ...tangible , but ...some other	D) earthly, ethereal scene	Logical Conclusion

Incorrect Choices & Common Patterns		
Evidence	Incorrect keywords	Tone & Concept
The rolling foothills ...tangible and comprehensible, but ...some other and purer world.	A) short, long distance	"The rolling foothills ... tangible" refers to earthly and "but ...some other" refers to intangible
	B) fictional world	
	C) a safe place	
	E) foreigners' worldview	

Q35. Pattern 3: Summary Question

Question Keywords: Which of Alps' features does the author mainly describes in paragraph 3?

Step 1	Step 2	Step 3
Keywords from the Passage	Keywords from Answer	Tone & Concept
vision may not resist the insistent call to explore	D) people's desire	Synonym

Incorrect Choices & Common Patterns		
Evidence	Incorrect keywords	Tone & Concept
One who has seen this vision may not resist the insistent call to explore the mountain world, to discover what lies beyond the frowning battlements that guard this other realm.	A) skepticism	People's desire to climb the mountain is the main theme of the third paragraph
	B) stylistic	
	C) the historical	
	E) the symbolic meaning	

Q36. Pattern 2: Main Idea Question

Question Pattern: is best understood to mean as
Question Keywords: Let us…to be drawn." in lines 5-7 where everything is

Step 1	Step 2	Step 3
Keywords from the Passage	Keywords from Answer	Tone & Concept
knowable to be entirety and absolute.	A) homogeneous	Synonym

Incorrect Choices & Common Patterns		
Evidence	Incorrect keywords	Tone & Concept
Let us suppose, by way of hypothesis, the knowable to be entirety and absolute.	B) beyond analytical	Not Supported by the passage
	C) measured by data	
	D) tangible	
	E) intangible	

Q37. Pattern 3: Summary Question

Question Pattern: The author suggests that
Question Keywords: the term "knowable" (line 2) is an entity that should be

Step 1	Step 2	Step 3
Keywords from the Passage	Keywords from Answer	Tone & Concept
knowable....mind, matter.	D) our mind and matter	Synonym
Incorrect Choices & Common Patterns		
Evidence	Incorrect keywords	Tone & Concept
knowable....if some belong to what we call the mind and others to what we call matter.	A) scientific boundary	insufficient information
	B) ordinary life	insufficient information
	C) all theories.	not stated
	E) excluded, mind matter	Opposite

Q38. Pattern 3: Summary Question

Question Pattern: EXCEPT
Question Keywords: All of the following elements can be classified as a knowable entirety

Step 1	Step 2	Step 3
Keywords from the Passage	Keywords from Answer	Tone & Concept
the pleasure they give us	C) person watching movie	it can't be homogeneous
Incorrect Choices & Common Patterns		
Evidence	Incorrect keywords	Tone & Concept
(TOPIC) Let us suppose, by way of hypothesis, the knowable to be entirely and absolutely homogeneous. Things may be classified according to their <u>color</u>, their shape, their <u>weight,</u> the <u>pleasure they give us</u>, their quality of being alive or <u>dead,</u>	A) color	C) is opposite concept
	B) mortality	
	D) character in a movie	
	E) weight	

Q39. Type 2: Inference Question [Pattern 1: Local Question] {Category A}

Question Pattern: it can be interpreted as
Question Keywords: In line 17, when the author says "acting fantastically",

Step 1	Step 2	Step 3
Keywords from the Passage	Keywords from Answer	Tone & Concept
a criterion <u>Otherwise, acting fantastically.</u>	C) randomly	opposite to criterion

Incorrect Choices & Common Patterns		
Evidence	Incorrect keywords	Tone & Concept
it must be supposed that we shall do so by <u>means of a criterion. Otherwise, we should only be acting fantastically.</u>	A) theoretically	A), B) D), E) are all positive.
	B) empirically	C) randomly is negative as
	D) wonderfully	"otherwise, acting fantastically" is
	E) magically	negative.

The author uses the word, 'fantastically' to compare the difference between criterion (the group) and the other (non-group). Therefore, fantastically must be a negative word.

Q40. Pattern 3: Summary Question

Question Pattern: the author suggests which of the following?
Question Keywords: In the last paragraph (lines 13-17),

Step 1	Step 2	Step 3
Keywords from the Passage	Keywords from Answer	Tone & Concept
so many divisions are possible, we stop	D) only blur the lines	Logical Conclusion

Incorrect Choices & Common Patterns		
Evidence	Incorrect keywords	Tone & Concept
Since so many divisions are possible, at which shall we stop and say: this is the one which corresponds exactly to the opposition of mind and matter? The choice is not easy to make.	A) impossible	A) is Too extreme word usage
	B) adding knowable	B) is Opposite
	C) there's no division	C) is Not Supported by the passage
	E) not necessarily	

"Since so many divisions are possible, at which shall we stop" can be interpreted as the current criterion will only blur the lines.

Test 4 ABSOLUTE PATTERNS for the Analogy Section

Q31. Absolute Pattern 7: Association (Characteristic) Pattern

E is the best answer

Counterfeit is fake money; Forgery is a fake art.

Choice A is wrong because a resemblance is a positive value.

Q32. Absolute Pattern 7: Association (Characteristic) Pattern

A is the best answer.

Cat chases rat as lion chases zebra. In that sense, they are both associated each other in characteristics.

B is out because they are flipped over.

C is wrong because people eat beef, not cow

Q33. Absolute Pattern 1: Production (Cause-Effect) Pattern

B is the best answer.

Music and cacophony both produce sound. However, one causes melody; another causes noise.

Q34. Absolute Pattern 7: Association (Characteristic) Pattern

A is the best answer

Arduous means difficult, and usually refers to a difficult physical work. (physical) Poignant means sorrow, and usually refers to difficult time. (mental)

Q35. Absolute Pattern 6:Purpose (Job/Tool) Pattern

E is the best answer

A midwife is a traditional caregiving practice, just as a nurse is a modern caregiving practice. In that sense, they both practice the same job.

Q36. Absolute Pattern 6:Purpose (Job/Tool) Pattern

E is the best answer

The purpose of a striker is to make a goal, just as the purpose of sleep is to rest.

Q37. Absolute Pattern 2: Part-Whole Pattern

C is the best answer

The toilet bowl is a part of a bathroom, as the sink is a part of a kitchen.

Choice A, B are flipped over.

Q38. Absolute Pattern 7: Association (Characteristic) Pattern

D is the best answer

A close-up in a movie and an excerpt from a book focus and summarize the scene.

Q39. Absolute Pattern 5: Degree Pattern

A is the best answer.

The rookie is a young player. A cub is a baby bear. They grow and become a captain player and a bear.

Q40. Absolute Pattern 6:Purpose (Job/Tool) Pattern

A is the best answer. (A passive act)

The function of a bandage is to prevent bleeding; the function of a dam is to prevent flooding.

Choice B is flipped over.

Choice D is ruled out because police are human and do not contain the same concept as bandage or dam.

Q41. Absolute Pattern 6:Purpose (Job/Tool) Pattern

B is the best answer

The fan circulates the air in a room; wall insulates air. They both have a similar function—controlling the air and the temperature.

Q42. Absolute Pattern 2: Part-Whole Pattern

C is the best answer

A gaggle is a group of goose as school is a group of fish.

(A), (B) are ruled out because they are human and word order is flipped over.

Q43. Absolute Pattern 6:Purpose (Job/Tool) Pattern

B is the best answer

The function of the wrap is to conceal. The function of storage is to preserve.

Choice C, E are out because they are different characters

Q44. Absolute Pattern 6:Purpose (Job/Tool) Pattern

E is the best answer

A blade cuts; A needle stitches.

Choice B is a Part-Whole Pattern.

Choice D is flipped over.

Q45. Absolute Pattern 7: Association (Characteristic) Pattern

A is the best answer.

Pound and liter are both measurements for weight and volume respectively.

Q46. Absolute Pattern 6:Purpose (Job/Tool) Pattern

B is the best answer.

A serial number is the identification of an item; a domain address is the identification of a website.

Q47. Absolute Pattern 4: Synonym Pattern

A is the best answer

Epoch and era are synonyms as stanza and paragraph are the same category.

Q48. Absolute Pattern 13: Mental-Physical Pattern

C is the best answer

Intelligence and myth are mental concepts as Brawn and ancient temple are physical concept.

A) is the Production Pattern.

B) is the Degree Pattern.

D) is the Part-Whole Pattern.

E) has no pattern.

Q49. Absolute Pattern 7: Association (Characteristic) Pattern

C is the best answer

Grace goes to Queen, and wizened goes to an old lady.

Choice E is wrong because King is male

Q50. Absolute Pattern 1: Production (Cause-Effect) Pattern

C is the best answer

Brewing produces coffee; baking produces bread.

E is ruled out because crayon is not edible.

Q51. Absolute Pattern 7: Association (Characteristic) Pattern

D is the best answer

Only an airline itinerary shows the expiry dates.

Q52. Absolute Pattern 7: Association (Characteristic) Pattern

C is the best answer.

There is an old saying, "silence is gold; time is money."

Q53. Absolute Pattern 6:Purpose (Job/Tool) Pattern

B is the best answer.

Painter uses a brush as editor uses a pen

Q54. Absolute Pattern 6:Purpose (Job/Tool) Pattern + 13: Mental-Physical Pattern

E is the best answer

The school is for knowledge, just as the church is for prayer.
C, and D are flipped over and do not possess the mental concept like education or prayer.

Q55. Absolute Pattern 8: Shape Pattern

B is the best answer

Imagine chandelier hanging on the ceiling and bat in a cave.

D), E) are flipped over.

Q56. Absolute Pattern 7: Association (Characteristic) Pattern

C is the best answer

Swamp is wet as desert is arid, creating the same climatic category.

Q57. Absolute Pattern 7: Association (Characteristic) Pattern

B is the best answer

Baseball and Sprint are both sports and both are played on diamond and track. In that sense, they both share the same characteristics.

Q58. Absolute Pattern 3: Antonym (Positive-Negative) Pattern

C is the best answer.

happiness (positive) to sadness (negative) = amiable (positive) to antagonism (negative)

For A), B), D), although they share the same antonym (opposite) patterns, they do not contain Positive-Negative Patterns.

Q59. Absolute Pattern 3: Antonym (Positive-Negative) Pattern

A is the best answer.

Secret is opposite to exposure as intangible is opposite to tangible.

Q60. Absolute Pattern 7: Association (Characteristic) Pattern

D is the best answer

Brave is the symbol of lion as trembling dance is the symbol of honey bee.

Test 4 Recap

Central Ideas/Theme Question

Central Ideas is usually located at the conclusion sentence, where the author (narrator/character) most likely re-emphasizes his thesis (argument) at the end of the passage.

The key to find the answer is to identify the tone or emotional state within the concluding paragraph, especially in the last sentence.

Analyzing Overall Structure

The original purpose of this question is to ask structural relationships between the paragraphs. Given the extensive reading scope remains the same as central idea question, you should, to analyze the overall text structure, be hoovering up the entire passage to observe its hardware (the organization of the passage) rather than the software (the context).

Analyzing Word Choice

Every word-in-context question carries synonym or antonym in the same line. This clue word bears either a positive-negative tone or physical-mental concept For instance, if the keyword (s) you found from the text is a mental concept, the choice with the physical concept—no matter how great the gravity pulls you up to that option—is incorrect choice.

SSAT
Reading & Verbal Practice
Test 5

ALL THE LOGIC AND RULES
BEHIND THE EVERY SINGLE
SSAT QUESTION

Test 5 Reading Section
Time: 40 Minutes, 40 Questions

Directions: Each reading passage is followed by questions about it. Answer the questions that follow a passage on the basis of what is stated or implied in that passage.

Questions 1-6 are based on the following passage.

Line
　　The ordinary run of men live among phenomena of which they know nothing and care less. They see bodies fall to the earth, they hear sounds, they kindle fires, they see the heavens roll above them, but of the causes and inner working of the whole they are ignorant, and with their ignorance they are content. "Understand the structure of a soap-bubble?" said a cultivated

5　literary man whom I know; "I wouldn't cross the street to know it!"
And if this is a prevalent attitude now, what must have been the attitude in ancient times, when mankind was emerging from savagery, and when history seems composed of harassments by wars abroad and revolutions at home?

　　In the most violently disturbed times indeed, those with which ordinary history is mainly

10　occupied, science is quite impossible. It needs as its condition, in order to flourish, a fairly quiet, untroubled state, or else a cloister or university removed from the din and bustle of the political and commercial world. In such places it has taken its rise, and in such peaceful places and quiet times true science will continue to be cultivated. The great bulk of mankind must always remain, I suppose, more or less careless of scientific research and scientific result,

15　except in so far as it affects their modes of locomotion, their health and pleasure, or their purse.

1

In the first paragraph, the author most likely suggests that the ordinary men cannot

A) imagine the nature
B) prophesize the future
C) see the cause of phenomena
D) conceptualize the scientific theory
E) suppose the abnormality in nature

2

The quote in line 5, "I wouldn't.. know it contains the meaning of

A) triviality
B) significance
C) distinctiveness
D) rarity
E) eccentricity

CONTINUE

3

In his discussion of scientific research, the author positions "revolution" in line 8 as

(A) disapproval

B) surprise

C) uncertainty

D) curiosity

E) approval

4

The author characterizes "the structure of a soap-bubble" in line 4 as

(A) ignorance

B) appearance

C) frustration

D) phenomena

E) quiet

5

According to the author, "a cloister" in line 11 can be viewed as a place where

(A) important human achievement is realized

B) harmful events like war develop

C) monks and nuns practice religion

D) important phenomenon is observed

E) revolution can occur

6

"it" mentioned in line 5 most nearly refers to

A) science

B) ignorance

C) structural phenomena

D) the person who developed soap bubbles

(E) a soap-bubble

Questions 7-12 are based on the following passage.

Line

Mr. Phileas Fogg lived, in 1872, at No. 7, Saville Row, Burlington Gardens.

He was one of the most noticeable members of the Reform Club, which made him always to

avoid attracting attention; an enigmatical personage, about whom little was known,

except that he was a polished man of the world. People said that he resembled Byron--at least

5 that his head was Byronic; but he was a bearded, tranquil Byron, who might live on a

thousand years without growing old.

Certainly an Englishman, it was more doubtful whether Phileas Fogg was a Londoner. He

was never seen on 'Change, nor at the Bank, nor in the counting-rooms of the "City" He

certainly was not a manufacturer; nor was he a merchant or a gentleman farmer.

10 He belonged, in fact, to none of the numerous societies which swarm in the English

capital. The way in which he got admission to this exclusive club was simple enough.

He was recommended by the Barings, with whom he had an open credit. His cheques were

regularly paid at sight from his account current, which was always flush.

CONTINUE

7

The literary device used in line 2-3, "He was…
attention" is

A) paradox

B) simile

C) allusion

D) extended metaphor

E) metaphor

8

In line 3, "enigmatical" most nearly means

A) clear

B) arrogant

C) modest

D) rich

E) cryptic

9

In context, "the Barings" in line 12 is best understood
as a

A) a family member of Mr. Phileas Fogg

B) a member of the exclusive club

C) Mr. Phileas Fogg's patron

D) a regular Englishman

E) a banker

10

The author uses the expression "people said...growing
old" (lines 4-6) to implies Mr. Phieas'

A) instructional nature

B) having no sentiments

C) aristocratic behavior

D) reclusive nature

E) enigmatic appearance

11

In line 6, "without growing old" suggests that the
narrator believes Mr. Phileas is

A) maintaining composure that contributes his
   consistent appearance

B) unwilling to acknowledge his age

C) incapable of acting like an adult

D) inclined to act like an old person

E) experiencing anti-aging symptom

12

The narrator describes Mr.Phileas in paragraph 2 as

A) a mysterious person

B) an arrogant person

C) a less desirable person to get close to

D) a respectful person

E) a suitable person to be friend with

CONTINUE

Questions 13-18 are based on the following passage.

Line   We have progressed appreciably beyond the days of the old horseless carriage, which, it will be
remembered, retained even the dashboard. To-day the modern automobile somewhat resembles,
in its outlines, across between a decapod locomotive and a steam fire-engine, or at least
something concerning the artistic appearance of which the layman has very grave doubts.

5   The control of a restive horse, a cranky boat, or even a trolley-car on rails is difficult enough
for the inexperienced, and there are many who would quail before making the attempt; but to the
novice in charge of an automobile, some serious damage is likely enough to occur within an
incredibly short space of time, particularly if he does not take into account the tremendous force
and power which he controls merely by the moving of a tiny lever, or by the depressing of a

10   pedal.

Any one interested in automobiles should know something of the literature of the subject,
which, during the last decade, has already become formidable.

13

The tone of the "old horseless carriage" and the modern automobile" mentioned in the first paragraph is best characterized as a pair of, respectively,

A) beautiful and practical

B) wistful and artistic

C) dismayed and identical

D) ambivalent and advanced

E) progressive and conventional

14

According to the statement "concerning...doubts (line 4) the author suggests that automobile

A) should not be viewed as an artistic object

B) is no longer viewed as an artistic object

C) does not appeal to regular folks

D) regular folks focus so much on the artistic aspect

E) there is not much difference between appearance

CONTINUE

15

The second paragraph mainly points out that

A) the automobile at this stage is not reliable

B) the technology is advancing fast

C) the layman should not operate automobile

D) the automobile possesses tremendous power

E) a great deal of skill is required to control automobile

16

According to the passage, the early inventors of the automobile were mainly interested in transforming

A) the rails for a trolley-car

B) the massive weight of the steam engine

C) roads and highways

D) the pricy structure of the automobile

E) the appearance of the vehicle body

17

In line 12, "formidable" means

A) unfinished but improved

B) very popular

C) beautiful

D) technically advanced

E) impressively grown

18

The primary purpose of the passage is to

A) illustrate the principle mechanism of automobile

B) discuss the early attempt to advance automobile

C) bolster some great automobile inventors 'efforts

D) summarize a particular experiment

E) speculate the future automobile

CONTINUE

Questions 19-24 are based on the following passage.

Line
One of the greatest of modern philosophers--the founder of that system of scientific philosophy which traces the processes of evolution in every department, whether physical or intellectual--has devoted a chapter of his "First Principles" of the new system to the consideration of the multiplication of the effects of the various forces, social and other, which
5 are continually modifying this wonderful and mysterious universe of which we form a part. Herbert Spencer, himself an engineer, there traces the wide-spreading, never-ceasing influences of new inventions.

The power of the steam-engine, and its inconceivable importance as an agent of civilization, has always been a favorite theme with philosophers and historians as well as poets.
10 As Religion has always been, and still is, the great moral agent in civilizing the world, and as Science is the great intellectual promoter of civilization, so the Steam-Engine is, in modern times, the most important physical agent in that great work. It would be superfluous to attempt to enumerate the benefits which it has conferred upon the entire human race and their work, for such an enumeration would include an addition to every comfort and the creation of almost every luxury that we now enjoy.

19

The primary purpose of the passage is to

A) celebrate wide applications of the steam-engine
B) celebrate the inventor of the steam-engine
C) introduce the scientific philosophy
D) speculate the future of the steam-engine
E) explain the conceptual gap between philosophers and engineers

20

According to the passage, Herbert Spencer was

A) the inventor of steam engine
B) the 19th century historian
C) the most respected entrepreneur in the19th century
D) the founder of modern philosophy
E) the person with more than one profession

21

In lines 8-9, the author mentions "philosophers, historians, and poets." in order to

A) show the attention to the particular invention
B) undermine the steam engine's practicality
C) epitomize a uniqueness of steam engine
D) bolster the author's academic interest
E) show various applications of a unique invention

22

Which of the following industries or person can best refute the author's argument "It would be...enjoy" (lines 12-14)

A) singer at the nightclub
B) gasoline producers
C) the fishing industry
D) automobile salesman
E) children's clothing manufacturers

CONTINUE

23

It can be inferred from the passage that in the second chapter of his book, Herbert Spencer would probably describe

A) the philosophical approach to the influences of new inventions

B) ancient Greek philosophers

C) western religion in the 19th century

D) science and politics

E) the theory of steam engine

24

The author's overall tone concerning the steam engine is

A) conversational

B) sarcastic

C) appeal to emotion

D) analytical

E) celebratory

Questions 25-30 are based on the following passage.

Line   The integration of the armed forces was a momentous event in our military and national history; it represented a milestone in the development of the armed forces and the fulfillment of the democratic ideal. The experiences in World War I and the postwar pressures generated by the civil rights movement compelled all the services--Army, Navy, Air Force, and Marine

5   Corps--to reexamine their traditional practices of segregation. While there were differences in the ways that the services moved toward integration, all were subject to the same demands, fears, and prejudices and had the same need to use their resources in a more rational and economical way. All of them reached the same conclusion: traditional attitudes toward minorities must give way to democratic concepts of civil rights.

10   If the integration of the armed services now seems to have been inevitable in a democratic society, it nevertheless faced opposition that had to be overcome and problems that had to be solved through the combined efforts of political and civil rights leaders and civil and military officials.

CONTINUE

25

It can be inferred that the most influential social group in the integrated armed force movement was

A) Impressionist painters after the WWI

B) school teachers' union

C) African-American women

D) white Navy widowers

E) WWII army veterans

26

The author describes "political and civil rights leaders" (line 16) as an example of social groups that

A) shared the same resources

B) made decisions to the integration

C) took advantage of the integration

D) supported the integration

E) took various criticism during the integration

27

It can be inferred from the passage that

A) there was no integrated armed force before the WWI

B) the postwar pressures was the single stimulus for the integrated armed force movement

C) the integrated armed force combined mainly two services: Army and Navy

D) Integrated armed force movement influenced around the world

E) the military history parallels to the democratic history of the country

28

Which of the following factors ignited the need for the integrated armed force?

I. WWII

II. The postwar movement

III. Civil rights movement

A) I, II only

B) II, III only

C) III only

D) I.II, III

E) I only

29

The passage mainly suggests that

A) there was no absolute unanimity toward the complete integration

B) the ability to integrate armed force was limited by democratic principles

C) integrating all the previously segregated armed forces was in fact impractical

D) the segregated armed force was in fact predominately favored in society

E) there were some regretful results after the integration

30

The primary purpose of the passage is to

A) demonstrate the author's belief that integrated armed force was inevitable

B) introduce the concept of the integrated armed force

C) describe an alternative interpretation of the integrated armed force

D) indicate the important differences between the integrated and segregated armed force

E) justify social groups' reaction against the integrated armed force

CONTINUE

Questions 31-35 are based on the following passage.

Line   I've got an office in the Daily Standard building and sometimes when things are slow in my line--theatrical bookings--I drift upstairs and talk to the guy who writes the column, The Soldier's Friend, for the Standard.

        On this particular morning I walked into his office and found it empty so I sat down and
5   waited, figuring he was downstairs getting a mug of coffee. After I cleaned my nails and glanced through Jake's mail I propped my feet up on the desk and relaxed. Things in my line were strictly stinkeroo. I sighed and moodily contemplated my uncreased trouser legs and thought of my non-existent bank balance.

        The door opened and I heard a shuffle of footsteps on the floor. I tipped my derby back and
10 looked up, expecting to see Jake, but the office was empty. The door was standing open and I scratched my head. Maybe it had blown open.

        "Hello," a voice said.

        My feet came down from the desk with a crash. I sat up straight and stared about the small room. "Who said that?" I demanded.

15 "I did. I'm right here." It was the same voice and I jerked my head in the direction of the sound. For an instant I didn't see a thing. But then, my eyes seemed suddenly to focus, and I saw a tall, lanky young man standing a few feet from me. light suit.

        "Can you see me now?" he asked, and his voice sounded strained, as if he were exerting himself in some manner.

31

The narrator in the first paragraph appears to be

A) bored

B) companionable

C) aggressive

D) diligent

E) curious

32

It can be inferred from the first paragraph that the occupation of the narrator is

A) a tour arrangement guide

B) the Jake's manager

C) a magazine columnist

D) an office cleaner

E) a book editor

CONTINUE

33

The author's difficulty to identify the stranger in lines 9-15 was probably caused by the

A) unfamiliar voice

B) physical contact with the stranger

C) unanticipated change of mood

D) refusal to react to reality

E) daydreaming

34

In line 19, "exerting himself some manner" primarily serves to

A) show the stranger's initial uneasy feeling

B) reveal the narrator's discomfort

C) highlight the stranger's height

D) show some polite gesture

E) indicate a significant turning point of the relationship

35

In line 6, "stinkerro" suggests that the narrator values his jobs as

A) frivolous

B) flexible

C) smelly

D) scholarly

E) important

CONTINUE

Questions 36-40 are based on the following passage.

Line The considerable degree of decorative and artistic skill attained by the so-called Mound-Builders, as evidenced by many of the relics that have been exhumed from the mounds, has not failed to arrest the attention of archeologists. Among them, indeed, are found not a few who assert for the people conveniently designated as above a degree of artistic skill very far

5 superior to that attained by the present race of Indians as they have been known to history. In fact, this very skill in artistic design, asserted for the Mound-Builders, as indicated by the sculptures they have left, forms an important link in the chain of argument upon which is based the theory of their difference from and superiority to the North American Indian.

 Eminent as is much of the authority which thus contends for an artistic ability on the part of

10 the Mound-Builders far in advance of the attainments of the present Indian in the same line, the question is one admitting of argument; and if some of the best products of artistic handicraft of the present Indians be compared with objects of a similar nature taken from the mounds, it is more than doubtful if the artistic inferiority of the latter-day Indian can be substantiated. Deferring, however, for the present, any comparison between the artistic ability

15 of the Mound-Builder and the modern Indian, attention may be turned to a class of objects from the mounds, notable, indeed, for the skill with which they are wrought, but to be considered first in another way and for another purpose than mere artistic comparison.

36

Throughout the passage, the author presents "Mound-Builders" as a

A) mentors

B) surprising technicians

C) scholarly designers

D) inferior manufacturers

E) reclusive builders

37

The primary obstacle the author faces from the inferiority of the products made by the latter-day Indian can be resolved by

A) looking for a different purpose of the products

B) interpreting a scholarly hypothesis

C) finding a new evidence

D) gathering the best products of the latter-day Indian

E) maintaining the same emotional attachment

CONTINUE

38

The primary purpose of the passage is to

A) compare the sculptures of Mound-Builders from those of later-day Indians

B) position the sculptures of Mound-Builder above the later-day Indian

C) teach a lesson learned from Mound-Builder to the later-day Indian

D) describe the skills used in the process of sculpting

E) celebrate the sophisticated technique of Mound-Builders

39

In line 17, "substantiated" means

A) required

B) vary

C) basic

D) essential

E) proven

40

The author agrees with all of the following points EXCEPT

A) It is a proper way to investigate a different purpose between the products made by the Mound-Builders and the modern Indian

B) The products of Mound-Builder impressed the later-Indian

C) Some authorities assume that the artistic ability of the Mound-Builder exceeds that of the present Indian

D) Archeologists are fascinated by the Mound-Builders' artistic skills

E) Comparing artistic ability of the Mound-Builder to that of modern Indian requires more than artistic skill

STOP

If you finish before time is called,
you may check your work on this section.

Do not turn to the next section.

Test 5 Verbal Section   30 MINUTES, 60 QUESTIONS

Directions: the synonym questions ask you to find the most appropriate synonym to the question.

The analogy questions ask you to find the most appropriate analogy to the question.
Select the answer that best matches to the question.

Synonym Sample Question:

Q: SUPERIOR

A higher rank

B inferior

C considerable

D supermarket

E supper

A) is the best answer because the synonym for superior is higher rank.

B) is incorrect because it applies the 'opposite concept.

C) and E) are irrelevant words.

D) is incorrect because it applies physical concept to mental concept

---

Test 5 Synonym questions 1 to 30

1. RAUCOUS

(A) harsh

(B) mellow

(C) deep

(D) flexible

(E) comfort

2. PROSPER

(A) advance

(B) propel

(C) unsuccessful

(D) profuse

(E) professional

3. ADULTERATE

(A) fully grown

(B) contaminate

(C) adultery

(D) pure

(E) adulate

4. TACTFUL

(A) skillful

(B) diplomatic

(C) fixed

(D) technique

(E) stream

5. REMOTE

(A) far away

(B) satellite

(C) orbit

(D) travel

(E) control

CONTINUE

6. CONCISE

(A) short

(B) dictionary

(C) cut

(D) together

(E) skill

7. PRUDENT

(A) pure

(B) discreet

(C) ingenuity

(D) reckless

(E) provisional

8. AMPLE

(A) medium

(B) a lot

(C) fruit

(D) ambiguous

(E) scarce

9. AUDACIOUS

(A) hearing

(B) radio

(C) equipped

(D) audience

(E) bold

10. HINDER

(A) progress

(B) hindsight

(C) protect

(D) lofty

(E) delay

11. AESTHETIC

(A) beauty

(B) showy

(C) theoretic

(D) study

(E) funny

12. FOSTER

(A) terminate

(B) prevent

(C) promote

(D) stymie

(E) halt

13. PREVAIL

(A) Stipend

(B) defeat

(C) lonely

(D) premeditate

(E) win

14. AFFABLE

(A) friendly

(B) affectation

(C) fabulous

(D) disloyal

(E) easy

15. AFFECTATION

(A) artificial

(B) natural

(C) behavior

(D) impression

(E) intention

CONTINUE

16. BROOD

(A) confident

(B) offspring

(C) bloody

(D) focus

(E) share

17. POTENT

(A) weak

(B) delivery

(C) powerful

(D) motionless

(E) great

18. ENTICE

(A) band

(B) tight

(C) engender

(D) tempt

(E) affinity

19. UNCANNY

(A) natural

(B) spontaneity

(C) sympathy

(D) affluent

(E) eerie

20. SUFFICIENT

(A) affluent

(B) poor

(C) good

(D) subversive

(E) prosper

21. AGENDA

(A) program

(B) book

(C) gender

(D) agrarian

(E) aggregation

22. FLOUNDER

(A) inundate

(B) flower

(C) stumble

(D) scent

(E) odor

23. AGNOSTIC

(A) believer

(B) non-believer

(C) adherent

(D) follower

(E) geology

24. EAGERNESS

(A) alacrity

(B) serendipity

(C) iconoclast

(D) pivot

(E) crestfallen

25. To assert without proof

(A) epicure

(B) cosmopolitan

(C) allege

(D) husbandry

(E) equanimity

CONTINUE

26. SATURATE

(A) salt

(B) soak

(C) dry

(D) wet

(E) semiarid

27. UNINVOLVED

(A) halcyon

(B) juxtapose

(C) demagogue

(D) double entendre

(E) aloof

28. CLARIFY

(A) dubious

(B) hard to understand

(C) explain

(D) mirror

(E) nostalgia

29. TYRANT

(A) president

(B) king

(C) dictator

(D) medicine

(E) subject

30. MOBILIZE

(A) vehicle

(B) transport

(C) activate

(D) stop

(E) engine oil

Analogy Sample Question:

Q: River is to Ocean as:

A better is to good

B rain is to cloud

C father is to mother

D city is to country

E fork is to spoon

D is the correct answer. Just as the river is smaller than the Ocean, the city is smaller than the country. The pattern applied in this question is the Degree Pattern (small to big)

A) is incorrect because the word order is flipped over.

B) is incorrect because it applies the production pattern (cloud produces rain)

C), E) are incorrect because they apply the Antonym patterns.

Test 5 Analogy questions 31 to 60

31. Martin Luther King Jr. is to peace as Hitler is to

(A) generous

(B) chancellor

(C) German

(D) army

(E) catastrophe

CONTINUE

UNAUTHORIZED COPYING OR REUSE OF ANY PART OF THIS PAGE IS ILLEGAL

32. Cane is to rain as

(A) bear is to hibernate

(B) snow is to melt

(C) contemporary is to modern

(D) old is to umbrella

(E) mountain is to river

33. Score is to game as egg is to

(A) boil

(B) sunnyside up

(C) chicken

(D) fragile

(E) yolk

34. Seven colors is to rainbow as

(A) flower is to Spring

(B) winter is to snow

(C) pilot is to parachute

(D) choreographer is dancer

(E) bland is to soup

35. Clicking is to flicking as lion is to

(A) peek

(B) laxity

(C) Zion

(D) symbol

(E) help

36. Mime is to dime as pale is to

(A) green

(B) gale

(C) drama

(D) dollar

(E) unhealthy

37. Poor is door as rare is to

(A) beer

(B) rich

(C) hair

(D) dread

(E) usual

38. Sand is to hand as complex is to

(A) body

(B) foot

(C) beach

(D) simple

(E) reflex

39. Production is to process as

(A) opera is to baritone

(B) study is to exam

(C) business is to money

(D) play is to scene

(E) construction is to wood

40. Dragonfly is to insect as dragon is

(A) fly

(B) myth

(C) fire

(D) reptile

(E) strong

41. Army is to accruement as chef is to

(A) dish

(B) cook

(C) hand

(D) utensil

(E) kitchen

CONTINUE

42. Spider is to web as
(A) medicine is to cure
(B) bee is to honey
(C) beaver is to dam
(D) supermarket owner is to grocery
(E) accident is to victim

43. Lieutenant is sapling as tree is to
(A) public
(B) grass
(C) private
(D) wood
(E) communal

44. Preface is to book as
(A) macaroni is to pasta
(B) hero is to legend
(C) appetizer is to meal
(D) capital is to state
(E) mail is to envelope

45. Music is to earphone as star is to
(A) microscope
(B) telescope
(C) book
(D) cosmology
(E) moon

46. Protagonist is to antagonist as
(A) hero is to villain
(B) dream is to real
(C) school is to office
(D) house is to factory
(E) deity is to god

47. Horny is to sticky as
(A) gas is to mileage
(B) candle is to wax
(C) car is to mirror
(D) bee is to honey
(E) sweet is to glue

48. Citadel is to invasion as
(A) fly is to screen door
(B) coffee is to lid
(C) goal is to keeper
(D) fire is to insulator
(E) cathedral is to prayer

49. Snow is to melt as
(A) beach is to sunburn
(B) rain is to raincoat
(C) cement is to harden
(D) read is to sleepy
(E) movie is to scene

50. Producer is to TV program as
(A) teacher is to student
(B) barber is to scissor
(C) traveler is to sightseeing
(D) driver is to bus
(E) director is to movie

51. Evil is to god as
(A) man is to woman
(B) baby is to adult
(C) north pole is to south pole
(D) junk is to sedan
(E) spider is to fly

CONTINUE

52. F is to A+ as

(A) sky is to sky

(B) fish is to bird

(C) salt is to sugar

(D) volcano is to eruption

(E) poison is to medicine

53. Rich is to poor as

(A) servant is to king

(B) opaque is to transparent

(C) victory is to defeat

(D) heat is to cold

(E) doctor is to patient

54. Sanitation is contamination as

(A) pious is to religious

(B) noise is to music

(C) movie is to music

(D) evil is to benign

(E) work is to procrastinate

55. Flour is to bread

(A) alphabet is to word

(B) handcuff is to police

(C) ice cream is to desert

(D) lemon is lemonade

(E) sunglass is to sun

56. Sunscreen is to burn as

(A) bulwark is to castle

(B) thermometer is to heat

(C) bulwark is to enemy

(D) saving is to invest

(E) bandage is to cut

57. Even is to math as

(A) jargon is to English

(B) slang is to English

(C) onomatopoeia is to English

(D) simile is to English

(E) climax is to English

58. Column is to building as

(A) buttress is to pantheon

(B) architect is to hammer

(C) plan is to schedule

(D) weird is to strange

(E) stone is to concrete

59. Neutron is to atom as yellow is to

(A) pigment

(B) paint

(C) red

(D) old

(E) disease

60. Bear is to ursine as

(A) fish is to piscine

(B) rat is to equine

(C) cow is to porcine

(D) pig is to bovine

(E) dog is to feline

CONTINUE

STOP

If you finish before time is called,
you may check your work on this section.

Do not turn to the next section.

Test 5

ABSOLUTE PATTERNS

TEST 5
READING SECTION

Please refer to the Reading Section Absolute Pattern Analysis next page

THE SYNONYM QUESTIONS TEST 5 NO.1 ~ 30   THE ANALOGY QUESTIONS TEST 5 NO. 31 ~ 60

1	A	16	B
2	A	17	C
3	B	18	D
4	A	19	E
5	A	20	A
6	A	21	A
7	B	22	C
8	B	23	B
9	E	24	A
10	E	25	C
11	A	26	B
12	C	27	E
13	E	28	C
14	A	29	C
15	A	30	C

Please refer to the Analogy Section Absolute Pattern

Analysis in page 292

UNAUTHORIZED COPYING OR REUSE OF ANY PART OF THIS PAGE IS ILLEGAL

Test 5

ABSOLUTE PATTERNS for the Reading Section

Q1. Pattern 2: Main Idea Question

Question Pattern: In the first paragraph, the author most likely suggests that
Question Keywords: the ordinary men cannot

Step 1	Step 2	Step 3
Keywords from the Passage	Keywords from Answer	Tone & Concept
causes and inner working, the whole they, ignorant	C) see the cause	Synonym
Incorrect Choices & Common Patterns		
Evidence	Incorrect keywords	Tone & Concept
but of the causes and inner working of the whole they are ignorant, and with their ignorance they are content.	A) imagine	D) is Too extreme word usage
	B) prophesize	
*The author believes that ordinary people are ignorant to the causes and inner working of the whole phenomenon.	D) scientific theory	
	E) abnormality	

Q2. Type 2: Inference Question [Pattern 1: Local Question] {Category A}

Question Pattern: The quote in | **Question Keywords:** in line 5, "I wouldn't.. know it!"

Step 1	Step 2	Step 3
Keywords from the Passage	Keywords from Answer	Tone & Concept
"Triviality (insignificance) of the issue"	A) triviality	Synonym
Incorrect Choices & Common Patterns		
Evidence	Incorrect keywords	Tone & Concept
"I wouldn't cross the street to know it!" means people would not labor to find out the cause of phenomenon due to triviality.	B) significance	Not Supported by the passage
	C) distinctiveness	
	D) rarity	
	E) eccentricity	

Q3. Pattern 7: Understanding Attitude / Tone

Question Pattern: In his discussion of the author, positions
Question Keywords: scientific research, "revolution" in line 8 as

Step 1	Step 2	Step 3
Keywords from the Passage	Keywords from Answer	Tone & Concept
violently disturbed times, science, impossible.	A) disapproval	Similar Concept

Incorrect Choices & Common Patterns		
Evidence	Incorrect keywords	Tone & Concept
In the most <u>violently disturbed times</u> indeed, those with which ordinary history is mainly occupied, <u>science is quite impossible. It needs as its condition, in order to flourish, a fairly quiet, untroubled state.</u>	B) surprise C) uncertainty D) curiosity E) approval	it is evident the author's attitude towards revolution is negative because the revolution is the same as the disturbance.

Q4. Type 1: Example Question [Pattern 1: Local Question] {Category A}

Question Pattern: The author characterizes,
Question Keywords: "the structure of a soap-bubble" in line 4

Step 1	Step 2	Step 3
Keywords from the Passage	Keywords from Answer	Tone & Concept
phenomena, understand the structure of a soap	D) phenomena	phenomena (inner workings)

Incorrect Choices & Common Patterns		
Evidence	Incorrect keywords	Tone & Concept
Understand the structure of a soap-bubble?"	A) ignorance	Negative
	B) appearance	Opposite to inner workings
	C) frustration	Negative
	E) quiet	Unrelated word usage

Q5. Pattern 2: Main Idea Question

Question Pattern: According to the author, can be viewed as a place where
Question Keywords: "a cloister" in line 11,

Step 1	Step 2	Step 3
Keywords from the Passage	Keywords from Answer	Tone & Concept
a fairly quiet, untroubled state, taken its rise	A) human achievement	Positive, the essence of the concept

Incorrect Choices & Common Patterns		
Evidence	Incorrect keywords	Tone & Concept
a fairly quiet, untroubled state, or else a cloister or university removed from the din and bustle of the political and commercial world. In such places it has taken its rise	B) harmful C) monks and nuns D) phenomenon E) revolution	The passage tone is positive. B) is negative. E) "revolution" is also referred to the disturbance to science. C) is Too literal Implication D) is Not Supported by the passage

Q6. Pattern 3: Summary Question

Question Pattern: most nearly refers to
Question Keywords: "it" mentioned in line 5

Step 1	Step 2	Step 3
Keywords from the Passage	Keywords from Answer	Tone & Concept
"Understand the **structure** of a soap-bubble?"	C) structural phenomena	Synonym

Incorrect Choices & Common Patterns		
Evidence	Incorrect keywords	Tone & Concept
"Understand the **structure** of a soap-bubble?" said a cultivated literary man whom I know; "I wouldn't cross the street to know **it!**"	A) science B) ignorance D) the person E) a soap-bubble	E) is wrong because the main point is the "structure" or science behind the bubble, not the soap-bubble.

Q7. Pattern 5: Word-In-Context Question

Question Pattern: The literary device used in is   **Question Keywords:** line 2-3, "He was...attention"

Step 1	Step 2	Step 3
Keywords from the Passage	Keywords from Answer	Tone & Concept
most noticeable, **always to avoid**	A) paradox	It represents the paradox

Incorrect Choices & Common Patterns		
Evidence	Incorrect keywords	Tone & Concept
He was one of the **most noticeable** members of the Reform Club, which made him **always to avoid** A) attracting attention	B) simile	The sentence displays contradicting situation. Therefore, it is a paradox
	C) allusion	
	D) extended metaphor	
	E) metaphor	

A) Simile: a figure of speech that directly compares two different things using "as" or "like."

C) Allusion: an expression designed to call something to mind without mentioning it

D) Extended metaphor: a comparison between two unlike things that continues throughout a series of sentences in a paragraph

E) Metaphor: a comparison between two things that aren't alike

Q8. Pattern 5: Word-In-Context Question

Question Pattern: most nearly means   **Question Keywords:** In line 3, "enigmatical"

Step 1	Step 2	Step 3
Keywords from the Passage	Keywords from Answer	Tone & Concept
always to avoid, **enigmatical, little was known**	E) cryptic	Synonym

Incorrect Choices & Common Patterns		
Evidence	Incorrect keywords	Tone & Concept
always to avoid attracting attention; an **enigmatical** personage, about whom **little was known**, except that he was a polished man of the world. * Enigmatic = cryptic (very little known)	A) clear	Unrelated word usage
	B) arrogant	
	C) modest	
	D) rich	

UNAUTHORIZED COPYING OR REUSE OF ANY PART OF THIS PAGE IS ILLEGAL

Q9. Type 2: Inference Question [Pattern 1: Local Question] {Category A}

Question Pattern: In context, is best understood as a   **Question Keywords:** "the Barings" in line 12

Step 1	Step 2	Step 3
Keywords from the Passage	Keywords from Answer	Tone & Concept
open credit. His cheques regularly paid	E) a banker	Logical conclusion

Incorrect Choices & Common Patterns		
Evidence	Incorrect keywords	Tone & Concept
He was recommended by the Barings, with whom <u>he had an open credit. His cheques were regularly paid at sight from his account current</u>, which was always flush.	A) a family	Not Supported by the passage
	B) member, exclusive club	
	C) patron	
	D) a regular Englishman	

Q10. Type 2: Inference Question [Pattern 1: Local Question] {Category A}

Question Pattern: The author uses the expression to implies
Question Keywords: "people said...growing old" (lines 4-6), Mr. Phieas'

Step 1	Step 2	Step 3
Keywords from the Passage	Keywords from Answer	Tone & Concept
he resembled Byron, live on a thousand years	E) enigmatic appearance	Similar Concept

Incorrect Choices & Common Patterns		
Evidence	Incorrect keywords	Tone & Concept
People said that <u>he **resembled Byron**--at least that his head was Byronic</u> (APPEARANCE); but he was a bearded, tranquil Byron who might <u>live on a thousand years without growing old</u> (ENIGMATIC)	A) instructional nature	Not Supported by the passage
	B) having no sentiments	
	C) aristocratic behavior	
	D) reclusive nature	

Q11. Pattern 7: Understanding Attitude / Tone

Question Pattern: suggests that the narrator believes
Question Keywords: In line 6, "without growing old" , Mr. Phileas is

Step 1	Step 2	Step 3
Keywords from the Passage	Keywords from Answer	Tone & Concept
tranquil Byron, live on a thousand years	A) consistent appearance	Similar Concept

Incorrect Choices & Common Patterns		
Evidence	Incorrect keywords	Tone & Concept
tranquil Byron, who might live on a thousand years without growing old. *tranquil = composure	B) unwilling	Not Supported by the passage
	C) incapable of	
	D) act like an old person	
	E) anti-aging symptom	

Q12. Pattern 3: Summary Question

Question Pattern: The narrator describes   **Question Keywords:** Mr. Phileas in paragraph 2 as

Step 1	Step 2	Step 3
Keywords from the Passage	Keywords from Answer	Tone & Concept
He belonged, in fact, to none of the numerous	A) a mysterious	he is an unknown person

Incorrect Choices & Common Patterns		
Evidence	Incorrect keywords	Tone & Concept
He belonged, in fact, to none of the numerous societies which swarm in the English capital.	B) an arrogant	Not Supported by the passage
	C) a less desirable	
	D) a respectful	
	E) a suitable person	

Q13. Pattern 3: Summary Question

Question Pattern: The tone of mentioned in the first paragraph is best characterized as a pair
Question Keywords: the "old horseless carriage" and the modern automobile"

Step 1	Step 2	Step 3
Keywords from the Passage	Keywords from Answer	Tone & Concept
remembered, artistic appearance of	B) wistful, artistic	Synonym
Incorrect Choices & Common Patterns		
Evidence	Incorrect keywords	Tone & Concept
We have progressed appreciably beyond the days of the old horseless carriage, which, it will be remembered, retained... (WISTFUL) To-day the modern automobile somewhat something concerning the artistic appearance of	A) beautiful, practical	Not Supported by the passage
	C) dismayed, identical	
	D) ambivalent, advanced	
	E) progressive, conventional	

Q14. Pattern 3: Summary Question

Question Pattern: According to the statement the author suggests that
Question Keywords: "concerning...doubts (line 4), automobile

Step 1	Step 2	Step 3
Keywords from the Passage	Keywords from Answer	Tone & Concept
artistic appearance, layman, very grave doubts	C) does not appeal	doesn't understand
Incorrect Choices & Common Patterns		
Evidence	Incorrect keywords	Tone & Concept
concerning the **artistic appearance** of which the **layman (regular folks)** has very grave **doubts** (does not understand). Regular folks do not see the aesthetic quality of auto mobile as the way the author views.	A) should not be viewed	Not Supported by the passage
	B) is no longer viewed	
	D folks focus so much	
	E) not much difference	

Q15. Pattern 2: Main Idea Question

Question Pattern: The second paragraph mainly points out that

Step 1	Step 2	Step 3
Keywords from the Passage	Keywords from Answer	Tone & Concept
some serious damage is likely enough to occur	E) skill is required	Similar Concept

Incorrect Choices & Common Patterns		
Evidence	Incorrect keywords	Tone & Concept
but to the novice in charge of an automobile, some serious damage is likely enough to occur within an incredibly short space of time,	A) automobile, not reliable	C) Too extreme word usage
	B) technology, advancing fast	B), D) are Inconsistent with
	C) layman should not	the question
	D) automobile, power	

Q16. Pattern 3: Summary Question

Question Pattern: According to the passage,
Question Keywords: the early inventors of the automobile were mainly interested in transforming

Step 1	Step 2	Step 3
Keywords from the Passage	Keywords from Answer	Tone & Concept
hopes that inventors ...for light road vehicles,	B) the massive weight	Similar Concept

Incorrect Choices & Common Patterns		
Evidence	Incorrect keywords	Tone & Concept
the early hopes that inventors had in connection with steam as a motive power for light road vehicles,	A) the rails	Not Supported by the passage
	C) roads	
	D) the pricy	
	E) the appearance	

Q17. Pattern 5: Word-In-Context Question

Question Pattern: means		**Question Keywords:** In line 12, "formidable"
Step 1	Step 2	Step 3
Keywords from the Passage	Keywords from Answer	Tone & Concept
has already become <u>formidable. (powerful)</u>	E) impressively grown	synonym

Incorrect Choices & Common Patterns		
Evidence	Incorrect keywords	Tone & Concept
Anyone interested in automobiles should know something of the <u>literature of the subject</u>, which, during the last decade, <u>has already become formidable.</u>	A) unfinished	Unrelated word usage
	B) very popular	
	C) beautiful	
	D) advanced	

Q18. Pattern 2: Main Idea Question

Question Pattern: The primary purpose of the passage is to		
Step 1	Step 2	Step 3
Keywords from the Passage	Keywords from Answer	Tone & Concept
Anyone interested in automobiles should know	B) advance automobile	Similar Concept

Incorrect Choices & Common Patterns		
Evidence	Incorrect keywords	Tone & Concept
Always refer to the last sentence of the passage for the main purpose question. The passage discusses early attempt to advance automobile.	A) mechanism	A), C) Minor Issues
	C) inventors 'efforts	D), E) Not Supported by the passage
	D) a particular experiment	
	E) future automobile	

Q19. Pattern 2: Main Idea Question

Question Pattern: The primary purpose of the passage is to

Step 1	Step 2	Step 3
Keywords from the Passage	Keywords from Answer	Tone & Concept
The power of the steam-engine	A) steam-engine	the main idea

Incorrect Choices & Common Patterns		
Evidence	Incorrect keywords	Tone & Concept
1> For the primary purpose question, you should focus on the topic sentence and find key words. 2> The most repeated words in that area and throughout the passage should be the answer.	B) inventor	A) is Minor Issue
	C) scientific philosophy	B) It's not about inventor
	D) future	D) Predicting the Future is always incorrect
	E) philosophers	E) is not mentioned

Q20. Type 2: Inference Question [Pattern 1: Local Question] {Category A}

Question Pattern: According to the passage,   **Question Keywords:** Herbert Spencer was

Step 1	Step 2	Step 3
Keywords from the Passage	Keywords from Answer	Tone & Concept
philosophers... himself an engineer	E) more than one profession	He was philosopher and engineer.

Incorrect Choices & Common Patterns		
Evidence	Incorrect keywords	Tone & Concept
One of the greatest of modern philosophers--the founder of that system of scientific philosophy which traces .... Herbert Spencer, himself an engineer.	A) the inventor	Not Supported by the passage
	B) historian	
	C) the most respected	
	D) the founder	

Q21. Pattern 3: Summary Question

Question Pattern: in order to
Question Keywords: In lines 8-9, the author mentions "philosophers, historians, and poets."

Step 1	Step 2	Step 3
Keywords from the Passage	Keywords from Answer	Tone & Concept
has always been a favorite theme	A) widely held attention	Similar Concept

Incorrect Choices & Common Patterns		
Evidence	Incorrect keywords	Tone & Concept
The power of the steam-engine, and its inconceivable importance as an agent of civilization, has always been a favorite theme with philosophers and historians as well as	B) undermine	B) Negative
	C) uniqueness of steam engine	C), E) Unrelated word usage
	D) author's academic	
	E) show various applications	

Q22. Type 2: Inference Question [Pattern 1: Local Question] {Category A}

Question Pattern: can best refute the author's argument
Question Keywords: Which of the following industries or person "It would be...enjoy" (lines 12-14)

Step 1	Step 2	Step 3
Keywords from the Passage	Keywords from Answer	Tone & Concept
support of this wonderful machine.	A) singer at the nightclub	Logical Conclusion

Incorrect Choices & Common Patterns		
Evidence	Incorrect keywords	Tone & Concept
We cannot examine the methods and processes of any branch of industry without discovering, somewhere, the assistance and support of this wonderful machine.	B) gasoline producers	Singer is not using steam power to manufacture her voice.
	C) fishing industry	
	D) automobile salesman	
	E) clothing manufacturers	

Q23. Type 2: Inference Question [Pattern 1: Local Question] {Category A}

Question Pattern: It can be inferred from the passage that

Question Keywords: in the second chapter of his book, Herbert Spencer would probably describe

Step 1	Step 2	Step 3
Keywords from the Passage	Keywords from Answer	Tone & Concept
chapter of his "First Principles", engineer	A) philosophical, inventions	Logical Conclusion
Incorrect Choices & Common Patterns		
Evidence	Incorrect keywords	Tone & Concept
has devoted a chapter of his "First Principles" of the new system to the consideration of the multiplication of the effects of the various forces. Herbert Spencer, himself an engineer	B) ancient Greek	B), C), D) Not Supported by the passage
	C) western religion	E) Although he put much weight on steam engine, "theory" is Too extreme
	D) science and politics	
	E) the theory, steam engine	

Q24. Pattern 2: Main Idea Question

Question Pattern: The author's overall tone of the steam engine is

Step 1	Step 2	Step 3
Keywords from the Passage	Keywords from Answer	Tone & Concept
The power of the steam-engine, favorite theme	E) celebratory	Synonym
Incorrect Choices & Common Patterns		
Evidence	Incorrect keywords	Tone & Concept
The author's main purpose is to present the immense contribution of steam power and the underpinning scientific philosophy. Therefore, it is C. Celebratory = appreciative.	A) conversational	D) The overall tone can be analytical. However, the question asks the author's overall tone concerning the steam engine.
	B) sarcastic	
	C) appeal to emotion	
	D) analytical	

Q25. Type 2: Inference Question [Pattern 1: Local Question] {Category A}

Question Pattern: It can be inferred from the passage that one of the most
Question Keywords: influential social groups in the integrated armed force movement was

Step 1	Step 2	Step 3
Keywords from the Passage	Keywords from Answer	Tone & Concept
reexamine traditional <u>practices of segregation</u>	C) African-American women	Logical Conclusion

Incorrect Choices & Common Patterns		
Evidence	Incorrect keywords	Tone & Concept
The experiences in World War I and the postwar pressures generated by the civil rights movement compelled all the services--Army, Navy, Air Force, and Marine Corps--to reexamine their traditional practices of segregation.	A) Impressionist painters B) school teachers' D) white Navy widowers E) WWII army veterans	The main theme is integrated armed force, not artist (A) school teachers (B), (D) white (E) it was after WWI

Q26. Type 1: Example Question [Pattern 1: Local Question] {Category A}

Question Pattern: The author describes, as an example of
Question Keywords: "political and civil rights leaders" (line 16) social groups that

Step 1	Step 2	Step 3
Keywords from the Passage	Keywords from Answer	Tone & Concept
through the combined efforts of	D) supported the integration	Synonym

Incorrect Choices & Common Patterns		
Evidence	Incorrect keywords	Tone & Concept
faced opposition that had to be overcome and problems that had to be solved through the combined efforts of political and civil rights leaders and civil and military officials.	A) shared, resources B) made decisions C) took advantage E) took various criticism	Not Supported by the passage E) is not the main purpose of the groups, but inevitable criticism they received.

Q27. Type 2: Inference Question [Pattern 1: Local Question] {Category A}

Question Pattern: It can be inferred from the passage that

Step 1	Step 2	Step 3
Keywords from the Passage	Keywords from Answer	Tone & Concept
The experiences in World War I	A) no, force before WWI	Logical Conclusion

Incorrect Choices & Common Patterns		
Evidence	Incorrect keywords	Tone & Concept
The experiences in World War I and the postwar pressures generated by the civil rights movement compelled all the services	B) postwar pressures, single	B) The experience of WWI was another cause.
	C) two services:	C) All the services--Army, Navy, Air Force, and Marine
	D) around the world	
	E) parallels, history	

Q28. Pattern 3: Summary Question

Question Pattern: Which of the following factors
Question Keywords: ignited the need for the integrated armed force?

Step 1	Step 2	Step 3
Keywords from the Passage	Keywords from Answer	Tone & Concept
The experiences in World War I	I. WWII	Logical Conclusion

Incorrect Choices & Common Patterns		
Evidence	Incorrect keywords	Tone & Concept
The experiences in World War I and the postwar pressures generated by the civil rights movement compelled all the services--Army, Navy, Air Force, and Marine Corps--to reexamine their traditional practices of segregation.	II. The postwar movement	It is WWI, not WWII. Therefore the answer is B) II, III only
	III. Civil rights movement	

Q29. Pattern 3: Summary Question

Question Pattern: The passage mainly suggests that

Step 1	Step 2	Step 3
Keywords from the Passage	Keywords from Answer	Tone & Concept
problems, had to be solved, efforts	A) no absolute unanimity	Synonym

Incorrect Choices & Common Patterns		
Evidence	Incorrect keywords	Tone & Concept
it nevertheless faced opposition that had to be overcome and problems that had to be solved through the combined efforts	B) limited by democratic principles	B) is not stated. C), D), E) are all Opposite to the fact.
	C) in fact impractical	
	D) the segregated armed force, favored	
	E) regretful results	

Q30. Pattern 2: Main Idea Question

Question Pattern: The primary purpose of the passage is to

Step 1	Step 2	Step 3
Keywords from the Passage	Keywords from Answer	Tone & Concept
The integration, momentous event	A) author's belief	Logical Conclusion

Incorrect Choices & Common Patterns		
Evidence	Incorrect keywords	Tone & Concept
The integration of the armed forces was a momentous event in our military and national history.	B) concept	Minor Issue
	C) alternative interpretation	Not Supported by the passage
	D) differences between integrated, segregated	
	E) justify social groups'	

Q31. Pattern 7: Understanding Attitude / Tone

Question Pattern: The narrator in the first paragraph appears to be

Step 1	Step 2	Step 3
Keywords from the Passage	Keywords from Answer	Tone & Concept
I sighed and moodily	A) bored	Synonym

Incorrect Choices & Common Patterns		
Evidence	Incorrect keywords	Tone & Concept
I sighed and moodily contemplated my uncreased trouser legs and thought of my non-existent bank balance.	B) companionable	Opposite
	C) aggressive	
	D) diligent	
	E) curious	

Q32. Type 2: Inference Question [Pattern 1: Local Question] {Category A}

Question Pattern: It can be inferred from the first paragraph that
Question Keywords: the occupation of the narrator is

Step 1	Step 2	Step 3
Keywords from the Passage	Keywords from Answer	Tone & Concept
my line--theatrical bookings– ~	A) a tour arrangement guide	Logical Conclusion

Incorrect Choices & Common Patterns		
Evidence	Incorrect keywords	Tone & Concept
I've got an office in the Daily Standard building and sometimes when things are slow in my line--**theatrical bookings**– ~ we can infer that the narrator's occupation	B) the Jake's manager	Not Supported by the passage
	C) a magazine columnist	
	D) an office cleaner	
	E) a book editor	

UNAUTHORIZED COPYING OR REUSE OF ANY PART OF THIS PAGE IS ILLEGAL

Q33. Type 2: Inference Question [Pattern 1: Local Question] {Category A}

Question Keywords: The author's difficulty to identify the stranger in lines 9-15 was probably caused by the

Step 1	Step 2	Step 3
Keywords from the Passage	Keywords from Answer	Tone & Concept
But then, my eyes seemed suddenly to focus,	E) daydreaming	Logical Conclusion

Incorrect Choices & Common Patterns		
Evidence	Incorrect keywords	Tone & Concept
"I did. I'm right here." It was the same voice and I jerked my head in the direction of the sound. For an instant I didn't see a thing.	A) unfamiliar voice B) physical contact C) unanticipated D) refusal	There are no other choices that suggest why he could not see the stranger at first, but daydreaming.

Q34. Pattern 7: Understanding Attitude / Tone

Question Pattern: primarily serves to   **Question Keywords:** In line 19, "exerting himself some manner"

Step 1	Step 2	Step 3
Keywords from the Passage	Keywords from Answer	Tone & Concept
sounded strained, he were exerting himself	A) initial uneasy feeling	Logical Conclusion

Incorrect Choices & Common Patterns		
Evidence	Incorrect keywords	Tone & Concept
"Can you see me now?" he asked, and his voice sounded strained, as if he were exerting himself in some manner.	B) narrator's discomfort C) stranger's height D) polite gesture E) relationship	The underlined sentence shows that the stranger tries to adjust his uneasy feeling.

Q35. Pattern 7: Understanding Attitude / Tone

Question Keywords: In line 6, "stinkerro" suggests that the narrator values his jobs as

Step 1	Step 2	Step 3
Keywords from the Passage	Keywords from Answer	Tone & Concept
Things in my line were strictly <u>stinkeroo., I sighed</u>	A) frivolous	Logical Conclusion

Incorrect Choices & Common Patterns		
Evidence	Incorrect keywords	Tone & Concept
Things in my line were strictly stinkeroo. I sighed and moodily contemplated my uncreased trouser legs and thought of my non-existent bank balance.	B) flexible	Throughout the passage, the narrative is laid on boredom. The narrator does not value his job highly.
	C) smelly	
	D) scholarly	
	E) important	

Q36. Pattern 7: Understanding Attitude / Tone

Question Pattern: Throughout the passage, the author presents
Question Keywords: "Mound-Builders" as a

Step 1	Step 2	Step 3
Keywords from the Passage	Keywords from Answer	Tone & Concept
<u>above a degree of artistic skill very far superior</u>	B) surprising technicians	Logical Conclusion

Incorrect Choices & Common Patterns		
Evidence	Incorrect keywords	Tone & Concept
Among them, indeed, are found not a few who assert for the people conveniently designated as <u>above a degree of artistic skill very far superior</u> to that attained by the present race of Indians as they have been known to history.	A) mentor	Not Supported by the passage. E) 'reclusive' means hiding or isolated from society, which is negative.
	C) scholarly designers	
	D) inferior manufacturers	
	E) reclusive builders	

Q37. Pattern 3: Summary Question

Question Pattern: The primary obstacle the author faces from the
Question Keywords: inferiority of the products made by the latter-day Indian can be resolved by

Step 1	Step 2	Step 3
Keywords from the Passage	Keywords from Answer	Tone & Concept
but to be considered first in another way	A) different purpose	Logical Conclusion

Incorrect Choices & Common Patterns		
Evidence	Incorrect keywords	Tone & Concept
but to be considered first in another way and for another purpose than mere artistic comparison.	B) interpreting a scholarly	The author suggests not to focus on the artistic skills alone.
	C) new evidence	
	D) best products	
	E) emotional attachment	

Q38. Pattern 7: Understanding Attitude / Tone

Question Pattern: The primary purpose of the passage is to

Step 1	Step 2	Step 3
Keywords from the Passage	Keywords from Answer	Tone & Concept
skill attained by Mound-Builders, attention	E) celebrate, technique	Synonym

Incorrect Choices & Common Patterns		
Evidence	Incorrect keywords	Tone & Concept
The considerable degree of decorative and artistic skill attained by the so-called Mound-Builders, not failed to arrest the attention of archeologists.	A) compare the sculptures	Minor Issue
	B) position, above	Minor Issue
	C) teach a lesson	Not Supported by the passage & Too specific
	D) describe the skills	

Q39. Pattern 5: Word-In-Context Question

Question Pattern: means   **Question Keywords:** In line 17, "substantiated"

Step 1	Step 2	Step 3
Keywords from the Passage	Keywords from Answer	Tone & Concept
it is more than doubtful ,can be substantiated.	E) proven	Synonym

Incorrect Choices & Common Patterns

Evidence	Incorrect keywords	Tone & Concept
it is more than doubtful if the artistic inferiority of the latter-day Indian **can be substantiated**.	A) required	substantiated' means proven.
	B) vary	
	C) basic	
	D) essential	

Q40. Pattern 3: Summary Question

Question Pattern: The author agrees with all of the following points EXCEPT

Step 1	Step 2	Step 3
Keywords from the Passage	Keywords from Answer	Tone & Concept
it is more than doubtful substantiated.	B) Mound-Builder impressed, later-Indian	

Incorrect Choices & Common Patterns

Evidence	Incorrect keywords	Tone & Concept
it is more than doubtful if the artistic inferiority of the latter-day Indian can be substantiated.	A) different purpose	There is no evidence that the products of Mound-Builder impressed the latter-Indian
	C) artistic ability, exceeds	
	D) Archeologists are fascinated	
	E) Comparing more than artistic skill	

UNAUTHORIZED COPYING OR REUSE OF ANY PART OF THIS PAGE IS ILLEGAL

Test 5 ABSOLUTE PATTERNS for the Analogy Section

Q31. Absolute Pattern 7: Association (Characteristic) Pattern

E is the best answer

Martin Luther King Jr. is the symbol of peace; Hitler is the symbol catastrophe.

Q32. Absolute Pattern 6: Purpose (Job/Tool) Pattern

D is the best answer

Old man uses a cane (tool) for a walk; Umbrella is a tool for rains.

Q33. Absolute Pattern 1: Production (Cause-Effect) Pattern

C is the best answer.

Game produces score as chicken produces egg

Q34. Absolute Pattern 1: Production (Cause-Effect) Pattern

A is the best answer.

Rainbow produces seven-colors; spring produces flowers.
B is flipped over.

Q35. Absolute Pattern 11: Homophony Pattern

C is the best answer

This type of question has nothing to do with a meaning or logic. It is all about the sound of words that it produces.

Clicking is to flicking as lion is to Zion

Q36. Absolute Pattern 11: Homophony Pattern

B is the best answer

Mime is to dime as pale is to gale

Q37. Absolute Pattern 11: Homophony Pattern

C is the best answer

poor is door as rare is to hair

Q38. Absolute Pattern 11: Homophony Pattern

E is the best answer.

Sand is to hand as complex is to reflex

Q39. Absolute Pattern 1: Production (Cause-Effect) Pattern

D is the best answer.

The process is a part of a production as a scene is a part of a play.

Q40. Absolute Pattern 7: Association (Characteristic) Pattern

B is the best answer

Dragonfly is categorized as (belongs to) an insect; Dragon is categorized as (belongs to) myth.

Choice A) "fly" is incorrect because, 'fly' is not corresponding to the question category "insect" in which dragonfly belongs to.

Q41. Absolute Pattern 6:Purpose (Job/Tool) Pattern

D is the best answer

Army uses accruements as a tool, just as the chef uses a utensil as a tool.

Choice E is wrong because the kitchen is not a tool. It's facility.

In other words, if chef uses kitchen army has to use army base (the same facility category).

Q42. Absolute Pattern 12: Active-Passive Pattern

C is the best answer

The question and (C) are both passive activities and both function as a shelter.

Choice A is a different category. Choice B is production pattern.

UNAUTHORIZED COPYING OR REUSE OF ANY PART OF THIS PAGE IS ILLEGAL

Q43. Absolute Pattern 5: Degree Pattern

C is the best answer   (big to small)

Lieutenant is a higher rank in the army than private. Tree is bigger than a sapling.

*Private (the low rank solider)

Q44. Absolute Pattern 7: Association (Characteristic) Pattern

C is the best answer.

The preface is the beginning of the book as the appetizer is beginning of the meal.

Q45. Absolute Pattern 6:Purpose (Job/Tool) Pattern

B is the best answer.

An earphone is a tool to listen to music; a telescope is a tool to see the stars.

Q46. Absolute Pattern 3: Antonym (Positive-Negative) Pattern

A is the best answer

B is wrong analogy because the opposite of real is unreal, not a dream.

Q47. Absolute Pattern 6:Purpose (Job/Tool) Pattern

E is the best answer

Honey makes food sweet; Glue makes things sticky.

Choice D doesn't work in any logical correlation.

Q48. Absolute Pattern 6:Purpose (Job/Tool) Pattern

E is the best answer

The purpose of a citadel is to protect from invasion. The purpose of the cathedral is for prayer

Choice B, D are flipped over.

Q49. Absolute Pattern 7: Association (Characteristic) Pattern

C is the best answer

Snow melts and cement gets harden.

Q50. Absolute Pattern 1: Production (Cause-Effect) Pattern

E is the best answer.

The producer produces TV program; director produces a movie in the same entertainment genre.

Q51. Absolute Pattern 3: Antonym (Positive-Negative) Pattern

D is the best answer.

Evil and god are negative and positive entities, just as junk is to a sedan.

Choice A, B, C have no clear +/- values.

Q52. Absolute Pattern 3: Antonym (Positive-Negative) Pattern

E is the best answer

F and A+ are directly opposite and have a negative and positive value.

No other choices have that pattern but (E).

Q53. Absolute Pattern 3: Antonym (Positive-Negative) Pattern

C is the best answer

Choice A and B are flipped over.

Choice D and E have no positive and negative relations.

Q54. Absolute Pattern 3: Antonym (Positive-Negative) Pattern

E is the best answer

Sanitation and contamination are positive-negative relations. Choice E) work and procrastinate are also positive-negative.

Q55. Absolute Pattern 1: Production (Cause-Effect) Pattern

D is the best answer

Flour produces bread, just as lemon produces lemonade

Choice A is wrong because they are not the food category.

Q56. Absolute Pattern 6:Purpose (Job/Tool) Pattern

C is the best answer.

Sunscreen protects skin from burning. Bulwark protects enemies.

Q57. Absolute Pattern 7: Association (Characteristic) Pattern

D is the best answer.

Both Even in math and simile in literature work on the same principle.

Q58. Absolute Pattern 6:Purpose (Job/Tool) Pattern

A is the best answer

Column supports a building and buttress supports a pantheon.

Q59. Absolute Pattern 2: Part-Whole Pattern

A is the best answer.

Neutron is a part of the atom, just as yellow is a part of pigment.

Q60. Absolute Pattern 7: Association (Characteristic) Pattern

A is the best answer

Bear belongs to ursine, fish is a group of piscine.

Test 5 Recap

Negative question

When question contains a word, such as EXCEPT, NOT, LEAST, UNLIKE, or 'I, II, III, IV,' it is called "Negative question".

The negative question is difficult. This type of question consumes twice of your time and energy while significantly reducing your chance to get the correct answer that eventually hampers your overall time management during the test.

Consider this question as the universal type question and save it for last.

The crucial point is to train yourself to view the perspective from the opposite situation.

That is, you need to find keywords and the proper tone of the text and then reverse the tone and the value of the keywords.

SSAT HACKERS

SSAT

Reading & Verbal Practice

Test 6

ALL THE LOGIC AND RULES

BEHIND THE EVERY SINGLE

SSAT QUESTION

Test 6 Reading Section
Time: 40 Minutes, 40 Questions

Directions: Each reading passage is followed by questions about it. Answer the questions that follow a passage on the basis of what is stated or implied in that passage.

Questions 1-6 are based on the following passage.

Line In a splendid chamber of the Palais Royal, formerly styled the Palais Cardinal, a man was sitting in deep reverie, his head supported on his hands, leaning over a gilt and inlaid table which was covered with letters and papers. Behind this figure glowed a vast fireplace alive with leaping flames; great logs of oak blazed and crackled on the polished brass andirons

5 whose flicker shorn upon the superb habiliments of the lonely tenant of the room, which was illumined grandly by twin candelabra rich with wax-lights.

Any one who happened at that moment to contemplate that red simar--the gorgeous robe of office--and the rich lace, or who gazed on that pale brow, bent in anxious meditation, might, in the solitude of that apartment, combined with the silence of the ante-chambers and the

10 measured paces of the guards upon the landing-place, have fancied that the shade of Cardinal Richelieu lingered still in his accustomed haunt.

It was, alas! the ghost of former greatness. France enfeebled, the authority of her sovereign contemned, her nobles returning to their former turbulence and insolence, her enemies within her frontiers--all proved the great Richelieu no longer in existence.

15

1

The primary function of the first paragraph is to
A) describe a man's specific concerns
B) describe the setting of a place
C) describe the difference between the Palais Royal and palais Cardinal
D) account for the charismatic appeal of a man
E) explain why the Palais Cardinal changed its name to Palais Royal

2

It can be inferred from the passage that
A) the Palais Royal was used for defense
B) the Palais Royal was known for its haunted place
C) Cardinal Richelieu had a condescending nature
D) Palais Roayl was the part of Palais Cardinal
E) the Palais Royal is not currently occupied by Cardinal Richelieu

CONTINUE

3

The tone of the passage is

A) didactic

B) pensive

C) ominous

D) baffle

E) sardonic

4

The passage portrays the Cardinal Richelieu as the

A) knowledgeable scholar

B) defeated authority

C) adventurous explorer

D) revered clergyman

E) ignorant ruler

5

The relationships between the second and the third paragraph can be described respectively as the

A) physical characteristic and mentality of Palais Cardinal

B) depiction of time and place

C) current state and the future

D) myth about the place and the reality

E) sense of misconception and the revelation

6

"Any one" in line 7 is portrayed as being

A) overly sentimental

B) deeply complex

C) regretful

D) simplistic

E) fantasized

CONTINUE

Questions 7-12 are based on the following passage.

Line

While the world pays respectful tribute to Rembrandt the artist, it has been compelled to wait until comparatively recent years for some small measure of reliable information concerning Rembrandt the man. The sixteenth and seventeenth centuries seem to have been very little concerned with personalities. There were no newspapers to record his doings and,

5   if he chanced to be an artist, it was nobody's business to set down the details of his life. Sometimes a diarist chanced to pass by and to jot down a little gossip, quite unconscious of the fact that it would serve to stimulate generations yet unborn, but, for the most part, artists who did great work in a retiring fashion and were not honoured by courts and princes as Rubens was, passed from the scene of their labours with all the details of their sojourn

10 unrecorded.

Rembrandt was fated to suffer more than mere neglect, for he seems to have been a light-hearted, headstrong, extravagant man, with no capacity for business. He had not even the supreme quality, associated in doggerel with Dutchmen, of giving too little and asking too much. Consequently, he died poor and enfeebled.

15 Shakespeare has put into Mark Antony's mouth the statement that "the evil that men do lives after them," and this was very much the case with Rembrandt van Ryn. His first biographers seem to have no memory save for his undoubted recklessness, his extravagance, and his debts. living.

7

Which of the following statements about Rembrandt is true?

A) He lived in the era when people deeply concerned about artists' personal lives

B) His artistic genius was motivated from his persona

C) He was honoured by the courts of his time.

D) He enjoyed fame when he was alive

E) Until recently we scarcely had any information about Rembrandt as the man

8

The author characterizes our knowledge about the personal life of Rembrandt as

A) limited

B) abundant

C) divisive

D) objective

E) more false than true

CONTINUE

9

The word "gossip" in line 6 is to describe the

A) way people treated Rembrandt as the man

B) proof that he was being bullied

C) respect he enjoyed in his community

D) people's tendency to treat Rembrandt as a mediocre artist

E) strongly held opinion among folks

10

The author uses Shakespeare's quote in the last paragraph to illustrate how

A) well Rembrandt is remembered today

B) little Rembrandt is remembered today

C) falsely Rembrandt is remembered today

D) Rembrandt's attitude in his life affected the posthumous fame

E) undoubtedly great artist Rembrandt was

11

The author assumes Rembrandt's persona as

A) carefree

B) strict in his expenditures

C) adventurous

D) strict and disciplined

E) wise in financial matters

12

The author of the passage would be most interested in learning which of the following?

A) The masterpiece Rembrandt left after his death

B) An illustration about the era when Rembrandt lived

C) Some examples that describe the conventional wisdom of Dutchmen

D) The life of Shakespeare

E) The food Rembrandt enjoyed

CONTINUE

Questions 13-18 are based on the following passage.

Line

The excavations conducted by the Greek Archeological Society at Athens from 1883 to 1889 have laid bare the entire surface of the Acropolis, and shed an unexpected light upon the early history of Attic art. Many questions which once seemed unanswerable are now definitively answered, and, on the other hand, many more compelling questions have been raised. When, in
5 1886, Dörpfeld unearthed the foundations of a great temple close by the southern side of the Erechtheion, all questions concerning the exact site, the ground-plan, and the elevation of the great temple of Athena were decided once for all. On these points little or nothing can be added to what has been done, and Dörpfeld's results must be accepted as final and certain.

The history of the temple presents, however, several questions, some of which seem still
10 undecided. When was the temple built? Was it all built at one time? Conflicting answers to nearly all of these questions have appeared since the discovery of the temple. Only the first question has received one and the same answer from all. The material and the technical execution of the peripteros (building contained within the peristyle only) of the temple show conclusively that this part, at least, was erected in the time of Peisistratos.
15

13

The parenthesis in line 13 (the building…peristyle only) is mainly used to

A) emphasize the previous statement
B) set limit to the previous statement
C) demonstrate the example
D) explain the historical significance
E) demystify the precision of the excavation

14

The primary purpose of the passage is to

A) show growing concern about the excavation
B) regret some misconception
C) analyze the excavated site
D) reveal the current limitation
E) speculate about the future excavation

15

The author views "all questions" mentioned in line 6 with

A) appreciation about their complete revelation
B) ambivalence about their scholastic merits
C) curiosity about their future effects
D) skepticism about the complete revelation
E) disdain for their fabrications

16

The tone of the phrase "only the first question" mentioned in line 11 is

A) insincere
B) emphatic
C) pensive
D) evasive
E) endearing

CONTINUE

17

Which of the following situation is most analogoues to "Many questions...raised. (lines 3-4)

A) A detective story finally reveals the murderer.

B) A reader is stimulated by the clue presented from the following chapter

C) A customer tried a taster wine eagers to buy several bottles

D) A school boy conducts a science homework at his father's company research lab

E) A school teacher who corrected some minor grammar errors from a student's essay later found it was plagiarized from the Internet

18

The author's attitude toward Dörpfeld can best be described as

A) genuinely puzzled

B) hostile

C) solemnly respectful

D) generally indifferent

E) measured acceptance

Questions 19-24 are based on the following passage.

Line

If Sally Ann knows more about weaving than Elijah," reasoned eleven-year-old Susan with her father, "then why don't you make her overseer?"

"It would never do," replied Daniel Anthony as a matter of course. "It would never do to have a woman overseer in the mill."

5   This answer did not satisfy Susan and she often thought about it. To enter the mill, to stand quietly and look about, was the best kind of entertainment, for she was fascinated by the whir of the looms, by the nimble fingers of the weavers, and by the general air of efficiency. Admiringly she watched Sally Ann Hyatt, the tall capable weaver from Vermont. When the yarn on the beam was tangled or there was something wrong with the machinery, Elijah, the

10   overseer, always called out to Sally Ann, "I'll tend your loom, if you'll look after this." Sally Ann never failed to locate the trouble or to untangle the yarn. Yet she was never made overseer, and this continued to puzzle Susan.

Although women freeholders had voted in some of the colonies as late as 1807, just as in England in the fifteenth franchise had gradually found its way into the statutes, women's rights

15   as citizens were ignored, in spite of the contribution they had made to the defense and development of the new nation.

CONTINUE

19

It can be inferred from the passage that Elijah is

A) an unskillful person

B) a male worker

C) reluctant to the millwork

D) has a natural sense for weaving

E) exhausted by the millwork

20

Daniel Anthony's reply in lines 3-4, " it would... ..mill" implies that

A) woman are not allowed to take the higher role

B) Sally does not truly appreciate her work

C) His daughter's personal preference should not be involved in business

D) he likes Elijah better than Sally

E) he is keenly aware of man's superiority at weaving

21

The passage is viewed from Susan as

A) a girl condescendingly tolerant to the millworkers' clumsy operation

B) a girl experiencing a harsh millwork condition

C) a girl troubled by the situation

D) an adult recollecting her old memories

E) a detached observer

22

In the final paragraph, the author points out the identity of women as

A) a part of a property like cattle

B) the freeholders who enjoyed superiority to male

C) the citizens who helped found the new nation

D) family members without officially granted identity

E) individuals who contributed most in defense and development of the new nation

23

The primary purpose of the passage is to introduce

A) an early stage of life of a historical figure

B) the people given unequal treatment because of gender bias

C) the friendship between Sally Ann and Elijah

D) the patriarch society maintained in the 19th century

E) the historical overview of gender inequality

24

Which of the following aspects in the early 19th century is addressed in the passage?

A) Some female were allowed to vote

B) The citizenship were granted to some women

C) Some wealthier women could purchase their citizenships

D) Many women felt insecurity about their jobs

E) The experience from the mill became the stimulant to Susan's later feminism activity

CONTINUE

Questions 25-30 are based on the following passage.

Line   The life of Frederick Douglass, recorded in the pages which follow, is not merely an
example of self-elevation under the most adverse circumstances; it is, moreover, a noble
vindication of the highest aims of the American anti-slavery movement. The real object of
that movement is not only to disenthrall, it is, also, to bestow upon the Negro the exercise of
5   all those rights, from the possession of which he has been so long debarred.
But this full recognition of the colored man to the right, and the entire admission of the same
to the full privileges, political, religious and social, of manhood, requires powerful effort on
the part of the enthralled, as well as on the part of those who would disenthrall them. The
people at large must feel the conviction, as well as admit the abstract logic, of human
10   equality; the Negro, for the first time in the world's history, brought in full contact with high
civilization, must prove his title first to all that is demanded for him; in the teeth of unequal
chances, he must prove himself equal to the mass of those who oppress him--therefore,
absolutely superior to his apparent fate. to their relative ability.

25

The author describes the life of Frederick Douglass as the man

A) most people do not fully appreciate
B) who believed self-elevation is everything
C) accomplished impossibility
D) possessed pragmatic knowledge
E) who was recognized later for his feminism
   activity

26

Which of the following examples belongs to "a noble vindication" mentioned in line 2?

A) Escalate tension between the Negro and slave
   owners
B) Appeal to the psychology and logic
C) Take back all the rights by power
D) Train the Negro soldiers
E) Encourage domestic fight

27

The passage as a whole primarily serves as

A) a discussion of the antislavery activities
B) a case study of atypical biography
C) a survey of the historical figure
D) a brief examination of the revered figure
E) an overview of early slavery in America

28

Which of the following aspects concerning Fredrick Douglas is NOT addressed in the passage?

A) His ultimate goal was to emancipate the Negro
B) He was seeking to take all the rights that had been
   denied to the Negro
C) The privilege to participate in politics was the
   ultimate goal he demanded
D) He wanted to influence on white slave owners
E) He believed the enthralled had superior ability

CONTINUE

29

"all those rights" in line 5 includes and represents

A) the right to vote

B) the full political rights of the Negro and women

C) the full political, religious and social rights of all countries

D) the full political, religious and social rights of the Negro

E) the movement to disenthrall

30

In line 8, "those" most nearly refers to

A) the entire humanity

B) the aboriginal

C) the entire black people

D) all black community

E) anti-slavery activists

Questions 31-35 are based on the following passage.

Line   Portland Is a very beautiful city of 60,000 inhabitants. It is perhaps true of many of the growing cities of the West, that they do not offer the same social advantages as the older cities of the East. But this is principally the case as to what may be called boom cities, where the larger part of the population is of that floating class which follows in the line of temporary

5   growth for the purposes of speculation, and in no sense applies to those centers of trade whose prosperity is based on the solid foundation of legitimate business.

   As the metropolis of a vast section of country, having broad agricultural valleys filled with improved farms, surrounded by mountains rich in mineral wealth, and boundless forests of as fine timber as the world produces, the cause of Portland's growth and prosperity is the trade

10   which it has as the center of collection and distribution of this great wealth of natural re-sources, and it has attracted, not the boomer and speculator, who find their profits in the wild excitement of the boom, but the merchant, manufacturer, and investor, who seek the surer if slower channels of legitimate business and investment. These have come from the East. They came as seeking a better and wider field to engage in the same occupations they had followed

15   in their Eastern homes, and bringing with them all the love of polite life which they had acquired there, have established here a new society, equaling in all respects that which they left behind.

CONTINUE ➤

31

It can be inferred from the first paragraph that the West

A) had more inhabitants than the East

B) was socially less privileged than the East

C) had fewer boom cities

D) improved faster than the East

E) had a fewer legal enterprises

32

In line 4, the author describes the "floating class" as the people

A) had the similar business foundation of the cities

B) who became the majority of the city

C) who were rapidly evolving as the business foundation

D) who often traveled to the East

E) who were regarded as the potential predators of the business in the West

33

The passage categorizes the major occupations of the West businessmen EXCEPT

A) investor

B) manufacturer

C) merchant

D) timber processor

E) gold seeker

34

In line 6, "legitimate business," the narrator values which of the following most?

A) the size of wealth

B) the vision of the business

C) the faithful minds of the businessmen

D) the extended history

E) a unique type of the business

35

The author's attitude toward "These have come from the East" in line 13 is to

A) disdain for their opportunistic speculation

B) show their superior ability

C) praise their decision for relocation

D) subtly scorn their disgraceful occupations

E) question their identity

CONTINUE

Questions 36-40 are based on the following passage.

Line   Sand constitutes from 1/3 to 1/2 of the volume of concrete; when a large amount of concrete is to be made a contractor cannot, therefore, afford to guess at his source of sand supply. A long haul over poor roads can easily make the sand cost more than the stone per cubic yard of concrete. Engineers commonly specify that sand for concrete shall be clean and sharp, and

5   silicious in character for the highest quality concrete. Neither sharpness nor excessive cleanliness is worth seeking after if it involves much expense. Tests show conclusively that sand with rounded grains makes quite as strong a mortar, other things being equal, as does sand with angular grains. The admixture with sand of a considerable percentage of loam or clay is also not the unmixed evil it has been supposed to be. These experiments demonstrate

10   conclusively that loam and clay in sand to the amount of 10 to 15 per cent result in minimal material reduction in the strength of mortars made with this sand as compared with mortars made with the same sand after washing. There can be no doubt but that for much concrete work the expense entailed in washing sand is an unnecessary one.

36

According to the author, clay as a concrete material is

A) a debatable issue

B) an alternative

C) the superior quality

D) an impractical method

E) a frivolous issue

37

The term "unmixed evil" in line 9 mainly suggests the

A) mild acceptance

B) concern for deterioration

C) disadvantages outweigh advantages

D) inaccuracy of mixture

E) spiritual aspect of architecture

38

Which of the followings make the ideal concrete?

A) 1/3 of the best quality cleaned and sharp sand

B) 1/3 of cheap rounded sand

C) thoroughly washed cheap sand

D) 1/3 of clay

E) 1/2 of loam

CONTINUE

39

The passage states that when builders buy sand they should consider which of the following first?

A) the quality of sand

B) the quality of concrete

C) the road condition

D) the quality of stone

E) the volume of materials other than sand

40

Which of the followings would be the first consideration for the concrete builders in choosing their sand?

A) the sharpness of sand

B) the cost of sand

C) silicious

D) the admixture of sand

E) the cleanness of sand

Test 6 Verbal Section   30 MINUTES, 60 QUESTIONS

Directions: the synonym questions ask you to find the most appropriate synonym to the question.

The analogy questions ask you to find the most appropriate analogy to the question.
Select the answer that best matches to the question.

Synonym Sample Question:

Q: SUPERIOR

A higher rank

B inferior

C considerable

D supermarket

E supper

A) is the best answer because the synonym for superior is higher rank.

B) is incorrect because it applies the 'opposite concept.

C) and E) are irrelevant words.

D) is incorrect because it applies physical concept to mental concept

---

Test 6 Synonym questions 1 to 30

1. MODIFY
(A) model
(B) copy
(C) adhere
(D) alter
(E) mobilize

2. IMPLICATE
(A) divide
(B) disconnect
(C) imply
(D) conflict
(E) duplicate

3. ITEMIZE
(A) enumerate
(B) article
(C) lining
(D) confine
(E) idiomatic

4. VACILLATE
(A) vary
(B) unmoving
(C) value
(D) vocal
(E) fluctuate

5. REVITALIZE
(A) healthy
(B) bring back to life
(C) living
(D) release
(E) render

CONTINUE

6. VERIFY

(A) authenticate

(B) veracity

(C) heartfelt

(D) sound

(E) obtain

7. RUMINATE

(A) forget

(B) ponder

(C) illuminate

(D) light

(E) roomy

8. ALLUSION

(A) direct

(B) reference

(C) avoid

(D) distance

(E) condone

9. ALTRUISM

(A) generosity

(B) alternation

(C) change

(D) truthfulness

(E) alter ego

10. AMBIENCE

(A) mood

(B) unpleasantness

(C) ambulance

(D) noise

(E) emergency

11. SLUGGISH

(A) agile

(B) slow

(C) independent

(D) clear

(E) steadfast

12. GLEE

(A) happiness

(B) sadness

(C) benevolence

(D) syndication

(E) mood

13. SCURRY

(A) stew

(B) funny

(C) tempt

(D) inactive

(E) rush

14. COWER

(A) cow like

(B) diffident

(C) obey

(D) stupid

(E) endanger

15. HOSTILE

(A) hospitalize

(B) heal

(C) aggressive

(D) medical

(E) lenient

CONTINUE

16. EXTENSION

(A) delay

(B) cut short

(C) vast

(D) immaculate

(E) stipple

17. ROYAL

(A) regal

(B) declare

(C) creep

(D) invite

(E) name

18. LUNGE

(A) clear

(B) move briskly

(C) organ

(D) lung

(E) thrust

19. UNCLEAR

(A) ambiguous

(B) stalemate

(C) prosaic

(D) dormant

(E) patrician

20. IMPROVE

(A) recalcitrant

(B) ameliorate

(C) inadvertent

(D) proxy

(E) auspicious

21. BIG

(A) austere

(B) augment

(C) frugal

(D) fraternal

(E) gesticulate

22. TALKATIVE

(A) furtive

(B) gregarious

(C) genteel

(D) fraternal

(E) garrulous

23. INTIMATE

(A) lovely

(B) pacify

(C) friendly

(D) threaten

(E) interval

24. FROWN

(A) fish

(B) shrimp

(C) disapproval

(D) approval

(E) fame

25. CONCEITED

(A) nebulous

(B) lionize

(C) proud

(D) hidden

(E) centered

CONTINUE

UNAUTHORIZED COPYING OR REUSE OF ANY PART OF THIS PAGE IS ILLEGAL

26. DECIDE

(A) tactic

(B) resolve

(C) rash

(D) meeting

(E) reconciliation

27. COMPREHENSIVE

(A) understanding

(B) covering everything

(C) proposal

(D) polite

(E) refined

28. PERSISTENT

(A) tenacious

(B) obedient

(C) clumsy

(D) strong

(E) ample

29. DIDACTIC

(A) teach

(B) dialect

(C) divisive

(D) intended to learn

(E) propel

30. FOOLISH

(A) imprudent

(B) glut

(C) grandiloquent

(D) free

(E) unjustified

Analogy Sample Question:

Q: River is to Ocean as:

A better is to good

B rain is to cloud

C father is to mother

D city is to country

E fork is to spoon

D is the correct answer. Just as the river is smaller than the Ocean, the city is smaller than the country. The pattern applied in this question is the Degree Pattern (small to big)

A) is incorrect because the word order is flipped over.

B) is incorrect because it applies the production pattern (cloud produces rain)

C), E) are incorrect because they apply the Antonym patterns.

Test 6 Analogy questions 31 to 60

31. Circle is to octagon as

(A) land is to sky

(B) rectangle is to pentagon

(C) nice is to ugly

(D) bait is to fish

(E) root is to radius

CONTINUE

32. Table is to chair as

(A) man is to woman

(B) fork is to knife

(C) north is to south

(D) submarine is to jet

(E) surrealism is to existentialism

33. verbal is to oral as cartography is to

(A) map

(B) book

(C) music

(D) art

(E) business

34. Mountain is to vantage point as

(A) land is to people

(B) mall is to stores

(C) north pole is to penguin

(D) ocean is to fish

(E) lighthouse is to lamp

35. Shadow is to glim as chilly is to

(A) dazzle

(B) warm

(C) hot

(D) scorch

(E) parch

36. Antipathy is to sympathy as

(A) aversion is to love

(B) fail to vengeance

(C) man is to adult

(D) sugar is to salt

(E) tyrant is to autocrat

37. Piggybank is to coins as

(A) flowers is to vase

(B) garden is to flowers

(C) taxi is to driver

(D) bus is to passenger

(E) hostage is to ransom

38. Wedding dress is to bliss as

(A) President is to Whitehouse

(B) school is to principal

(C) memento is to nostalgia

(D) doctor is to patient

(E) scholar is to research

39. Hard work is to success as

(A) study is to test

(B) company is to profit

(C) sand is to beach

(D) shelter is to homeless

(E) legend is to dragon

40. Ransom is to hostage as

(A) milk is to baby

(B) money is to bank

(C) audience is to ticket

(D) student is to graduate

(E) verdict is to judge

41. Flower is to scent as spoiled milk is to

(A) stomachache

(B) garbage

(C) pungent

(D) fragrant

(E) spoil

CONTINUE

42. Dancer is to audience as

(A) professor is to faculty

(B) director is to producer

(C) coach is to crowd

(D) doctor is to surgery

(E) monitor is to screen

43. murder is to genocide as to gun is to

(A) police

(B) soldier

(C) tank

(D) destroy

(E) license

44. Improve is to ameliorate as

(A) promise is to pact

(B) oyster is to crab

(C) casual is to official

(D) farce is to humor

(E) canoe is to boat

45. Platform is to passenger as classroom is to

(A) teacher

(B) flag

(C) blackboard

(D) student

(E) chair

46. money is to employee as

(A) shower is to bath

(B) Christian is to church

(C) country is to president

(D) Pesticide is to insect

(E) dancer is to tip

47. Notice is to warning as suspension is to

(A) student

(B) education

(C) grounded

(D) expel

(E) study

48. Heart is to body as

(A) wheel is to car

(B) clothes is to wardrobe

(C) dishes is to table

(D) fish is to tank

(E) sun is to solar system

49. Students is to school as refugee is to

(A) cave

(B) hotel

(C) mansion

(D) asylum

(E) jail

50. Sizzling is to steak as

(A) squeaking is to door

(B) flicking is to finger

(C) stomping is to fist

(D) gulping is to water

(E) shooting is to gun

51. Skunk is to camouflage as butterfly is to

(A) strip

(B) zebra

(C) defense

(D) odor

(E) scent

CONTINUE

52. Transition is to alteration as

(A) marathon is to sprint

(B) poem is to anecdote

(C) story is to song

(D) start is to initiation

(E) ocean is to sky

53. Agile is to brisk as monitor is to

(A) electricity

(B) color

(C) check

(D) computer

(E) TV

54. Insignificant is to crucial as

(A) food is to hunger

(B) money is to estate

(C) planet is to earth

(D) loose is to tight

(E) pianist is to recital

55. Europa is to Earth as Jupiter is to

(A) star

(B) solar

(C) Sun

(D) Moon

(E) land

56. Cheese is to mould as

(A) investigator is to conceal

(B) police is to chase

(C) firefighter is to fire

(D) milk is to spoil

(E) copier is to print

57. Storybook is to picture as sausage is to

(A) ketchup

(B) long

(C) refrigerator

(D) food

(E) meat

58. psychologist is to Biologist as mind

(A) life

(B) science

(C) study

(D) school

(E) doctors

59. Stem is to accelerate as

(A) cell is to organism

(B) tree is to flower

(C) letter is to word

(D) journal is to novel

(E) curb is to develop

60. Decibel is to sound as magnitude as

(A) strength

(B) earthquake

(C) Mach

(D) kilo

(E) volcano

STOP

If you finish before time is called,
you may check your work on this section.

Do not turn to the next section.

Test 6

ABSOLUTE PATTERNS

TEST 6
READING SECTION

Please refer to the Reading Section Absolute Pattern Analysis next page

THE SYNONYM QUESTIONS
TEST 6 NO.1 ~ 60

THE ANALOGY QUESTIONS
TEST 6 NO. 31 ~ 60

Please refer to the Analogy Section Absolute Pattern Analysis in page 341

1	D	16	A
2	C	17	A
3	A	18	E
4	E	19	A
5	B	20	B
6	A	21	B
7	B	22	E
8	B	23	C
9	A	24	C
10	A	25	C
11	B	26	B
12	A	27	B
13	E	28	A
14	E	29	A
15	C	30	A

Test 6

ABSOLUTE PATTERNS for the Reading Section

Q1. Pattern 2: Main Idea Question

Question Pattern: The primary function of the first paragraph is to

Step 1	Step 2	Step 3
Keywords from the Passage	Keywords from Answer	Tone & Concept
In a splendid chamber, man	B) a setting	Logical Conclusion

Incorrect Choices & Common Patterns		
Evidence	Incorrect keywords	Tone & Concept
In a novel, the opening paragraph normally describes the setting of a place and the main character.	A) man's concerns	The primary function of the first paragraph is to describe the setting of a place. The others are Not Supported by the passage
	C) Palais Royal, palais Cardinal	
	D) charismatic appeal	
	E) Palais Cardinal changed	

Q2. Type 2: Inference Question [Pattern 1: Local Question] {Category A}

Question Pattern: It can be inferred from the passage that

Step 1	Step 2	Step 3
Keywords from the Passage	Keywords from Answer	Tone & Concept
It was, alas! the ghost of former greatness.	E) is not currently occupied	Logical Conclusion

Incorrect Choices & Common Patterns		
Evidence	Incorrect keywords	Tone & Concept
It was, alas! the ghost of former greatness. we can infer that the Palais Royal is not currently occupied by Cardinal Richelieu	A) Palais Royal defense	Not Supported by the passage
	B) Palais Royal, haunted	
	C) Cardinal, condescending	
	D) Palais Roayl, part of Palais	

Q3. Pattern 7: Understanding Attitude / Tone

Question Pattern: The tone of the passage is

Step 1	Step 2	Step 3
Keywords from the Passage	Keywords from Answer	Tone & Concept
gazed on that pale brow, anxious, haunt. ghost	C) ominous	Logical Conclusion

Incorrect Choices & Common Patterns		
Evidence	Incorrect keywords	Tone & Concept
who gazed on that pale brow, bent in anxious meditation, might, in the solitude of ... shade of Cardinal Richelieu lingered still in his accustomed haunt. It was, alas! the ghost of former greatness.	A) didactic	If you combine all these underlined portions of the sentences...
	B) pensive	
	D) baffle	
	E) sardonic	

Q4. Pattern 3: Summary Question

Question Pattern: The passage portrays   **Question Keywords:** the Cardinal Richelieu as

Step 1	Step 2	Step 3
Keywords from the Passage	Keywords from Answer	Tone & Concept
France enfeebled, the authority ,contemned,	B) defeated authority	Logical Conclusion

Incorrect Choices & Common Patterns		
Evidence	Incorrect keywords	Tone & Concept
France enfeebled, the authority of her sovereign contemned,	A) knowledgeable	Not Supported by the passage
	C) adventurous explorer	
	D) revered clergyman	
	E) ignorant ruler	

Q5. Pattern 4: Relationship Question

Question Keywords: The relationships between the second and the third paragraph

Step 1	Step 2	Step 3
Keywords from the Passage	Keywords from Answer	Tone & Concept
any one fancied, ghost	E) misconception, revelation	Logical Conclusion

Incorrect Choices & Common Patterns		
Evidence	Incorrect keywords	Tone & Concept
Any one, ...fancied that the shade of Cardinal Richelieu lingered still in his accustomed haunt. (<u>paragraph 2: the sense of misconception</u>) It was, alas! the ghost of former greatness. (<u>paragraph 3: revelation</u>)	A) physical characteristic	Not Supported by the passage
	B) time and place	
	C) future	
	D) myth	

Q6. Pattern 7: Understanding Attitude / Tone

Question Keywords: "Any one" in line 7 is portrayed as being

Step 1	Step 2	Step 3
Keywords from the Passage	Keywords from Answer	Tone & Concept
Anyone who happened might... have fancied	E) fantasized	Synonym

Incorrect Choices & Common Patterns		
Evidence	Incorrect keywords	Tone & Concept
Anyone who happened might... have fancied that the shade of Cardinal Richelieu lingered still in his accustomed haunt.	A) overly sentimental	Not Supported by the passage
	B) deeply complex	
	C) regretful	
	D) simplistic	

Q7. Pattern 3: Summary Question

Question Pattern: Which of the following statements about   **Question Keywords:** Rembrandt is true?

Step 1	Step 2	Step 3
Keywords from the Passage	Keywords from Answer	Tone & Concept
small measure, information, Rembrandt	E) we scarcely had any information	Logical Conclusion

Incorrect Choices & Common Patterns		
Evidence	Incorrect keywords	Tone & Concept
until comparatively recent years for some small measure of reliable information concerning Rembrandt the man.	A) people, concerned, artists'	A), C), D) are Opposite B) is not stated
	B) His artistic genius	
	C) honoured by the courts	
	D) He enjoyed fame	

Q8. Pattern 3: Summary Question

Question Pattern: The author characterizes

Question Keywords: our knowledge about the personal life of Rembrandt as

Step 1	Step 2	Step 3
Keywords from the Passage	Keywords from Answer	Tone & Concept
small measure, information, Rembrandt	A) limited	Logical Conclusion

Incorrect Choices & Common Patterns		
Evidence	Incorrect keywords	Tone & Concept
Topic sentence: While the world pays respectful tribute to Rembrandt the artist, it has been compelled to wait until comparatively recent years for some small measure of reliable information concerning Rembrandt the man.	B) abundant	The author characterizes our knowledge about the personal life of Rambrandt as limited.
	C) divisive	
	D) objective	
	E) more false than true	

Q9. Type 1: Example Question [Pattern 1: Local Question] {Category A}

Question Pattern: The word, is to describe		**Question Keywords:** "gossip" in line 6
Step 1	Step 2	Step 3
Keywords from the Passage	Keywords from Answer	Tone & Concept
it was nobody's business, his life. gossip	A) the way people treated	Logical Conclusion
Incorrect Choices & Common Patterns		
Evidence	Incorrect keywords	Tone & Concept
if he chanced to be an artist, <u>it was nobody's business to set down the details of his life.</u> Sometimes a diarist chanced to pass by and to jot down a little gossip	B) being bullied	They are all Too extreme word usage in one way or another.
	C) the respect	
	D) mediocre artist	
	E) a strongly, opinion	

Q10. Type 1: Example Question [Pattern 1: Local Question] {Category A}

Question Pattern: The author uses to illustrate how

Question Keywords: Shakespeare's quote in the last paragraph

Step 1	Step 2	Step 3
Keywords from the Passage	Keywords from Answer	Tone & Concept
<u>His first biographers, have no memory</u>	B) little Rembrandt, remembered	Logical Conclusion
Incorrect Choices & Common Patterns		
Evidence	Incorrect keywords	Tone & Concept
this was very much the case with Rembrandt van Ryn. <u>His first biographers seem to have no memory save for his undoubted recklessness, his extravagance, and his debts. living.</u>	A) Rembrandt, remembered	The author uses Shakespeare's quote in the last paragraph to illustrate how little Rembrandt is remembered today.
	C) falsely Rembrandt	
	D) Rembrandt's attitude	
	E) great artist Rembrandt	

UNAUTHORIZED COPYING OR REUSE OF ANY PART OF THIS PAGE IS ILLEGAL

Q11. Pattern 7: Understanding Attitude / Tone

Question Keywords: The author assumes Rembrandt's persona as

Step 1	Step 2	Step 3
Keywords from the Passage	Keywords from Answer	Tone & Concept
a light-hearted,	A) carefree	Synonym

Incorrect Choices & Common Patterns		
Evidence	Incorrect keywords	Tone & Concept
Rembrandt ... a light-hearted, headstrong, extravagant man, with no capacity for business.	B) strict expenditures	The underlined portions clarifies that he was a carefree person.
	C) adventurous	
	D) strict and disciplined	
	E) wise	

Q12. Type 2: Inference Question [Pattern 1: Local Question] {Category A}

Question Pattern: The author of the passage would be most interested in learning which of the following?

Step 1	Step 2	Step 3
Keywords from the Passage	Keywords from Answer	Tone & Concept
Rembrandt the man.	E) food Rembrandt enjoyed	Logical Conclusion

Incorrect Choices & Common Patterns		
Evidence	Incorrect keywords	Tone & Concept
for some small measure of reliable information concerning Rembrandt the man.	A) The masterpiece	Opposite
	B) the era	Too broad concept
* "Rembrandt the man" means the personal life of Rembrandt	C) wisdom of Dutchmen	Unrelated word usage
	D) The life of Shakespeare	Unrelated items

Q13. Pattern 6: Understanding Structure of the Passage

Question Pattern: The parenthesis is mainly used to
Question Keywords: in line 13 (the building…peristyle only)

Step 1	Step 2	Step 3
Keywords from the Passage	Keywords from Answer	Tone & Concept
(building contained within the peristyle **only**)	B) set limit	Logical Conclusion
Incorrect Choices & Common Patterns		
Evidence	Incorrect keywords	Tone & Concept
(building contained within the peristyle only)	A) emphasize, previous	Not Supported by the passage
	C) demonstrate, example	
	D) significance	
	E) demystify	

Q14. Pattern 2: Main Idea Question

Question Pattern: The primary purpose of the passage is to

Step 1	Step 2	Step 3
Keywords from the Passage	Keywords from Answer	Tone & Concept
the temple presents, however, several questions	D) current limitation	Logical Conclusion, Mental
Incorrect Choices & Common Patterns		
Evidence	Incorrect keywords	Tone & Concept
The history of the temple presents, however, several questions, some of which seem still undecided.	A) concern, excavation	Physical concept
	B) regret	Not Supported by the passage
	C) analyze	
	E) future excavation	

The passage is about the questions unresolved after the excavation, a mental concept. (A) is the concern about the actual physical site.

Q15. Pattern 7: Understanding Attitude / Tone

Question Pattern: The author views **Question Keywords:** "all questions" mentioned in line 6 with

Step 1	Step 2	Step 3
Keywords from the Passage	Keywords from Answer	Tone & Concept
presents, however, several questions,	D) skepticism	Synonym

Incorrect Choices & Common Patterns		
Evidence	Incorrect keywords	Tone & Concept
The history of the temple presents, however, several questions, some of which seem still undecided.	A) appreciation	The author is skeptical about the revelation. B) ambivalence means puzzled. The author is clear about what is good and bad.
	B) ambivalence	
	C) curiosity	
	E) disdain	

Q16. Pattern 7: Understanding Attitude / Tone

Question Pattern: The tone of the phrase
Question Keywords: "only the first question" mentioned in line 11 is

Step 1	Step 2	Step 3
Keywords from the Passage	Keywords from Answer	Tone & Concept
Only the first question, received one	B) emphatic	emphatic = absolute

Incorrect Choices & Common Patterns		
Evidence	Incorrect keywords	Tone & Concept
Only the first question has received one and the same answer from all.	A) insincere	The author emphasizes only one. The tone is empathic or absolute
	C) pensive	
	D) evasive	
	E) endearing	

Q17. Type 3: Analogy Question [Pattern 1: Local Question] {Category A}

Question Pattern: Which of the following situation is most analogous to
Question Keywords: "Many questions...raised. (lines 3-4)

Step 1	Step 2	Step 3
Keywords from the Passage	Keywords from Answer	Tone & Concept
Many questions many more compelling	E) grammar errors, plagiarized	Logical Conclusion

Incorrect Choices & Common Patterns		
Evidence	Incorrect keywords	Tone & Concept
E) A school teacher who corrected some minor grammar errors from a student's essay later found it was plagiarized from the Internet	A), B), D) have no same logic	The logic employed here is a small to big increment with a negative tone.
	C) has the same logic but positive tone.	

Q18. Pattern 7: Understanding Attitude / Tone

Question Pattern: The author's attitude toward, can best be described as
Question Keywords: Dörpfeld

Step 1	Step 2	Step 3
Keywords from the Passage	Keywords from Answer	Tone & Concept
however, several questions, still undecided.	E) measured acceptance	Logical Conclusion

Incorrect Choices & Common Patterns		
Evidence	Incorrect keywords	Tone & Concept
Dörpfeld's results must be accepted as final and certain. (ACCEPTANCE) The history of the temple presents, however, several questions, some of which seem still undecided. (MEASURED)	A) genuinely puzzled	Not Supported by the passage
	B) hostile	
	C) solemnly respectful	
	D) generally indifferent	

Q19. Type 2: Inference Question [Pattern 1: Local Question] {Category A}

Question Pattern: It can be inferred from the passage
Question Keywords: that Elijah is

Step 1	Step 2	Step 3
Keywords from the Passage	Keywords from Answer	Tone & Concept
"It would never do to have a woman overseer	B) a male worker	Logical Conclusion
Incorrect Choices & Common Patterns		
Evidence	Incorrect keywords	Tone & Concept
The father's reply "It would never do to have a woman overseer in the mill." shows that Elijah is male.	A) an unskillful person	Not Supported by the passage
	C) reluctant	
	D) natural sense	
	E) exhausted	

Q20. Type 2: Inference Question [Pattern 1: Local Question] {Category A}

Question Pattern: implies that
Question Keywords: Daniel Anthony's reply in lines 3-4, " it would.....mill"

Step 1	Step 2	Step 3
Keywords from the Passage	Keywords from Answer	Tone & Concept
"It would never do," woman overseer	A) woman are not allowed	Logical Conclusion
Incorrect Choices & Common Patterns		
Evidence	Incorrect keywords	Tone & Concept
"It would never do," "It would never do to have a woman overseer in the mill."	B) appreciate her work	Not Supported by the passage
	C) personal preference	
	D) he likes Elijah	
	E) he is keenly aware	

Q21. Pattern 3: Summary Question

Question Pattern: The passage is viewed from   **Question Keywords:** Susan as

Step 1	Step 2	Step 3
Keywords from the Passage	Keywords from Answer	Tone & Concept
reasoned eleven-year-old Susan	C) a girl troubled by the situation	Logical Conclusion

Incorrect Choices & Common Patterns		
Evidence	Incorrect keywords	Tone & Concept
If Sally Ann knows more about weaving than Elijah," reasoned eleven-year-old Susan	A) condescendingly	The entire passage is written from the view of young Susan Anthony.
	B) experiencing a harsh millwork	
	D) an adult	
	E) a detached	"detached" means indifferent

Q22. Pattern 3: Summary Question

Question Pattern: In the final paragraph, the author points out
Question Keywords: the identity of women as

Step 1	Step 2	Step 3
Keywords from the Passage	Keywords from Answer	Tone & Concept
Women, was not endowed citizenship.	D) family, without identity	Synonym

Incorrect Choices & Common Patterns		
Evidence	Incorrect keywords	Tone & Concept
women's rights as citizens were ignored, in spite of the contribution they had made to the defense and development of the new nation. Women during this era was not endowed citizenship.	A) a property like cattle	Not Supported by the passage
	B) superiority to male	
	C) citizens	
	E) contributed most	

Q23. Pattern 2: Main Idea Question

Question Pattern: The primary purpose of the passage is to introduce

Step 1	Step 2	Step 3
Keywords from the Passage	Keywords from Answer	Tone & Concept
reasoned eleven-year-old Susan	A) an early stage of life	Logical Conclusion
Incorrect Choices & Common Patterns		
Evidence	Incorrect keywords	Tone & Concept
This passage describes a young Susan Anthony's early experience at the mill where she observed woman's limited role regardless of talent.	B) people	Not Supported by the passage
	C) friendship	
	D) patriarch	
	E) historical overview	

Q24. Pattern 3: Summary Question

Question Pattern: Which of the following aspects is addressed in the passage?
Question Keywords: in the early 19th century

Step 1	Step 2	Step 3
Keywords from the Passage	Keywords from Answer	Tone & Concept
Although women freeholders had voted	A) Some female, vote	Synonym
Incorrect Choices & Common Patterns		
Evidence	Incorrect keywords	Tone & Concept
Lines10-11: Although women freeholders had voted in some of the colonies as late as 1807,	B) The citizenship, women	Not Supported by the passage
	C) Some wealthier women	
	D) insecurity about their jobs	
	E) Susan's later feminism	

Q25. Pattern 3: Summary Question

Question Pattern: The author describes
Question Keywords: the life of Frederick Douglass as

Step 1	Step 2	Step 3
Keywords from the Passage	Keywords from Answer	Tone & Concept
a noble vindication of the highest aims	C) accomplished impossibility	Logical Conclusion

Incorrect Choices & Common Patterns		
Evidence	Incorrect keywords	Tone & Concept
"The life of Frederick Douglass, is <u>not merely an example of self-elevation under the most adverse circumstances…</u>"a noble vindication of the highest aims	A) people do not appreciate	Negative
	B) self-elevation is everything	Insufficient information
	D) pragmatic knowledge	Not Supported by the passage
	E) feminism activity	

E) cannot be the answer because, although known fact, it is not stated in the passage.

Q26. Type 2: Inference Question [Pattern 1: Local Question] {Category A}

Question Pattern: Which of the following examples belongs to
Question Keywords: "a noble vindication" mentioned in line 2?

Step 1	Step 2	Step 3
Keywords from the Passage	Keywords from Answer	Tone & Concept
a noble vindication	B) Appeal to the psychology	the mental concept

Incorrect Choices & Common Patterns		
Evidence	Incorrect keywords	Tone & Concept
it is, moreover, a noble vindication of the highest aims of the American anti-slavery movement. *"Noble" means showing fine personal and high moral principles and ideals.	A) Escalating tension	the physical concept
	C) Take, by power	
	D) Train the Negro soldiers	
	E) domestic fight	

Q27. Pattern 2: Main Idea Question

Question Pattern: The passage as a whole primarily serves as

Step 1	Step 2	Step 3
Keywords from the Passage	Keywords from Answer	Tone & Concept
The life of Frederick Douglass	D) revered figure	Logical Conclusion

Incorrect Choices & Common Patterns		
Evidence	Incorrect keywords	Tone & Concept
The life of Frederick Douglass, recorded in the pages which follow, is not merely an example	A) discussion of activities	Too broad
	B) atypical biography	Negative
	C) a survey	Not Supported by the passage
	E) an overview	

Q28. Pattern 3: Summary Question

Question Pattern: Which of the following aspects concerning is NOT addressed in the passage?
Question Keywords: Fredrick Douglas

Step 1	Step 2	Step 3
Keywords from the Passage	Keywords from Answer	Tone & Concept
The real object, is not only to disenthrall,	A) goal, emancipate	Logical Conclusion

Incorrect Choices & Common Patterns		
Evidence	Incorrect keywords	Tone & Concept
The real object of that movement is not only to disenthrall, as well as on the part of those who would disenthrall them

(D) the underlined portion may include the white slave holders. | B) take all the rights | E) is true statement based on the last sentence "absolutely superior to his apparent fate. to their relative ability." |
	C) participate in politics	
	D) influence on white	
	E) superior ability	

Q29. Pattern 3: Summary Question

Question Keywords: "all those rights" in line 5 includes and represents

Step 1	Step 2	Step 3
Keywords from the Passage	Keywords from Answer	Tone & Concept
entire admission of the same to the full privileges,	D) full rights the Negro	Logical Conclusion

Incorrect Choices & Common Patterns		
Evidence	Incorrect keywords	Tone & Concept
But this full recognition of the colored man to the right, and the entire admission of the same to the full privileges, political, religious and social, of manhood, requires powerful effort on the part of the enthralled	A) the right to vote B) women C) rights of all countries E) disenthrall	A), E) are too limited; therefore, insufficient. B), C) are not mentioned

Q30. Type 2: Inference Question [Pattern 1: Local Question] {Category A}

Question Pattern: most nearly refers to   **Question Keywords:** In line 8, "those"

Step 1	Step 2	Step 3
Keywords from the Passage	Keywords from Answer	Tone & Concept
the part of those who would disenthrall them.	E) anti-slavery activists	Logical Conclusion

Incorrect Choices & Common Patterns		
Evidence	Incorrect keywords	Tone & Concept
requires powerful effort on the part of the enthralled, as well as on the part of those who would disenthrall them.	A) the entire humanity B) the aboriginal C) the entire black people D) all black community	Not Supported by the passage

Q31. Type 2: Inference Question [Pattern 1: Local Question] {Category A}

Question Pattern: It can be inferred from the first paragraph that
Question Keywords: the West

Step 1	Step 2	Step 3
Keywords from the Passage	Keywords from Answer	Tone & Concept
do not offer the same social advantages as, East.	B) less privileged	Logical Conclusion
Incorrect Choices & Common Patterns		
Evidence	Incorrect keywords	Tone & Concept
It is perhaps true of many of the growing cities of the <u>West, that they do not offer the same social advantages as the older cities of the East.</u>	A) more inhabitants	Not Supported by the passage
	C) fewer boom cities	
	D) improved faster	
	E) fewer legal enterprises	

Q32. Pattern 3: Summary Question

Question Pattern: the author describes   **Question Keywords:** In line 4, the "floating class" as the people

Step 1	Step 2	Step 3
Keywords from the Passage	Keywords from Answer	Tone & Concept
<u>boom cities, larger population, floating class</u>	B) majority of the city	Logical Conclusion
Incorrect Choices & Common Patterns		
Evidence	Incorrect keywords	Tone & Concept
But this is principally the case as to what may be called <u>boom cities, where the larger part of the population is of that floating class</u>	A) similar business foundation	Not Supported by the passage
	C) business foundation	
	D) traveled often	
	E) the potential predators	

Q33. Pattern 3: Summary Question

Question Pattern: The passage categorizes, EXCEPT
Question Keywords: the major occupations of the West businessmen

Step 1	Step 2	Step 3
Keywords from the Passage	Keywords from Answer	Tone & Concept
not the boomer and speculator, find their profits	E) gold seeker	Logical Conclusion
Incorrect Choices & Common Patterns		
Evidence	Incorrect keywords	Tone & Concept
collection and distribution of this great wealth of <u>natural resources, and it has attracted, not the boomer and speculator, who find their profits in the wild excitement of the boom, but the merchant, manufacturer, and investor,</u>	A) investor B) manufacturer C) merchant D) timber processor	These people are mentioned as the foundation of business

Q34. Pattern 3: Summary Question

Question Pattern: suggests that the narrator
Question Keywords: In line 6, "legitimate business" values most?

Step 1	Step 2	Step 3
Keywords from the Passage	Keywords from Answer	Tone & Concept
<u>prosperity is based on the solid foundation</u>	D) extended history	Logical Conclusion
Incorrect Choices & Common Patterns		
Evidence	Incorrect keywords	Tone & Concept
and in no sense applies to those centers of trade <u>whose prosperity is based on the solid foundation of legitimate business.</u>	A) size of wealth B) vision of the business C) faithful minds E) unique type	"solid foundation of legitimate business" shouldn't be A) "size" or B) "vision" C) and E) are too broad.

UNAUTHORIZED COPYING OR REUSE OF ANY PART OF THIS PAGE IS ILLEGAL

Q35. Pattern 7: Understanding Attitude / Tone

Question Pattern: The author's attitude toward

Question Keywords: "These have come from the East" in line 13 is to

Step 1	Step 2	Step 3
Keywords from the Passage	Keywords from Answer	Tone & Concept
the love of polite life, here a new society	C) praise, relocation	Logical Conclusion

Incorrect Choices & Common Patterns		
Evidence	Incorrect keywords	Tone & Concept
They came as seeking a better and wider field to engage in the same occupations they had followed in their Eastern homes, and bringing with them all the love of polite life which they had acquired there, have established here a new society	A) disdain B) superior ability D) subtly scorn E) question	A), D), E) are all Negative B) is not stated. The passage is positive about their relocation.

Q36. Pattern 3: Summary Question

Question Pattern: According to the author,   **Question Keywords:** clay as a concrete material is

Step 1	Step 2	Step 3
Keywords from the Passage	Keywords from Answer	Tone & Concept
clay is also not the unmixed evil	B) an alternative	Logical Conclusion

Incorrect Choices & Common Patterns		
Evidence	Incorrect keywords	Tone & Concept
clay is also not the unmixed evil it has been supposed to be	A) a debatable C) the superior D) an impractical E) a frivolous	All of them are negative. "not the unmixed evil" is positive.

Q37. Pattern 5: Word-In-Context Question

Question Pattern: The term, mainly suggests   **Question Keywords:** "unmixed evil" in line 9

Step 1	Step 2	Step 3
Keywords from the Passage	Keywords from Answer	Tone & Concept
clay is also not the unmixed evil	A) mild acceptance	Positive

Incorrect Choices & Common Patterns		
Evidence	Incorrect keywords	Tone & Concept
clay is also not the unmixed evil it has been supposed to be.	B) concern	B),C) and D) are all Negative. "not the unmixed evil" is positive.
	C) disadvantages	
	D) inaccuracy	
	E) spiritual	

Q38. Pattern 3: Summary Question

Question Keywords: Which of the followings make the ideal concrete?

Step 1	Step 2	Step 3
Keywords from the Passage	Keywords from Answer	Tone & Concept
rounded grains makes quite as strong a mortar	B) 1/3 of cheap	Logical Conclusion

Incorrect Choices & Common Patterns		
Evidence	Incorrect keywords	Tone & Concept
<u>Neither sharpness nor excessive cleanliness is worth seeking after if it involves much expense. Tests show conclusively that sand with rounded grains makes quite as strong a mortar.</u>	A) best quality	D), E) loam and clay in sand to the amount of 10 to 15 percent result, not 1/3 or 1/2, which make 33% ~50 %
	C) thoroughly washed	
	D) 1/3 of clay	
	E) 1/2 of loam	

Q39. Pattern 3: Summary Question

Question Pattern: The passage states that they should consider which of the following first?
Question Keywords: when builders buy sand

Step 1	Step 2	Step 3
Keywords from the Passage	Keywords from Answer	Tone & Concept
poor roads	C) the road condition	Synonym
Incorrect Choices & Common Patterns		
Evidence	Incorrect keywords	Tone & Concept
A long haul over poor roads can easily make the sand cost more	A) the quality of sand	They can consider these after the road condition.
	B) the quality of concrete	
	D) the quality of stone	
	E) other than sand	

Q40. Pattern 3: Summary Question

Question Pattern: Which of the followings would be
Question Keywords: the first consideration for the concrete builders?

Step 1	Step 2	Step 3
Keywords from the Passage	Keywords from Answer	Tone & Concept
expense.	B) cost of sand	Synonym
Incorrect Choices & Common Patterns		
Evidence	Incorrect keywords	Tone & Concept
Neither sharpness nor excessive cleanliness is worth seeking after if it involves much expense.	A) sharpness of sand	
	C) silicious	
	D) admixture of sand	
	E) cleanness of sand	

Test 6 ABSOLUTE PATTERNS for the Analogy Section

Q31. Absolute Pattern 8: Shape Pattern

B is the best answer

Circle, octagon, rectangle, and pentagon are all shape.

Q32. Absolute Pattern 7: Association (Characteristic) Pattern

B is the best answer

Table and chair always go together as a pair, so do fork and knife as a silverware.

Choice A is a human category. The other choices do not work as a pair.

Q33. Absolute Pattern 4: Synonym Pattern

A is the best answer.

Verbal and oral are synonym, and cartography and map are synonyms.

Q34. Absolute Pattern 6:Purpose (Job/Tool) Pattern

E is the best answer.

The purpose of vantage point on mountains is to look out, the purpose of a lamp in a lighthouse is to look out.

Q35. Absolute Pattern 5: Degree Pattern

B is the best answer

Both shadow and glim are mild degrees, and both chilly and warm are mild degree.

The remaining words choices are all extreme.

Q36. Absolute Pattern 5: Degree Pattern

A is the best answer (small to big)

Antipathy (dislike) goes to aversion (hate a lot), and sympathy (like) goes to love (like a lot).

Q37. Absolute Pattern 7: Association (Characteristic) Pattern + 15: Syntax Pattern

B is the best answer

Piggybank is filled with coins, just as a garden is filled with flowers.

Choice A is flipped over.

Choice D "passenger" is a singular, while coins and flowers are plural.

Q38. Absolute Pattern 13: Mental-Physical Pattern

C is the best answer

Wedding dress creates a feeling of (bliss, so does memento to nostalgia.

The same mental patterns

Q39. Absolute Pattern 6:Purpose (Job/Tool) Pattern

B is the best answer.

The purpose of hard work is for success, so is company for profit.

Q40. Absolute Pattern 7: Association (Characteristic) Pattern

C is the best answer.

Hostage needs to pay ransom to be free; audience needs to a buy ticket to get in the show.

Q41. Absolute Pattern 7: Association (Characteristic) Pattern

C is the best answer

The scent from flowers and the pungent smell from a spoiled milk are associated with smell.

Q42. Absolute Pattern 7: Association (Characteristic) Pattern

C is the best answer

A dancer performs in front of the audience, so does coach in front of the crowd.

The audience and the crowd are the same category.

Q43. Absolute Pattern 5: Degree Pattern

C is the best answer

Murder to genocide, a massive race killing, involves a greater degree of killing.

Gun to tank involves a greater degree of fatality.

Q44. Absolute Pattern 4: Synonym Pattern

D is the best answer

Improve and ameliorate are a synonym; farce and humor are a synonym.

(A) is official and unofficial pattern.

(B) is the same sea animal category.

(E) is a part-whole pattern.

Q45. Absolute Pattern 7: Association (Characteristic) Pattern

D is the best answer

A platform is where passengers are waiting for a train; A classroom is where students are waiting for a class.

Choice A is wrong because both passenger and student are the same category—receiving a service, while a teacher and a locomotive operator are the same category—offering a service.

Q46. Absolute Pattern 7: Association (Characteristic) Pattern

E is the best answer.

Dancer takes tips; employee takes money.

Q47. Absolute Pattern 5: Degree Pattern

D is the best answer.

The warning is a stronger degree than Notice. Expel is a stronger degree than suspension.

Q48. Absolute Pattern 8: Shape Pattern

E is the best answer

The heart is at the center of our body, as the sun is at the center of solar system.

Q49. Absolute Pattern 6:Purpose (Job/Tool) Pattern

D is the best answer

School teaches students, and asylum protects refugees.
Refugees do not use A) cave, B) hotel, C) mansion, or E) jail.

Q50. Absolute Pattern 11: Homophony Pattern

A is the best answer

Steak makes sizzling sound so does door to squeaking.

Q51. Absolute Pattern 6:Purpose (Job/Tool) Pattern

D is the best answer.

Skunk uses odor to protects itself, and butterfly uses camouflage.

Q52. Absolute Pattern 4: Synonym Pattern

D is the best answer

Transition and alteration are a synonym; start and initiation are a synonym.

Q53. Absolute Pattern 4: Synonym Pattern

C is the best answer.

Agile and brisk are a synonym; monitor and check are a synonym.

Q54. Absolute Pattern 5: Degree Pattern

D is the best answer.   (Weak to strong)

Insignificant (weak) is to crucial (strong); loose (weak) is to tight (strong)

Choice A is not the same category

Q55. Absolute Pattern 7: Association (Characteristic) Pattern

D is the best answer.

Europa is the moon of Jupiter. (moon or satellite)

Q56. Absolute Pattern 1: Production (Cause-Effect) Pattern

D is the best answer

Mould is produced when cheese gets rotten; spoiled milk is produced when a milk gets bad.

Q57. Absolute Pattern 2: Part-Whole Pattern

E is the best answer

Pictures are a part of the storybook as meat is a part of sausage.

Q58. Absolute Pattern 6:Purpose (Job/Tool) Pattern

A is the best answer

The job of psychologists is to study people's mind; the job of biologists is to study life (living organs).

Q59. Absolute Pattern 4: Synonym Pattern

E is the best answer

Stem and curb; accelerate and develop are synonyms.

Q60. Absolute Pattern 7: Association (Characteristic) Pattern

A is the best answer.

Decibel is the measurement of sound, just as magnitude to strength

UNAUTHORIZED COPYING OR REUSE OF ANY PART OF THIS PAGE IS ILLEGAL

Test 6 Recap

SSAT Questions Rely Heavily on the Contradictory Conjunction

Transitional word or phrase, especially contradictory subordinating conjunction or conjunctive adverbial phrase become a flashpoint.

Consciously finding and focusing on them as you read the passage will give you vast opportunity to locate the answer promptly and accurately.

But	However	Yet	Still	Although
Despite	Even though	In contrast	In spite of	Instead of
Nevertheless	On the contrary	On the other hand	Rather than	Granted

Inference Questions

The inference questions mainly starts with the phrase such as
  - The author implies that
  - The narrator feels that
  - According to the passage, the narrator is likely that

The nature of the inference question is to draw the conclusion based on reasoning analysis.

One key factor in solving the inference question is to cancel out the options that are written in the passage.

Inference question must be distinguished from the local type descriptive question (e.g. "The author mainly describes in line 10...")

Since the question asks us to seek out what is being suggested, instead of what is written on the passage, it is crucial to eliminate any options that literally resemble the phrase or sentence from the passage.

SSAT
Reading & Verbal Practice
Test 7

ALL THE LOGIC AND RULES

BEHIND THE EVERY SINGLE

SSAT QUESTION

UNAUTHORIZED COPYING OR REUSE OF ANY PART OF THIS PAGE IS ILLEGAL

Test 7 Reading Section
Time: 40 Minutes, 40 Questions

Directions: Each reading passage is followed by questions about it. Answer the questions that follow a passage on the basis of what is stated or implied in that passage.

Questions 1-6 are based on the following passage.

Line

The Habsburg Empire is built upon centuries-old traditions of reaction and violence. Its present power is presumably based on the alliance which Bohemia and Hungary concluded with Austria against the Turkish peril in 1526. The Czechs freely elected the Habsburgs to the throne of Bohemia which remained a fully independent state. But soon the Habsburgs began to violate the liberties of Bohemia which they were bound by oath, and this

5   led finally to the fateful Czech revolution of 1618. At the battle of the White Mountain in 1620 the Czechs suffered a defeat and were cruelly punished for their rebellion. In 1627 Ferdinand II. greatly curtailed the administrative rights of Bohemia, yet he did not dare to deprive her entirely of her independence. In his "Renewed Ordinance of the Land" Ferdinand declared the Bohemian crown to be hereditary in the House of Habsburg, and reserved

10   legislative power to the sovereign, remained valid, notwithstanding all subsequent arbitrary centralizing measures taken by the Habsburgs. state to-day.

1

The opening sentence focuses on the Habsburg Empire's

A) geographic isolation

B) ethnic diversity

C) vastness of the territory

D) struggle for survival

E) centuries-old traditions

2

In line 2-3 (Its present power…1526), the author does which of the followings?

A) speculates about the development

B) describes an actual fact with the evidence

C) cites an authority

D) discusses an important criticism

E) questions an old hypothesis

CONTINUE

3

From the Habsburg' point of view, the outcome of the Czech revolution of 1618 was

A) fortuitous

B) disappointing

C) accidental

D) foreboding

E) foreseeable

4

According to the passage, which state benefited most by the Turkish peril in 1526?

A) Habsburg

B) Bohemia

C) Hungary

D) Czech

E) Turkey itself

5

From the Bohemian's point of view, the outcome of the Czech revolution of 1618 was

A) fortuitous

B) disappointing

C) accidental

D) progressive

E) foreseeable

6

The last sentence suggests that Ferdinad II's approach to Bohemian was a part of

A) challenge

B) compromise

C) preparation for another war

D) trust

E) boast

CONTINUE

Questions 7-12 are based on the following passage.

Line   Recent years have seen a remarkable improvement in the conditions of child life. In all civilized countries, but especially in England, statistics show only a mild decrease in infant mortality.

    Related to other countries' decrease in mortality a corresponding improvement is to be seen 5 in the physical development of children; they are physically finer and more vigorous. It has been the diffusion, the popularization of science, which has brought about such notable advantages. Mothers have learned to welcome the dictates of modern hygiene and to put them into practice in bringing up their children. Many new social institutions have sprung up and have been perfected with the object of assisting children and protecting them during the 10 period of physical growth. In this way what is practically a new race is coming into being, a race more highly developed, finer and more robust; a race which will be capable of offering resistance to insidious disease. What has science done to effect this? Science has suggested for us certain very simple rules by which the child has been restored as nearly as possible to conditions of a natural life, and an order and a guiding law have been given to the functions 15 of the body. It is science which suggested maternal feeding, the abolition of swaddling clothes, baths, life in the open air. Rules were also laid down for the measurement of food adapting it rationally to the physiological needs of the child's life.

7

The author's attitude in the first paragraph (lines 1-3) shifts from

A) regret to appreciation
B) optimism to concern
C) disappointment to restraint
D) ambivalence to outrage
E) bewilderment to courage

8

In the second paragraph, the author indicates all of the following EXCEPT

A) improvement of institutions
B) diversified opinions
C) improvement of hygiene
D) advancement of science
E) physical wellness of children

CONTINUE

9

The primary purpose of the passage is to emphasize the

A) proper way to educate working parents

B) power of science to child's development

C) importance of science in child education

D) finding a solution to decrease infant mortality

E) importance of hygiene

10

The passage indicates all the merits of science in nurturing child EXCEPT

A) complex and sophisticated rules

B) the food measurement

C) maternal feeding

D) a guiding law to the functions of the body

E) modern hygiene

11

The rhetorical question in line 12 (What has…this?) serves primarily to

A) advance alternative explanations

B) discredit the previous argument

C) evoke a hypothetical situation

D) call attention to the importance

E) question the feasibility

12

It can be inferred from the passage that the writer of the essay would be

A) an elementary school teacher

B) a nurse

C) a social scientist

D) an economist

E) a philosopher

CONTINUE ▷

Questions 13-18 are based on the following passage.

Line

Meanwhile, as he ministered, there was time to look about me. Where was I? It was not the Broadway; it was not Staten Island on a Saturday afternoon. The night was just over, and the sun on the point of rising. Yet it was still shadowy all about, the air being marvelously tepid and pleasant to the senses. Quaint, soft aromas like the breath of a new world--the fragrance of
5 unknown flowers, and the dewy scent of never-trodden fields drifted to my nostrils; and to my ears came a sound of laughter scarcely more human than the murmur of the wind in the trees, and a pretty undulating whisper as though a great concourse of people were talking softly in their sleep. I gazed about scarcely knowing how much of my senses or surroundings were real and how much fanciful, until I presently became aware the rosy twilight was broadening into day,
10 and under the increasing shine a strange scene was fashioning itself.

At first it was an opal sea I looked on of mist, shot along its upper surface with the rosy gold and pinks of dawn. Then, as that soft, translucent lake ebbed, jutting hills came through it, black and crimson, and as they seemed to mount into the air other lower hills showed through the veil with rounded forest knobs till at last the brightening day dispelled the mist, and as the rosy-colored
15 gauzy fragments went slowly floating away a wonderfully fair country lay at my feet, with a broad sea glimmering in many arms and bays in the distance beyond. It was all dim and unreal at first, the mountains shadowy, the ocean, the flowery fields between it and me vacant and shadowy. As my eyes cleared and day brightened it presently dawned upon me.

13

Line 1-2 (Meanwhile,…afternoon) indicates the narrator's

A) evocation

B) confusion

C) sadness

D) insecurity

E) complication

14

The passage indicates that the landscape was

A) nostalgic

B) vast and arid

C) remote

D) exotic

E) intimidating

CONTINUE

15

The narrator's mood conveys

A) optimism

B) entertainment

C) perseverance

D) ominous foreboding

E) wonder

16

In line 16 "It was all...at first" was mainly caused by

A) unusually familiar landscape

B) his dream he once had

C) nostalgia

D) monotony environment

E) darkness

17

The passage as a whole serves primarily to

A) show the humiliation the narrator felt

B) explore the new world

C) set the views and the inner mindsets of the narrator

D) differentiate between the real and unreal circumstances

E) weight the possibility to survive

18

The descriptions of the scene in the passage and the narrator's mood present a contrast between his

A) organized perception and chaotic place

B) confusion and graceful new world

C) pretension and ruggedness

D) volatile temperament and beautiful wilderness

E) sophistication and advanced artificiality

CONTINUE

Questions 19-24 are based on the following passage.

Line   Sara was such a little girl that one did not expect to see such a look on her small face. It would have been an old look for a child of twelve, and Sara Crewe was only seven. The fact was, however, that she was always dreaming and thinking odd things and could not herself remember any time when she had not been thinking things about grown-up people and the

5   world they belonged to. She felt as if she had lived a long, long time. At this moment she was remembering the voyage she had just made from Bombay with her father, Captain Crewe.

    She was thinking of the big ship, of the Lascars passing silently to and fro on it. She was thinking of what a queer thing it was that at one time one was in India in the blazing sun, and then in the middle of the ocean, and then driving in a strange vehicle through strange streets.

10   "Papa," she said in a low, mysterious little voice which was almost a whisper, "papa." What is it, darling?" Captain Crewe answered, holding her closer and looking down into her face. "What is Sara thinking of?""Is this the place?" Sara whispered, "Is it, papa? "Yes, little Sara, it is. We have reached it at last." And though she was only seven years old, she knew that he

15   felt sad when he said it. It seemed to her many years since he had begun to prepare her mind for "the place"

19

The description in lines 14-15 ("And though...said it.") suggests that Sara experienced a sense of

A) pressure

B) nervousness

C) self-esteem

D) joy

E) duty

20

The first paragraph primarily describes that Sara was

A) seeking to understand the world from the different perspective

B) escaping from the oppressive life

C) hoping to change a lifestyle

D) attempting to varying experiences

E) trying to find the answer to the world

CONTINUE ➤

21

The passage as a whole is viewed from the perspective of

A) seven-year-old Sara

B) one who knows the inner mindsets of Sara

C) a grown-up Sara recollecting her childhood

D) Sara in her dream

E) Sara's father

22

"The fact...long time" in lines 2-5 is most analogous to

A) a poor janitor dreaming of becoming a banker

B) a teacher rewarding one of his best students

C) a boy having a nightmare of getting caught by shoplifting

D) a girl teaching her grandpa how to write

E) a girl taking care of her sick mother

23

The narrator's description of the voyage suggests that

A) it provided some strange memories

B) it foreboded her fate

C) it brought some intense emotional transition

D) it made her proud of her father

E) it had little connection to Sara's memory

24

It can be inferred from the passage that Sara is going to

A) move into a new place

B) chase her dream in another country

C) extend her trip to India

D) travel alone

E) meet her mother

CONTINUE ▶

Questions 25-30 are based on the following passage.

Line   Several years ago, at the regular annual meeting of one of the major engineering societies, the president of the society, in the formal address with which he opened the meeting, gave expression to a thought so startling that the few laymen who were seated in the auditorium fairly gasped. What the president said in effect was that, since engineers had got the world

5   into war, it was the duty of engineers to get the world out of war. As a thought, it probably reflected the secret opinion of every engineer present, for, however innocent of intended wrong-doing engineers assuredly are as a group in their work of scientific investigation and development, the statement that engineers were responsible for the conflict then raging in Europe was absolute truth. I mention this merely to bring to the reader's attention the

10   tremendous power which engineers wield in world affairs.

    The profession of engineering--which, by the way, is merely the adapting of discoveries in science and art to the uses of mankind--is a peculiarly isolated one. But very little is known about it among those outside of the profession. Laymen know something about law, a little about medicine, quite a lot--nowadays--about metaphysics. But laymen know nothing about

15   engineering. Indeed, a source of common amusement among engineers is the peculiar fact that the average layman cannot differentiate between the man who runs a locomotive and the man who designs a locomotive. In ordinary parlance both are called engineers. Yet there is a difference between them--a difference as between day and night.
For one merely operates the results of the creative genius of the other.

25

Why does the President believe as he said in lines 4-5, ("What...war.")

A) Engineers conveyed their knowledge to war

B) War utilized engineers' knowledge without their consent

C) Engineers were insidiously supported war

D) War was ignited by engineers

E) Engineers are destructively innovative

26

Why did the few laymen in line 4 gasp?

A) They were not prepared to hear such a remark

B) They were not engineers

C) They thought engineers contributed positively to the war

D) The president justified the war

E) They didn't agree with what he said

CONTINUE ▶

27

"the tremendous power" (line 10), focuses primarily on which aspect of engineers?

A) Their practicality

B) Their perseverance

C) Their connection to politics

D) Their depth of knowledge

E) Their imagination

28

In line 16-17 ("the man...locomotive"), the author compares which of the followings as a pair?

A) engineering and non-engineering

B) familiarity and unfamiliarity

C) benefit and harm

D) practicality and impracticality

E) easy and difficult

29

The author refers "law, medicine, and metaphysics" in order to

A) understate engineering

B) compare relatively familiar subjects

C) entertain the audience with easier subjects

D) boast his knowledge in various fields

E) present the complexity of engineering

30

In the context of the passage, "For one...the other" (line 19) emphasizes

A) the need to distinguish between a locomotive operator and its designer

B) the willingness to train locomotive operators to become engineers

C) the immense power of engineering

D) the productive aspect of engineering

E) the complexity of engineering

CONTINUE

Questions 31-35 are based on the following passage.

Line

It would seem that Cicero's love for literature was inherited from his father. He too, we may conjecture, led the young Cicero to feel the Importance of a study of philosophy to serve as a corrective for the somewhat narrow rhetorical discipline of the time. Cicero's first systematic lessons in philosophy were given him by the Epicurean Phaedrus,

5 then at Rome because of the unsettled state of Athens, whose lectures he attended at a very early age, even before he had assumed the toga virilis. He is the only Epicurean, with, perhaps, the exception of Lucretius, whom the orator ever allows to possess any literary power.

Cicero soon abandoned Epicureanism, but his schoolfellow, T. Pomponius Atticus, received

10 more lasting impressions from the teaching of Phaedrus. At this time (i.e. before 88 B.C.) Cicero also heard the lectures of Diodotus the Stoic, with whom he studied chiefly, though not exclusively, the art of dialectic. This art, which Cicero deems so important to the orator that he calls it "abbreviated eloquence," was then the monopoly of the Stoic school.

31

In line 1 ("It would…his father.") the author makes use of which of the following?

A) Speculation

B) Allusion

C) Analogy

D) Confirmation

E) Euphemism

32

According to lines 2-3 (He too…of the time), Cicero learned first systemic philosophy that focuses on

A) grammar

B) system of speech

C) art of stoicism

D) poetry

E) historical citations

CONTINUE

33

Who would be most likely to learn "the art of dialectic" mentioned in line 22?

A) Merchant

B) Scientist

C) Poet

D) Farmer

E) Politician

34

In line 14, "the monopoly of the Stoic school" implies the education system was then

A) cooperative

B) diversified

C) limited

D) expansive

E) underdeveloped

35

Cicero himself would most likely agree with which of the following statement?

A) Epicureanism has its limit to demonstrate orator's skills

B) The ultimate literary power can be obtained through the art of dialectic

C) Literary skills are no less important than philosophy

D) Phaedrus earned more respect as orator than Lucretius

E) I respect both Diodotus and Phaedrus for their Epicureanism lecture

CONTINUE

Questions 36-40 are based on the following passage.

Line   Your letter of the 4th just to hand. How glad your letters make me; how glad I am to have

you to tell little things to. I intended to write you as soon as I came back from Green River, to

tell you of a girl I saw there; but there was a heap to do and I kept putting it off. I have

described the desert so often that I am afraid I will tire you, so I will leave that out and tell

5   you that we arrived in town rather late. The help at the hotel were having their supper in the

regular dining-room, as all the guests were out. They cheerfully left their own meal to place

ours on the table.

One of them interested me especially. She was a small person; I couldn't decide whether she

was a child or a woman. I kept thinking her homely, and then when she spoke I forgot every-

10   thing but the music of her voice,--it was so restful, so rich and mellow in tone, and

she seemed so small for such a splendid voice. Somehow I kept expecting her to squeak like a

mouse, but every word she spoke charmed me.

Before the meal was over it came out that she was the dish-washer. All the rest of the help had

finished their work for the day, but she, of course, had to wash what dishes we had been us-

15   ing.

The rest went their ways; and as our own tardiness had belated her, I offered to help her to

carry out the dishes. It was the work of only a moment to dry them, so I did that. She was so

small that she had to stand on a box in order to be comfortable while she washed the cups and

plates.

36

The narrator's attitude to "a girl" in the passage suggests that he is in the feeling of

A) sympathy

B) bewilderment

C) ambivalence

D) concern

E) love

37

In line 10, "the music of her voice", the narrator employs which of the following rhetorical device?

A) exaggeration

B) allusion

C) slang

D) metaphor

E) personification

CONTINUE

38

The narrator offered his help to the girl because he

A) was boredom

B) chanced to display his manhood

C) wished to show his appreciation for her music

D) was in love

E) concerned for her frailty

39

It can be inferred that this passage was taken from the part of

A) a correspondence letter

B) a magazine

C) a traveling journal

D) an autobiography

E) a love letter

40

Which of the following literary device is used for the statement "she seemed...splendid voice" (line 11)

A) paradox

B) juxtaposition

C) metaphor

D) simile

E) personification

Test 7 Verbal Section   30 MINUTES, 60 QUESTIONS

Directions: the synonym questions ask you to find the most appropriate synonym to the question.

The analogy questions ask you to find the most appropriate analogy to the question.
Select the answer that best matches to the question.

Synonym Sample Question:

Q: SUPERIOR

   A higher rank

   B inferior

   C considerable

   D supermarket

   E supper

A) is the best answer because the synonym for
   superior is higher rank.

B) is incorrect because it applies the 'opposite
   concept.

C) and E) are irrelevant words.

D) is incorrect because it applies physical concept
   to mental concept

Test 7 Synonym questions 1 to 30

1. CONGENIAL

(A) generational

(B) pleasant

(C) congratulation

(D) conventional

(E) hostile

2. CONJECTURE

(A) evidence

(B) summon

(C) expertise

(D) guess

(E) taste

3. CONSECRATE

(A) disloyal

(B) holy

(C) secretive

(D) consensus

(E) respite

4. VENERABLE

(A) respect

(B) aged

(C) dignity

(D) benevolent

(E) benign

5. PUERILE

(A) pure

(B) foolish

(C) child

(D) intelligent

(E) estimable

CONTINUE

6. LEVITY

(A) tender

(B) improper gaiety

(C) overly excited

(D) heavenly

(E) grave

7. FRUGAL

(A) husbandry

(B) wasteful

(C) fruitful

(D) attributive

(E) serious

8. AVOCATION

(A) vacation

(B) side job

(C) love to enjoy nature

(D) trip

(E) profession

9. CHARLATAN

(A) imposter

(B) unreal

(C) fake

(D) character

(E) Christian

10. ELUCIDATE

(A) dirty

(B) clear

(C) elusive

(D) hard to understand

(E) election

11. INDOLENT

(A) diligent

(B) Indonesian

(C) lazy

(D) cute

(E) indulgent

12. LUDICROUS

(A) serious

(B) ridiculous

(C) dictionary

(D) shiny

(E) ratio

13. CALLOW

(A) low in value

(B) expert

(C) shallow

(D) immature

(E) cow like

14. BLITHE

(A) literal in meaning

(B) bless

(C) two liters

(D) gloomy

(E) cheerful

15. MALIGN

(A) mad

(B) mail delivery

(C) slander

(D) praise

(E) linger

CONTINUE

16. POSTHUMOUS

(A) after death

(B) finally humorous

(C) delivery

(D) before death

(E) person's literary work

17. HEINOUS

(A) histrionic

(B) heroic

(C) hairy

(D) generous

(E) wicked

18. REFUTE

(A) futuristic

(B) repeating

(C) disapprove

(D) approve

(E) past

19. CURSORY

(A) hasty

(B) cautious

(C) curbing

(D) mouse

(E) deep apology

20. RETICENT

(A) money

(B) clothe

(C) un-talkative

(D) talkative

(E) very cheap

21. OPULENCE

(A) abundance

(B) lack

(C) opportunity

(D) flowing

(E) opposite

22. ARDUOUS

(A) door

(B) dangerous

(C) difficult

(D) duet

(E) easy

23. PALTRY

(A) serious

(B) trifling

(C) try out

(D) palpitate

(E) paypal

24. ABDUCT

(A) channel

(B) bring forth

(C) kidnap

(D) aqueduct

(E) homicide

25. TRACTABLE

(A) stubborn

(B) tractor related

(C) long road

(D) onerous

(E) easily controlled

CONTINUE

26. OBLITERATE

(A) obedience

(B) literal

(C) obligation

(D) destroy

(E) revamp

27. PRODIGIOUS

(A) enormous

(B) tiny

(C) professional

(D) amateur

(E) digital

28. HAUGHTY

(A) humble

(B) contempt

(C) height

(D) hauling

(E) mighty

29. EXACERBATE

(A) good

(B) bad

(C) worse

(D) better

(E) best

30. INCREDULOUS

(A) sincere

(B) skeptical

(C) incredible

(D) credit

(E) edible

Analogy Sample Question:

Q: River is to Ocean as:

A better is to good

B rain is to cloud

C father is to mother

D city is to country

E fork is to spoon

D is the correct answer. Just as the river is smaller than the Ocean, the city is smaller than the country. The pattern applied in this question is the Degree Pattern (small to big)

A) is incorrect because the word order is flipped over.

B) is incorrect because it applies the production pattern (cloud produces rain)

C), E) are incorrect because they apply the Antonym patterns.

Test 7 Analogy questions 31 to 60

31. Chicken is to dragon as food is to

(A) fried

(B) possibility

(C) myth

(D) fact

(E) fly

CONTINUE

32. Sky is to clouds as

(A) land is to eagle

(B) city is to busy

(C) farm is to fish

(D) factory is to medicine

(E) ocean is to wave

33. Punch is to bleeding as

(A) study is to exam

(B) fight is to win

(C) business is to success

(D) overheat is to burn

(E) rain is to cloudy

34. Mosquito is to insect as

(A) mammal is to man

(B) bean is to coffee

(C) soccer is to sport

(D) movie is to action

(E) woman is to girl

35. Fresh is to rotten as pill is to

(A) doctor

(B) poison

(C) chocolate

(D) drink

(E) water

36. King is to banquet as pianist is to

(A) ticket

(B) artist

(C) exhibition

(D) music

(E) recital

37. Heat is to vapor as

(A) diligent is to success

(B) mom is to sister

(C) fight is to argument

(D) work is to devotion

(E) library is to book

38. Counterfeit is to money as plastic is to

(A) human

(B) wood

(C) cheap

(D) truth

(E) valuable

39. Gloomy is to lugubrious as pleasant

(A) bored

(B) tired

(C) funny

(D) ecstatic

(E) joy

40. Rust is to metal as

(A) rotten is to apple

(B) old is to young

(C) bus is to bicycle

(D) clinic is to hospital

(E) employer is to employee

41. Rooster is to chicken as chimpanzee is to

(A) orangutan

(B) smart

(C) cage

(D) ape

(E) friendly

CONTINUE

42. Watch is to signal as time is to

(A) light

(B) lighthouse

(C) number

(D) predict

(E) measure

43. Hopeless is to victory as

(A) win is to draw

(B) rich is to poor

(C) police is to thief

(D) cancer is to die

(E) bird is to fish

44. Cast is to member as actor is to

(A) director

(B) staff

(C) movie

(D) family

(E) coach

45. Hammerhead is to grizzly as shark is to

(A) type

(B) natural

(C) aggressive

(D) bear

(E) tool

46. Fence is to neighbor as

(A) bank is to vault

(B) rain is to snow

(C) border is to country

(D) fire extinguisher is to the hallway

(E) buttress is to building

47. Paleontologist is to dinosaurs as psychologist is to

(A) economics

(B) law

(C) future

(D) wrong behavior

(E) mental

48. Podium is to medal as

(A) money is to work

(B) grade is to age

(C) school is to name

(D) religion is to language

(E) country is to continent

49. Anthropology is to civilization as animal is to

(A) ecology

(B) sociology

(C) zoology

(D) geology

(E) zoo

50. Fame is to movie star as

(A) poison is to cobra

(B) book is to author

(C) psychic is to fortune

(D) movie is to television

(E) history is to record

51. Chronic is to habitual as acute is to

(A) relation

(B) cost

(C) duration

(D) intensity

(E) period

CONTINUE

UNAUTHORIZED COPYING OR REUSE OF ANY PART OF THIS PAGE IS ILLEGAL

52. Day is to week as pint

(A) liter

(B) gram

(C) kilo

(D) pound

(E) cup

53. Articulate is to legible as speak is to

(A) paint

(B) hear

(C) law

(D) write

(E) draw

54. Circle is to bottle as

(A) square is to line

(B) arc is to area

(C) rectangle is to monitor

(D) cubic is to radius

(E) diameter is to pie

55 Manager is to store as editor is to

(A) film

(B) newsstand

(C) library

(D) society

(E) scholar

56. Excerpt is to story

(A) dessert is to dinner

(B) prologue is to concert

(C) autograph is to movie star

(D) journal is to student

(E) license is to driver

57. Garden flower is to grow as badge is to

(A) understand

(B) hang

(C) indicate

(D) collect

(E) sell

58. Hungry is to starvation as

(A) defect is to catastrophe

(B) diet is to hungry

(C) poison is to medicine

(D) insurance is to accident

(E) friend is to enemy

59. Area is to perimeter as

(A) animal is to species

(B) circle is to degree

(C) circle is to radius

(D) ice cream is to dessert

(E) detective story is to novel

60. Accuse is to prosecutor as

(A) cook is to mother

(B) work is to father

(C) search is to inspector

(D) teach is to student

(E) cure is to nurse

STOP

If you finish before time is called,
you may check your work on this section.

Do not turn to the next section.

Test 7

ABSOLUTE PATTERNS

TEST 7
READING SECTION

Please refer to the Reading Section Absolute Pattern Analysis next page

THE SYNONYM QUESTIONS
TEST 7 NO.1 ~ 30

1	B	16	A
2	D	17	E
3	B	18	C
4	A	19	A
5	B	20	C
6	B	21	A
7	A	22	C
8	B	23	B
9	A	24	C
10	B	25	E
11	C	26	D
12	B	27	A
13	D	28	B
14	E	29	C
15	C	30	B

THE ANALOGY QUESTIONS
TEST 7 NO. 31 ~ 60

Please refer to the Analogy Section Absolute Pattern Analysis in page 392

Test 7

ABSOLUTE PATTERNS for the Reading Section

Q1. Pattern 3: Summary Question

Question Pattern: The opening sentence focuses on   **Question Keywords:** the Habsburg Empire's

Step 1	Step 2	Step 3
Keywords from the Passage	Keywords from Answer	Tone & Concept
traditions of reaction and violence	D) Struggle for survival	Logical Conclusion

Incorrect Choices & Common Patterns		
Evidence	Incorrect keywords	Tone & Concept
The Habsburg Empire is built upon centuries -old traditions of reaction and violence.	A) geographic isolation	Unrelated issues with the opening sentence.
	B) ethnic diversity	
	C) vastness of territory	
	E) centuries-old traditions	

Q2. Pattern 3: Summary Question

Question Pattern: the author does which of the followings?
Question Keywords: In line 2-3 (Its present power…1526),

Step 1	Step 2	Step 3
Keywords from the Passage	Keywords from Answer	Tone & Concept
presumably based on	A) speculates	Logical Conclusion

Incorrect Choices & Common Patterns		
Evidence	Incorrect keywords	Tone & Concept
Its present power is presumably based on the alliance which Bohemia and Hungary concluded with Austria against the Turkish peril in 1526.	B) evidence	By using "presumably" the author uses his speculation. B), C) are Opposite D),E) are Negative.
	C) cites an authority	
	D) criticism	
	E) questions	

Q3. Pattern 3: Summary Question

Question Keywords: From the Habsburg' point of view, the outcome of the Czech revolution of 1618 was

Step 1	Step 2	Step 3
Keywords from the Passage	Keywords from Answer	Tone & Concept
the Czechs suffered a defeat	A) fortuitous	Logical Conclusion

Incorrect Choices & Common Patterns		
Evidence	Incorrect keywords	Tone & Concept
the Czechs suffered a defeat and were cruelly punished for their rebellion.	B) disappointing	It should be fortuitous to the Habsburg because it could maintain the control over Bohemia and Czech
	C) accidental	
	D) foreboding	
	E) foreseeable	

Q4. Pattern 3: Summary Question

Question Pattern: According to the passage,
Question Keywords: which state benefited most by the Turkish peril in 1526?

Step 1	Step 2	Step 3
Keywords from the Passage	Keywords from Answer	Tone & Concept
Its present power is ,based on the alliance which	A) Habsburg	Logical Conclusion

Incorrect Choices & Common Patterns		
Evidence	Incorrect keywords	Tone & Concept
Its present power is presumably based on the alliance which Bohemia and Hungary concluded with Austria against the Turkish peril in 1526. * In other words, the alliance between Bohemia and Hungary that concluded with Austria led the destruction of Turkey.	B) Bohemia	The Habsburg took all this advantage.
	C) Hungary	
	D) Czech	
	E) Turkey itself	

UNAUTHORIZED COPYING OR REUSE OF ANY PART OF THIS PAGE IS ILLEGAL

Q5. Pattern 3: Summary Question

Question Keywords: From the Bohemian's point of view, the outcome of the Czech revolution of 1618 was

Step 1	Step 2	Step 3
Keywords from the Passage	Keywords from Answer	Tone & Concept
Ferdinand II. greatly curtailed the administrative	B) disappointing	Logical Conclusion

Incorrect Choices & Common Patterns		
Evidence	Incorrect keywords	Tone & Concept
the Czechs suffered a defeat and were cruelly punished for their rebellion. Ferdinand II. greatly curtailed the administrative rights of Bohemia,	A) fortuitous C) accidental D) progressive E) foreseeable	It should be disappointing to the Bohemian because it lost the chance for independence.

Q6. Pattern 3: Summary Question

Question Pattern: The last sentence suggests that

Question Keywords: Ferdinad II's approach to Bohemian was a part of

Step 1	Step 2	Step 3
Keywords from the Passage	Keywords from Answer	Tone & Concept
yet he did not dare to deprive her entirely	B) compromise	Logical Conclusion

Incorrect Choices & Common Patterns		
Evidence	Incorrect keywords	Tone & Concept
Ferdinand II. greatly curtailed the administrative rights of Bohemia, yet he did not dare to deprive her entirely of her independence.	A) challenge C) another war D) trust E) boast	Not Supported by the passage

Q7. Pattern 6: Understanding Structure of the Passage

Question Pattern: The author's attitude in, shifts from   **Question Keywords:** the first paragraph (lines 1-3)

Step 1	Step 2	Step 3
Keywords from the Passage	Keywords from Answer	Tone & Concept
but , only a little bit of decrease in infant mortality.	B) optimism to concern	Logical sequence

Incorrect Choices & Common Patterns		
Evidence	Incorrect keywords	Tone & Concept
Recent years have seen a remarkable improvement (OPTIMISM) in the conditions of child life. In all civilized countries, **but** especially in England, statistics show only a little bit of decrease in infant mortality. (CONCERN)	A) regret to appreciation	Not Supported by the passage
	C) disappointment to restraint	
	D) ambivalence to outrage	
	E) bewilderment to courage	

Q8. Pattern 3: Summary Question

Question Pattern: In the second paragraph, the author indicates all of the following EXCEPT

Step 1	Step 2	Step 3
Keywords from the Passage	Keywords from Answer	Tone & Concept
A) institutions, C) hygiene, D) science, E) physical, children	B) diversified opinions	Synonyms

Incorrect Choices & Common Patterns		
Evidence	Incorrect keywords	Tone & Concept
to be seen in the physical development of children (E); they are physically finer and more vigorous. It has been the diffusion, the popularization of science (D), which has brought about such notable advantages. Mothers have learned to welcome the dictates of modern hygiene (C) and to put them into practice in bringing up their children. Many new social institutions (A) have sprung up	A) institutions	B) isn't mentioned.
	C) hygiene	
	D) advancement, science	
	E) physical, children	

UNAUTHORIZED COPYING OR REUSE OF ANY PART OF THIS PAGE IS ILLEGAL

Q9. Pattern 2: Main Idea Question

Question Pattern: The primary purpose of the passage is to emphasize the

Step 1	Step 2	Step 3
Keywords from the Passage	Keywords from Answer	Tone & Concept
What has science done to effect this?	B) power of science	Logical Conclusion

Incorrect Choices & Common Patterns		
Evidence	Incorrect keywords	Tone & Concept
What has science done to effect this? Science has suggested for us certain very simple rules by which the child has been restored as nearly as possible to conditions of a natural life,	A) educate, parents	These are all true statement, but Minor Issues
	C) child education	
	D) finding a solution	
	E) importance of hygiene	

For the main idea question, finding a meaningful transition words—rhetorical question in this passage—is the key to find the answer.

Q10. Pattern 3: Summary Question

Question Pattern: The passage indicates, EXCEPT

Question Keywords: all the merits of science in nurturing child

Step 1	Step 2	Step 3
Keywords from the Passage	Keywords from Answer	Tone & Concept
Science has suggested for us certain very simple rules (A)	A) complex rules	Opposite

Incorrect Choices & Common Patterns		
Evidence	Incorrect keywords	Tone & Concept
dictates of modern hygiene (E) Science has suggested for us certain very simple rules (A) by which the child has been restored, and an order and a guiding law have been given to the functions of the body. (D) it is science which suggested maternal feeding, (C) laid down the measurement of food (B)	B) food measurement	A) is Opposite
	C) maternal feeding	
	D) guiding law	
	E) modern hygiene	

Q11. Pattern 6: Understanding Structure of the Passage

Question Pattern: serves primarily to
Question Keywords: The rhetorical question in line 12 (What has...this?)

Step 1	Step 2	Step 3
Keywords from the Passage	Keywords from Answer	Tone & Concept
Science has suggested, certain very simple rules	D) call attention	the purpose of the rhetoric
Incorrect Choices & Common Patterns		
Evidence	Incorrect keywords	Tone & Concept
What has science done to effect this? Science has suggested for us certain very simple rules	A) advance alternative	This is a rhetorical question One of the purposes of the rhetorical question is to call attention to the issue.
	B) discredit	
	C) hypothetical	
	E) question	

Q12. Type 2: Inference Question [Pattern 1: Local Question] {Category A}

Question Pattern: It can be inferred from the passage that the writer of the essay would be

Step 1	Step 2	Step 3
Keywords from the Passage	Keywords from Answer	Tone & Concept
Rules were also laid down for ...the physiological	B) a nurse	Logical Conclusion
Incorrect Choices & Common Patterns		
Evidence	Incorrect keywords	Tone & Concept
Rules were also laid down for the measurement of food adapting it rationally to the physiological needs of the child's life.	A) school teacher	The passage is a well researched paper by the professional in infant nurturing.
	C) a social scientist	
	D) an economist	
	E) a philosopher	

Q13. Pattern 7: Understanding Attitude / Tone

Question Pattern: indicates the narrator's **Question Keywords:** Line 1-2 (Meanwhile,...afternoon)

Step 1	Step 2	Step 3
Keywords from the Passage	Keywords from Answer	Tone & Concept
Where was I? It was not the Broadway; it was not	B) confusion	Logical Conclusion

Incorrect Choices & Common Patterns		
Evidence	Incorrect keywords	Tone & Concept
Meanwhile, as he ministered, there was time to look about me. Where was I? It was not the Broadway; it was not Staten Island on a Saturday afternoon.	A) evocation	the narrator is confused.
	C) sadness	
	D) insecurity	
	E) complication	

Q14. Pattern 3: Summary Question

Question Pattern: The passage indicates that **Question Keywords:** the landscape was

Step 1	Step 2	Step 3
Keywords from the Passage	Keywords from Answer	Tone & Concept
the breath of a new world, never-trodden fields	D) exotic	Logical Conclusion

Incorrect Choices & Common Patterns		
Evidence	Incorrect keywords	Tone & Concept
Quaint, soft aromas like the breath of a new world-- the fragrance of unknown flowers, and the dewy scent of never-trodden fields drifted to my nostrils;	A) nostalgic	A), C) are Not Supported by the passage
	B) vast and arid	
	C) remote	B), E) are Negative
	E) intimidating	

Q15. Pattern 7: Understanding Attitude / Tone

Question Pattern: The narrator's mood conveys

Step 1	Step 2	Step 3
Keywords from the Passage	Keywords from Answer	Tone & Concept
fanciful, increasing shine, strange scene, fashioning	E) wonder	Logical Conclusion

Incorrect Choices & Common Patterns		
Evidence	Incorrect keywords	Tone & Concept
fanciful, until I presently became <u>aware the rosy twilight was broadening into day, and under the increasing shine</u> a <u>strange scene was fashioning itself</u>.	A) optimism	A), B) are scarcely mentioned.
	B) entertainment	
	C) perseverance	C), D) are Negative
	D) ominous foreboding	

Q16. Pattern 3: Summary Question

Question Pattern: was mainly caused by   **Question Keywords:** It was all...at first"

Step 1	Step 2	Step 3
Keywords from the Passage	Keywords from Answer	Tone & Concept
As my eyes cleared and day brightened	E) darkness	Logical Conclusion

Incorrect Choices & Common Patterns		
Evidence	Incorrect keywords	Tone & Concept
<u>It was all dim</u> and unreal at first, the mountains shadowy, the ocean unreal and <u>shadowy. As my eyes cleared and day brightened it presently dawned upon me.</u>	A) familiar landscape	He couldn't see it because it was dark.
	B) his dream	
	C) nostalgia	
	D) monotony	

Q17. Pattern 2: Main Idea Question

Question Pattern: The passage as a whole serves primarily to

Step 1	Step 2	Step 3
Keywords from the Passage	Keywords from Answer	Tone & Concept
Where was I? At first it was an opal sea	C) set the views, mindsets	Logical Conclusion

Incorrect Choices & Common Patterns		
Evidence	Incorrect keywords	Tone & Concept
Where was I? At first it was an opal sea	A) humiliation	The entire passage starts with the combination of the narrator's monologue and the reflection of his mindset. It also focuses on the views of the exotic world.
	B) explore	
	D) real and unreal	
	E) to survive	

Q18. Pattern 4: Relationship Question

Question Pattern: The descriptions of the scene in the passage and the narrator's mood present a contrast
Question Keywords: between his

Step 1	Step 2	Step 3
Keywords from the Passage	Keywords from Answer	Tone & Concept
Where was I? At first it was an opal sea	B) confusion and graceful	Logical Conclusion

Incorrect Choices & Common Patterns		
Evidence	Incorrect keywords	Tone & Concept
Where was I? At first it was an opal sea	A) organized	Not Supported by the passage
	C) pretension	
	D) volatile temperament	
	E) sophistication	

Q19. Pattern 7: Understanding Attitude / Tone

Question Pattern: The description in lines 14-15 ("And though...said it.") suggests that
Question Keywords: Sara experienced a sense of

Step 1	Step 2	Step 3
Keywords from the Passage	Keywords from Answer	Tone & Concept
From Sara's eyes, nervous feeling.	B) nervousness	Synonym

Incorrect Choices & Common Patterns		
Evidence	Incorrect keywords	Tone & Concept
And though she was only seven years old, she knew that he felt sad when he said it. The father was sad, not Sara. <u>From Sara's eyes it should have been nervous feeling.</u>	A) pressure	Not Supported by the passage
	C) self-esteem	
	D) joy	
	E) duty	

Q20. Pattern 3: Summary Question

Question Pattern: The first paragraph primarily describes   **Question Keywords:** that Sara was

Step 1	Step 2	Step 3
Keywords from the Passage	Keywords from Answer	Tone & Concept
<u>about grown-up people and the world</u>	A) different perspective	Logical Conclusion

Incorrect Choices & Common Patterns		
Evidence	Incorrect keywords	Tone & Concept
<u>could not herself remember any time when she had not been thinking things about grown-up people and the world they belonged to.</u>	B) escaping	Negative
	C) change a life	Not Supported by the passage
	D) varying experiences	
	E) the answer	

UNAUTHORIZED COPYING OR REUSE OF ANY PART OF THIS PAGE IS ILLEGAL

Q21. Pattern 6: Understanding Structure of the Passage

Question Pattern: The passage as a whole is viewed from the perspective of

Step 1	Step 2	Step 3
Keywords from the Passage	Keywords from Answer	Tone & Concept
Sara was such a little girl	B) one who knows	Logical Conclusion

Incorrect Choices & Common Patterns		
Evidence	Incorrect keywords	Tone & Concept
Sara was such a little girl	A) seven-year-old Sara	The narrator knows the inner mindsets of the little girl Sara.
	C) a grown-up Sara	
	D) Sara in her dream	
	E) Sara's father	

Q22. Type 3: Analogy Question [Pattern 1: Local Question] {Category A}

Question Pattern: is most analogous to   **Question Keywords:** "The fact...long time" in lines 2-5

Step 1	Step 2	Step 3
Keywords from the Passage	Keywords from Answer	Tone & Concept
she, been thinking things about grown-up people	A) a poor janitor dreaming	Logical Conclusion

Incorrect Choices & Common Patterns		
Evidence	Incorrect keywords	Tone & Concept
she was always dreaming and thinking ... thinking things about grown-up people. The analogy used implies the logic of (1) small to big and (2) positive concept of (3) one person.	B) a teacher rewarding	
	C) a boy having a nightmare	Negative
	D) a girl teaching	B), D), E) two people are involved.
	E) a girl taking care	

Q23. Pattern 3: Summary Question

Question Pattern: The narrator's description of the   **Question Keywords:** voyage suggests that

Step 1	Step 2	Step 3
Keywords from the Passage	Keywords from Answer	Tone & Concept
a queer thing it was that at one time one was in	A) strange memories	Synonym

Incorrect Choices & Common Patterns		
Evidence	Incorrect keywords	Tone & Concept
she was thinking of what a queer thing it was that at one time one was in India in the blazing sun.	B) it foreboded	Sara had a queer (strange) experience during the voyage.
	C) intense emotional	
	D) proud of her father	
	E) it had little connection	

Q24. Type 2: Inference Question [Pattern 1: Local Question] {Category A}

Question Pattern: It can be inferred from the passage that   **Question Keywords:** Sara is going to

Step 1	Step 2	Step 3
Keywords from the Passage	Keywords from Answer	Tone & Concept
Is this the place?"	A) new place	Logical Conclusion

Incorrect Choices & Common Patterns		
Evidence	Incorrect keywords	Tone & Concept
Is this the place?" Sara whispered, "Is it, papa? "Yes, little Sara, it is. We have reached it at last."	B) chase her dream	the conversation between Sara and father that Sara is going to move into a new place.
	C) extend her trip	
	D) travel alone	
	E) meet her mother	

Q25. Type 2: Inference Question [Pattern 1: Local Question] {Category A}

Question Keywords: Why does the President believe in lines 4-5, ("What...war.")

Step 1	Step 2	Step 3
Keywords from the Passage	Keywords from Answer	Tone & Concept
power which engineers wield in.	A) Engineers conveyed their knowledge	Logical Conclusion

Incorrect Choices & Common Patterns		
Evidence	Incorrect keywords	Tone & Concept
I mention this to bring to the reader's attention the <u>tremendous power which engineers wield in world affairs.</u>	B) without their consent	B) is Opposite
	C) Engineers were insidiously	C), D), E) are Too extreme word usage
	D) War was, by engineers	
	E) Engineers are destructively	

Q26. Type 1: Example Question [Pattern 1: Local Question] {Category A}

Question Keywords: Why did the few laymen in line 4 gasp?

Step 1	Step 2	Step 3
Keywords from the Passage	Keywords from Answer	Tone & Concept
, gave expression to a thought so startling	A) not prepared to hear	Logical Conclusion

Incorrect Choices & Common Patterns		
Evidence	Incorrect keywords	Tone & Concept
The president's speech was shocking revelation to the audience because they were not prepared to hear the secret opinion among engineers directly from the president	B) not engineers	B) Inconsistent with the question
	C) contributed positively	C),D), E) Not Supported by the passage
	D) The president justified	
	E) They didn't agree	

Q27. Pattern 3: Summary Question

Question Pattern: focuses primarily on which aspect of engineers?
Question Keywords: "the tremendous power" (line 10),

Step 1	Step 2	Step 3
Keywords from the Passage	Keywords from Answer	Tone & Concept
the tremendous power, engineers wield in world	A) practicality	Logical Conclusion

Incorrect Choices & Common Patterns		
Evidence	Incorrect keywords	Tone & Concept
I mention this merely to bring to the reader's attention the tremendous power which engineers wield in world affairs.	B) perseverance	Not Supported by the passage. D) is too weak and vague
	C) connection to politics	
	D) depth of knowledge	
	E) imagination	

Tremendous power refers to the engineers practicality to influence in world affairs.

Q28. Pattern 4: Relationship Question

Question Pattern: The author compares, as a pair of
Question Keywords: in line 16-17 ("the man…locomotive")

Step 1	Step 2	Step 3
Keywords from the Passage	Keywords from Answer	Tone & Concept
the man who runs, the man, designs	A) engineering and non-engineering	Logical Conclusion

Incorrect Choices & Common Patterns		
Evidence	Incorrect keywords	Tone & Concept
the man who runs a locomotive and the man who designs a locomotive.	B) familiarity and unfamiliarity	Not Supported by the passage
	C) benefit and harm	
	D) practicality and impracticality	
	E) easy and difficult	

Q29. Type 1: Example Question [Pattern 1: Local Question] {Category A}

Question Pattern: The author refers, in order to   **Question Keywords:** "law, medicine, and metaphysics"

Step 1	Step 2	Step 3
Keywords from the Passage	Keywords from Answer	Tone & Concept
But laymen know nothing, engineering.	E) complexity of engineering	Logical Conclusion

Incorrect Choices & Common Patterns		
Evidence	Incorrect keywords	Tone & Concept
Laymen know something about law, a little about medicine, quite a lot--nowadays-- about metaphysics. But laymen know nothing about engineering.	A) understate engineering C) entertain D) boast B) familiar subjects	B) is incorrect because this question put "law, medicine, and metaphysics" as an example

1> When a question asks an example sentence, the example itself doesn't contain any value nor the answer.

2> You should look up the main reason for the example. The main reason is presented after "But"

Q30. Type 1: Example Question [Pattern 1: Local Question] {Category A}

Question Pattern: In the context of the passage, emphasizes
Question Keywords: "For one...the other" (line 19)

Step 1	Step 2	Step 3
Keywords from the Passage	Keywords from Answer	Tone & Concept
laymen know nothing about engineering.	E) the complexity	Logical Conclusion

Incorrect Choices & Common Patterns		
Evidence	Incorrect keywords	Tone & Concept
laymen know nothing about engineering. *please refer to the explanation #29.	A) locomotive B) locomotive C) the immense power D) the productive aspect	A), B) Locomotive is not the main issue; therefore, the answer should not contain this word and treat as the keyword

Q31. Pattern 7: Understanding Attitude / Tone

Question Pattern: the author makes use of which of the following?

Question Keywords: In line 1 ("It would…his father.")

Step 1	Step 2	Step 3
Keywords from the Passage	Keywords from Answer	Tone & Concept
It would <u>seem</u> that	A) Speculation	Logical Conclusion

Incorrect Choices & Common Patterns		
Evidence	Incorrect keywords	Tone & Concept
It would <u>seem</u> that Cicero's love for literature was inherited from his father,	B) Allusion	The usage of a word "seem" makes his opinion based on speculation.
	C) Analogy	
	D) Confirmation	
	E) Euphemism	

Q32. Pattern 3: Summary Question

Question Pattern: According to

Question Keywords: lines 2-3 (He too...of the time), Cicero learned first systemic philosophy that focuses

Step 1	Step 2	Step 3
Keywords from the Passage	Keywords from Answer	Tone & Concept
rhetorical discipline of the time.	B) system of speech	Synonym

Incorrect Choices & Common Patterns		
Evidence	Incorrect keywords	Tone & Concept
He too, we may conjecture, led the young Cicero to feel the importance of a study of philosophy to serve as a corrective for the somewhat narrow rhetorical discipline of the time.	A) grammar	Rhetorical discipline means learning art of speech
	C) art of stoicism	
	D) poetry	
	E) historical citations	

Q33. Type 2: Inference Question [Pattern 1: Local Question] {Category A}

Question Keywords: Who would be most likely to learn "the art of dialectic" mentioned in line 22?

Step 1	Step 2	Step 3
Keywords from the Passage	Keywords from Answer	Tone & Concept
This art, important to <u>the orator</u>	E) Politician	Logical Conclusion

Incorrect Choices & Common Patterns		
Evidence	Incorrect keywords	Tone & Concept
This art, which Cicero deems so important to <u>the orator</u> that he calls it "abbreviated <u>eloquence</u> *One of the most important skills for politician should be possessing the skills of orator.	A) Merchant B) Scientist C) Poet D) Farmer	merchant, army, farmer or poet are not the group of people require the art of dialectic as much as a politician does.

Q34. Pattern 5: Word-In-Context Question

Question Pattern: implies
Question Keywords: In line 14, "the monopoly of the Stoic school" the education system was then

Step 1	Step 2	Step 3
Keywords from the Passage	Keywords from Answer	Tone & Concept
monopoly of the Stoic school	C) limited	Monopoly = exclusive or limited

Incorrect Choices & Common Patterns		
Evidence	Incorrect keywords	Tone & Concept
This art, which Cicero deems so important to the orator that he calls it "abbreviated eloquence," was then the monopoly of the Stoic school	A) cooperative B) diversified D) expansive E) underdeveloped	Not Supported by the passage

Q35. Type 2: Inference Question [Pattern 1: Local Question] {Category A}

Question Keywords: Cicero himself would most likely agree with which of the following statement?

Step 1	Step 2	Step 3
Keywords from the Passage	Keywords from Answer	Tone & Concept
Cicero soon abandoned Epicureanism	A) Epicureanism has its limit	Logical Conclusion

Incorrect Choices & Common Patterns		
Evidence	Incorrect keywords	Tone & Concept
Cicero soon abandoned Epicureanism	B) The ultimate literary power	B), C), D) are Not Supported by the passage
	C) Literary skills are no less	
	D) Phaedrus earned more respect	E) Diodotus is the teacher of the Art of dialectic.
	E) Diodotus, Epicureanism	

Q36. Type 2: Inference Question [Pattern 1: Local Question] {Category A}

Question Pattern: The narrator's attitude to, in the passage suggests that he is in the feeling of
Question Keywords: "a girl"

Step 1	Step 2	Step 3
Keywords from the Passage	Keywords from Answer	Tone & Concept
I kept thinking her homely, music of her voice,--	A) sympathy	Positive feeling

Incorrect Choices & Common Patterns		
Evidence	Incorrect keywords	Tone & Concept
One of them interested me especially. She was a small person; I couldn't decide whether she was a child or a woman. I kept thinking her homely, and then when she spoke, music of her voice,--	B) bewilderment	E) is incorrect because "was a child or a woman line 10" B),C),D) are all Opposite and Negative
	C) ambivalence	
	D) concern	
	E) love	

UNAUTHORIZED COPYING OR REUSE OF ANY PART OF THIS PAGE IS ILLEGAL

Q37. Pattern 5: Word-In-Context Question

Question Pattern: the narrator employs which of the following rhetorical device?

Question Keywords: In line 10, "the music of her voice",

Step 1	Step 2	Step 3
Keywords from the Passage	Keywords from Answer	Tone & Concept
I forgot everything but the music of her voice,--	D) metaphor	Synonym
Incorrect Choices & Common Patterns		
Evidence	Incorrect keywords	Tone & Concept
then when she spoke I forgot everything but the music of her voice,--	A) exaggeration	The narrator metaphorically describes her beautiful voice as music.
	B) allusion	
	C) slang	
	E) personification	

Q38. Pattern 3: Summary Question

Question Pattern: because he   **Question Keywords:** The narrator offered his help to the girl

Step 1	Step 2	Step 3
Keywords from the Passage	Keywords from Answer	Tone & Concept
and as our own tardiness had belated her,	A) was boredom	Logical Conclusion
Incorrect Choices & Common Patterns		
Evidence	Incorrect keywords	Tone & Concept
The rest went their ways; and as our own tardiness had belated her, I offered to help her to carry out the dishes.	B) display his manhood	Not Supported by the passage
	C) appreciation, music	
	D) was in love	
	E) concerned	

Q39. Type 2: Inference Question [Pattern 1: Local Question] {Category A}

Question Pattern: It can be inferred that this passage   **Question Keywords:** was taken from the part of

Step 1	Step 2	Step 3
Keywords from the Passage	Keywords from Answer	Tone & Concept
Your letter of the 4th just to hand.	A) correspondence letter	Logical Conclusion
Incorrect Choices & Common Patterns		
Evidence	Incorrect keywords	Tone & Concept
How glad your letters make me; how glad I am to have you to tell little things to.	B) a magazine	Not Supported by the passage
	C) a traveling journal	
	D) an autobiography	
	E) a love letter	

Q40. Pattern 5: Word-In-Context Question

Question Pattern: Which of the following literary device is used for the statement
Question Keywords: "she seemed...splendid voice" (line 11)

Step 1	Step 2	Step 3
Keywords from the Passage	Keywords from Answer	Tone & Concept
she seemed **so small** for such a **splendid** voice	A) paradox	Synonym
Incorrect Choices & Common Patterns		
Evidence	Incorrect keywords	Tone & Concept
and she seemed **so small** for such a **splendid** voice *Paradox: a self-contradictory statement	B) juxtaposition	Not Supported by the passage
	C) metaphor	
	D) simile	
	E) personification	

Test 7 ABSOLUTE PATTERNS for the Analogy Section

Q31. Absolute Pattern 7: Association (Characteristic) Pattern

C is the best answer

Chicken belongs to food category; dragon belongs to myth category.

Q32. Absolute Pattern 8: Shape Pattern

E is the best answer

Clouds in the sky and wave in the ocean are similar in color and shape.

Q33. Absolute Pattern 1: Production (Cause-Effect) Pattern

D is the best answer.

Punch produces bleeding; overheat produces burn. They are both Negative concept.

(E) has no Negative concept.

Q34. Absolute Pattern 2: Part-Whole Pattern

C is the best answer.

Mosquito is a part of the insect as soccer is a part of sports.

Q35. Absolute Pattern 3: Antonym (Positive-Negative) Pattern

B is the best answer

Fresh is an antonym to rotten; a pill is an antonym to poison.

Q36. Absolute Pattern 7: Association (Characteristic) Pattern

E is the best answer

King renders banquet; pianist renders recital.

Q37. Absolute Pattern 1: Production (Cause-Effect) Pattern

A is the best answer

Heat produces vapor as diligent produces success.

(B) mom produces baby, not a sister.

(C) is flipped over.

Q38. Absolute Pattern 7: Association (Characteristic) Pattern

B is the best answer

Counterfeit is an artificial (fake) money; plastic is an artificial while wood is real.

Q39. Absolute Pattern 5: Degree Pattern

D is the best answer

Gloomy (weak sadness) lugubrious (strong sadness); pleasant (weak sadness), ecstatic (strong sadness)

Q40. Absolute Pattern 5: Degree Pattern

A is the best answer.

Metal gets rust; apple gets rotten.

Q41. Absolute Pattern 2: Part-Whole Pattern

D is the best answer.

Rooster is a part of chicken; chimpanzee is a part of ape.

Q42. Absolute Pattern 6:Purpose (Job/Tool) Pattern

B is the best answer

The purpose (function) of a watch is to check time, the function of the lighthouse is to send a signal.

UNAUTHORIZED COPYING OR REUSE OF ANY PART OF THIS PAGE IS ILLEGAL

Q43. Absolute Pattern 3: Antonym (Positive-Negative) Pattern

B is the best answer

Hopeless is an antonym to victory as rich is an antonym to poor.

Choice C is a human concept, and there is no antonym concept. Police are to thief is the Purpose Pattern.

Choice D is incorrect because antonym to cancer is not dying. It's a Degree Pattern.

Choice E is wrong combination because antonym to a bird is not fish.

Q44. Absolute Pattern 2: Part-Whole Pattern

B is the best answer

Actor is a part of cast in a movie; member is a part of staff

Q45. Absolute Pattern 2: Part-Whole Pattern

D is the best answer

Hammerhead is a part (type) of Shark; grizzly is a part (type) of a bear.

Q46. Absolute Pattern 6:Purpose (Job/Tool) Pattern

C is the best answer.

A fence divides the neighbors as a border divides countries.

Q47. Absolute Pattern 6:Purpose (Job/Tool) Pattern

E is the best answer.

Paleontologist's job is to study dinosaurs; Psychologist's job is to study human mental

Q48. Absolute Pattern 8: Shape Pattern

B is the best answer

The podium is ranked by the colors of medals; grades are ranked by the age.

Q49. Absolute Pattern 6:Purpose (Job/Tool) Pattern

C is the best answer

The purpose of anthropology is to study of civilization; the purpose of zoology is to study animal.

Q50. Absolute Pattern 1: Production (Cause-Effect) Pattern

B is the best answer

Movie star creates fame; author creates books.
(A) is not the same human category.
(B), (E) There's no production relation.

Q51. Absolute Pattern 5: Degree Pattern

D is the best answer

Chronic pain is a habitual pain; acute pain is an intense pain that comes and goes quickly.

Q52. Absolute Pattern 5: Degree Pattern

A is the best answer (small to big)

Day is a part of week; pint is a part of liter

Q53. Absolute Pattern 4: Synonym Pattern

D is the best answer.

Articulate means speak clearly; legible means write clearly

Q54. Absolute Pattern 8: Shape Pattern

C is the best answer.

The bottle is a circle shape; the monitor is a rectangle shape.

UNAUTHORIZED COPYING OR REUSE OF ANY PART OF THIS PAGE IS ILLEGAL

Q55. Absolute Pattern 6:Purpose (Job/Tool) Pattern

A is the best answer

Manager works at a store; editor works for a film.

Q56. Absolute Pattern 7: Association (Characteristic) Pattern

B is the best answer

Excerpt introduces a story, as prologue introduces a concert.

Choice A is wrong because dessert comes after finishing the main meal

Q57. Absolute Pattern 7: Association (Characteristic) Pattern

C is the best answer

Garden grows flowers. That's the purpose of a garden. Badge indicates identity.

Q58. Absolute Pattern 5: Degree Pattern

A is the best answer

Hungry (weak) starvation (strong) ; defect (weak) catastrophe (strong)

Q59. Absolute Pattern 7: Association (Characteristic) Pattern

B is the best answer

Both the question and choice B are categorized as a measurement

Q60. Absolute Pattern 6:Purpose (Job/Tool) Pattern

C is the best answer.

Prosecutor's job is to accuse, as inspector's job is to search.

Test 7 Recap

Analyzing Purpose of Example

Summarizing and Identifying Explicit Meanings

This type of question can be represented by the cause-effect question.

When the transitional word, phrase, or clause like 'because,' 'in order to,' or 'as' are written in the question, try to search for transitional word or phrase from the passage that countermeasures the question such as 'as a result / but / however / yet / since / reason / although', etc.

SSAT

Reading & Verbal Practice

Test 8

ALL THE LOGIC AND RULES

BEHIND THE EVERY SINGLE

SSAT QUESTION

Test 8 Reading Section
Time: 40 Minutes, 40 Questions

Directions: Each reading passage is followed by questions about it. Answer the questions that follow a passage on the basis of what is stated or implied in that passage.

Questions 1-6 are based on the following passage.

Line   In undertaking a study of insects it is well first of all to know something about what they are, their general nature, appearance, habits and development. The insects comprise the largest group of animals on the globe. There are about four times as many different kinds of insects as all other kinds of animals combined. Insects vary greatly in size. Some are as large as small

5   birds, while others are so small that a thousand placed in one pile would not equal the size of a pea.

Insects are commonly spoken of as "bugs." This term, however, is properly used only when referring to the one order of insects which includes the sap and blood-sucking insects such as the chinch bug, bed-bug, squash bug, and the like. Then too, there are many so-called "bugs"

10   which are not insects at all. Spiders, thousand-legs, crawfishes and even earth-worms are often spoken of as bugs. Insects are variously formed, but as a rule the mature ones have three and only three pairs of legs, one pair of feelers, one pair of large eyes, and one or two pairs of wings. The body is divided into a head, thorax and abdomen. The head bears the eyes, feelers and mouth, the thorax bears the legs and wings, and the abdomen is made up of a number of

15   segments. The presence of wings at once decides whether or not it is an insect, for, aside from bats and birds, insects alone have true wings.

1

All of the followings are supported by the passage EXCEPT

A) Spiders can be grouped as insects but not as bugs
B) The terms 'bugs' and 'insects' cannot be used interchangeably.
C) Insects are categorized as the largest group of animal.
D) Insects and bugs are different species.
E) blood-sucking insects are bugs by some characteristics

2

The phrase mentioned in line 13, "only three pairs of legs" describes

A) a unique characteristic of all mature bugs
B) a unique characteristic of all insects
C) a type of difficulty to distinguish between bugs and insects
D) a mechanism only mature insect possesses
E) a part of the body often get confused with wings

CONTINUE

3

Which of the following does NOT comprise the part of insects' body?

A) Three pairs of eyes

B) Three pairs of legs

C) One pair of feelers

D) Two pairs of wings

E) One pair of ears

4

Which of following statements is NOT supported by the passage?

A) Some animals are legitimately called insects as well as bugs without distinction.

B) Some insects like spiders are wrongly categorized as bugs

C) Some bugs like spiders are wrongly categorized as insects.

D) Vast majority of animals are categorized as insect

E) Studying the general nature of insects is as important as studying their appearance.

5

Which of the following animal can be classified as both an insect and a bug?

A) Mosquito

B) Spider

C) Thousand-legs

D) Crawfishes

E) Earth-warms

6

In line 16, "abdomen" refers to which part of insects?

A) stomach

B) head

C) tail

D) legs

E) reproduction organ

CONTINUE

Questions 7-12 are based on the following passage.

Line   "I wonder when in the world you're going to do anything, Rudolf?" said my brother's wife.

"My dear Rose," I answered, laying down my egg-spoon, "why in the world should I do anything? My position is a comfortable one. I have an income nearly sufficient for my wants (no one's income is ever quite sufficient, you know), I enjoy an enviable social position: I am

5   brother to Lord Burlesdon, and brother-in-law to that charming lady, his countess. Behold, it is enough!"

"You are nine-and-twenty," she observed, "and you've done nothing but--"

"Knock about? It is true. Our family doesn't need to do things."

10 This remark of mine rather annoyed Rose, for everybody knows (and therefore there can be no harm in referring to the fact) that, pretty and accomplished as she herself is, her family is hardly of the same standing as the Rassendylls. Besides her attractions, she possessed a large fortune, and my brother Robert was wise enough not to mind about her ancestry. Ancestry is, in fact, a matter concerning which the next observation of Rose's has some truth.

15 "Good families are generally worse than any others," she said. Upon this I stroked my hair: I knew quite well what she meant. "I'm so glad Robert's is black!" she cried.

At this moment Robert (who rises at seven and works before breakfast) came in. He glanced at his wife: her cheek was slightly flushed; he patted it caressingly. "What's the matter, my dear?" he asked. "She objects to my doing nothing and having red hair," said I, in an injured

20 tone. "Oh! of course he can't help his hair," admitted Rose. "It generally crops out once in a generation," said my brother. "So does the nose. Rudolf has got them both."

7

Lines 20 ("Oh! of course...admitted Rose.") suggests that Rose admits that there's an inevitable fact in

A) personality
B) social status
C) hair color
D) family tradition
E) genetic inheritance

8

Throughout the passage, Rudolf emphasizes primarily about his?

A) profligacy
B) familiarity with uncomfortable living
C) resourcefulness
D) relationship with brother
E) unsuccessful marriage

CONTINUE

9

The parenthetical phrase in lines 10-11 (and there can't be…to the fact) primarily serves to

A) lament his current condition

B) introduce a new theory

C) challenge Rose's claim

D) emphasize a justification

E) state an exception

10

Compared to Rose's, Robert's remark "So does… both." (line 22) contains more

A) apologetic tone

B) assertive tone

C) analytic tone

D) invocative tone

E) humorous tone

11

Which of the following best reveals Rose's mood when she said "Oh! of course... his hair," (line 20)

A) remorse

B) fear

C) appreciation

D) celebration

E) bafflement

12

In line 20, "crops" most nearly refers to

A) farming

B) harvesting

C) occurring

D) remaining

E) showing

CONTINUE

Questions 13-18 are based on the following passage.

Line

The following recipes are not a mere marrowless collection of shreds and patches, and cuttings and pastings, but a bonâ fide register of practical facts,--accumulated by a perseverance not to be subdued or evaporated by the igniferous terrors of a roasting fire in the dog-days,--in defiance of the odoriferous and calefacient repellents of roasting, boiling, frying, and broiling;--moreover,

5 the author has submitted to a labor no preceding cookery-book-maker, perhaps, ever attempted to encounter,--having eaten each recipe before he set it down in his book.

They have all been heartily welcomed by a sufficiently well-educated palate, and a rather fastidious stomach. Numerous as are the receipts in former books, they vary little from each other, except in the name given to them; the processes of cookery are very few: I have

10 endeavored to describe each, in so plain and circumstantial a manner, as I hope will be easily understood, even by the amateur, who is unacquainted with the practical part of culinary concerns.

OLD HOUSEKEEPERS may think I have been tediously minute on many points which may appear trifling: my predecessors seem to have considered the RUDIMENTS of COOKERY quite

15 unworthy of attention. These little delicate distinctions constitute all the difference between a common and an elegant table, and are not trifles to the YOUNG HOUSEKEEPERS who must learn them either from the communication of others or blunder on till their own slowly accumulating and dear-bought experience teaches them.

A wish to save time, trouble and money to inexperienced housekeepers and cooks, and to bring

20 the enjoyments and indulgences of the opulent within each of the middle ranks of society, were my motives for publishing this book.

13

The passage as a whole

A) values cookery tradition over practicality

B) emphasizes the importance of creativity in cookery

C) urges the reader to be simplistic and adhere to the fundamental in cookery

D) instills readers to be scientific in meal preparation

E) promotes her book to be the bestseller

14

The author of the cookbook focused her main readers to be

A) cookbook editors

B) mothers preparing Thanksgiving meals

C) people with fastidious stomach

D) restaurant owners

E) experienced chef

CONTINUE

15

The author's main point in the first paragraph (lines 1-6) is that the cookbook

A) combined all the necessary data and information for great recipes

B) was made by the fine recipes that required perseverance and accumulation of knowledge

C) was obtained by many different professional chefs

D) carried the powerful, universally respected fine dining recipes

E) was prepared for those who are preparing for restaurant business

16

"OLD HOUSEKEEPERS...attention" (lines 13-15) implies that the author's predecessors have considered the cookery should focus on

A) some little delicate distinctions

B) every day meal

C) exquisite table

D) common table

E) basic cooking process

17

Which of the followings makes this cookbook unique?

A) the entire recipes are not a mere marrowless collection

B) patches, cuttings, and pastings were avoided

C) there have been heartily welcomed by many professional chefs

D) the author of the cookbook ate all the recipes in the book

E) the book contains recipes from former books

18

Which of the following situation is analogous to the claim "moreover, the author...book" (lines 5-6)

A) A chemistry teacher is offering a lecture to students based on the students' experiment outcome

B) A detective is interrogating a criminal based on the detective's instinct

C) A mother is preparing a Thanksgiving meal by referring to a note from her grandmother

D) A nurse is filling out a patient's record as she is checking at the patient's vitals.

E) A boy is writing his essay based on the school instruction

CONTINUE

Questions 19-24 are based on the following passage.

Line

It is not intended to advise against marriage, nor to draw the line too closely as to the don't-marry class, but simply to hint at the errors of some persons who match badly on so long a contract. The "yes or no" question is the vital one for all young people to answer. Some answer too soon, others wait too long, others never reach such a climax of happiness as to be invited by an eligible partner. The genius of selection is the rarest of faculties.

5

What most puzzles the will and makes us bear the ills we have is the theme of selection. A mother's or father's view of a suitor may be at variance with the daughter's wish and destroy the peace of both for a lifetime. But quite generally the real trouble arises from a spiteful choice or a hasty one, or one in some of the forms here mentioned. Should these hints prevent one unhappy marriage, they will well repay the little study that their brevity requires.

10

To avoid much lecturing, only two examples are given at any length, in the form of stories. These are as near to the real characters as the writer can safely relate them, being founded on actual romantic and unromantic marriages. As marriage is the first question that every family will discuss, it is well to treat it with exact candor. Don't marry for beauty merely.

15

Very few have a supply that would last a full dozen years in a married life that should continue for three decades. And, more than that, beauty is not the only requisite to happiness.

Very handsome people are almost always vain, often exacting, and generally live on their form, paying little or no attention to the rarer qualities of manhood or womanhood. If one seek beauty alone, he will find it in the fields and flowers and gardens, in paintings, art works, and

20

things of nature; while the real pleasures of life may be found in a thousand ways outside of the beauty.

19

By saying that " It is not intended to advise against marriage" (line 1), the author

A) revokes his later view on marriage

B) respects other's opinion about marriage

C) admits he has mixed view on marriage

D) defuses possible objection about his view on marriage

E) suggests an alternative explanation on his view on marriage

20

The author characterizes the main reason for unhappy marriage is rooted in

A) marry for mere beauty

B) romantic marriage

C) hasty choice

D) unromantic marriage

E) parents' preference

CONTINUE

21

All the statements represent "the real pleasures" in line 20 EXCEPT

A) A groom buying a cookbook for his bride

B) Finding the same hobbies between the partners

C) A mother helping a child doing a homework

D) A husband paints his wife's figure

E) A husband saves money for his wife's cosmetic surgery for her birthday present

22

In the passage, the author views beauty in marriage as

A) an admirable element in happy marriage

B) a grateful element that lasts full dozens of years

C) a value less than a garden

D) a value too abstract to define

E) not only the requisite but also happiness

23

In line 14, "it is well to treat it with exact candor" emphasizes the author's recognition of the

A) discovering sincerity is harder than discovering the beauty

B) nature of marriage often involves family interest

C) financial interest often blinds the right partner selection

D) happy marriage is impossible if the partner is chosen by the beauty

E) certain marriage requires more honest than beautify

24

In order to prevent the unhappy marriage, which of the following values should be considered most?

A) the unhindered interaction between two families

B) respecting the partner's privacy

C) approval from the parents

D) adhering to the partner's external appearance

E) making a considerate "yes" or "no" question

CONTINUE

Questions 25-30 are based on the following passage.

Line   At the foundation of all myths lies the mental process of personification, which finds expression in the rhetorical figure of human being. The definition of this, however, must be extended from the mere representation of inanimate things as animate, to include also the representation of irrational beings as rational, as in the "animal myths," a most common form
5   of religious story among primitive people.

   Some languages favor these forms of personification much more than others, and most of the American languages do so in a marked manner, by the broad grammatical distinctions they draw between animate and inanimate objects, which distinctions must invariably be observed. They cannot say "the boat moves" without specifying whether the boat is an
10 animate object or not, or whether it is to be considered animate, for rhetorical purposes, at the time of speaking.

The sounds of words have aided greatly in myth building. Names and words which are somewhat alike in sound,_paronyms_, as they are called by grammarians, may be taken or mistaken one for the other. Again, many myths spring from homonymy, that is, the sameness
15 in sound of words with difference in signification. Thus coatl, in the Aztec tongue, is a word frequently appearing in the names of divinities. It has three entirely different meanings, to wit, a serpent, a guest and twins. Now, whichever one of these was originally meant, it would be quite certain to be misunderstood, more or less, by later generations, and myths would arise to explain the several possible interpretations of the word--as, in fact, we find was the case.
20

25

The author's attitude toward "personification" in line 1 is based on the

A) solid evidence

B) logical argument

C) tentative acceptance

D) disturbing misconception

E) necessary speculation

26

The author mentions "personification" (line 1) as an example of the

A) dehumanizing aspect of all myths

B) gratification among some myth believers

C) ubiquitous quality of all myths

D) similar mentality shared by all nations that have myth

E) similar physical characteristics of the animal in myth

CONTINUE

27

Which of the following pair most likely resemble the description of homonymy?

A) Difficult and Easy

B) Again and Repeat

C) Basic and Fundamental

D) Boy and Boys

E) Be and Bee

28

The main reason for the statement "They cannot say the boat moves" (line 9) is that

A) the boat has yet to be subjected to an animate object

B) the message is understood in various forms without a clear implication

C) the grammatical definition should be mentioned first

D) they didn't see the actual boat moving

E) all boats are inanimate objects

29

The author implies that Aztec language has all the qualities EXCEPT

A) the written form of language

B) the lack of grammatical organization

C) the sounds of words

D) the reliance on myth for interpretation

E) the homonymy

30

The reference to "a serpent, a guest and twins" (line 17) primarily serves to

A) affirm the imaginative nature of myths

B) disparage the concept of homonymy

C) show the myth building is based on homonymy

D) support an alternative understanding of homonymy

E) illustrate a variety of extreme views on myths

CONTINUE

Questions 31-35 are based on the following passage.

Line   It has been said by a thoughtful writer that the subject of witchcraft has hardly received that place which it deserves in the history of opinions. There has been, of course, a reason for this neglect--the fact that the belief in witchcraft is no longer existent among intelligent people and that its history, in consequence, seems to possess rather an antiquarian than a living interest.

5 No one can tell the story of the witch trials of sixteenth and seventeenth century England without digging up a buried past, and the process of exhumation is not always pleasant. Yet the study of English witchcraft is more than an unsightly exposure of a forgotten superstition. There were few aspects of sixteenth and seventeenth century life that were not affected by the ugly belief. It is quite impossible to grasp the social conditions, it is impossible to understand

10 the opinions, fears, and hopes of the men and women who lived in Elizabethan and Stuart England, without some knowledge of the part played in that age by witchcraft. It was a matter that concerned all classes from the royal household to the ignorant denizens of country villages. Privy councilors anxious about their sovereign and thrifty peasants worrying over their crops, clergymen alert to detect the Devil in their own parishes, medical quacks eager to

15 profit by the fear of evil women, justices of the peace zealous to beat down the works of Satan --all classes, indeed--believed more or less sincerely in the dangerous powers of human creatures who had surrendered themselves to the Evil One. Witchcraft, in a general and vague sense, was something very old in English history. In a more specific and limited sense it is a comparatively modern phenomenon. This leads us to a

20 definition of the term. It is a definition that can be given adequately only in an historical way.

31

The passage as a whole is primarily concerned with the
A) problems faced by modern historians studying the witchcraft practice
B) pervasive impact of witchcraft in life
C) difficulties of debunking the witchcraft practice
D) earnest revelation of witchcraft practice
E) response from the early witchcraft

32

"the ugly belief" mentioned in line 9 most nearly refers to the belief of those
A) who practiced witchcraft
B) English witches
C) historians who deny witchcraft
D) modern people who unethically support witchcraft
E) naïve people accepted witches

CONTINUE

33

The author mentions "hopes" in lines 10 in order to point out the

A) pervasiveness nature of witchcraft

B) ignorance of those who believed in witchcraft

C) universal appeal of witchcraft

D) victims of witchcraft

E) condolence to those who believed in witchcraft

34

In retrospect, the author believes that the study of witchcraft has not been properly treated as it should have been because witchcraft practice

A) was not all bad

B) does not exist anymore

C) served its purpose more pervasively in people's lives

D) was treated more as psychology than as history

E) was practiced only in England

35

The passage provides information about witchcraft practiced in England in all the areas EXCEPT

A) the church

B) the court

C) farm

D) the government body

E) the army

CONTINUE

Questions 36-40 are based on the following passage.

Line

Art is a great thing. Maybe it is the greatest thing on earth. Wherever and whenever Nietzsche speaks about it he always does so loftily, and with reverence; while his position as an anchorite, and as an artist who kept aloof from the traffic for fame, allowed him to retain that innocence in his point of view, which he maintains is so
5 necessary in the treatment of such a subject.

As the children of an age in which Art is rapidly losing its prestige, we modern Europeans may perhaps feel a little inclined to purse our lips at the religious solemnity with which Nietzsche approaches this matter. So large a number of vital have been applied to the object of giving us entertainment in our large cities, that it is now no longer a simple matter to divorce
10 Art altogether in our minds from the category of things whose sole purpose is to amuse or please us.

Some there are, of course, who would repudiate this suggestion indignantly, and who would claim for Art a very high moral purpose. These moralists apart, however, it seems safe to say, that in the minds of most people to-day, Art is a thing which either leaves them utterly
15 unmoved, or to which they turn only when they are in need of distraction, of decoration for their homes, or of stimulation in their thought.

Leaving the discussion of Nietzsche's personal view of Art to the next lecture, I shall now first attempt, from his standpoint, a general examination of the condition of Art at the present day, which, though it will be necessarily rapid and sketchy, will, I hope, not prove inadequate for my purpose.

36

The primary purpose of the passage is to
A) convey the importance of art education
B) initiate the discussion of a general condition of Art
C) repudiate Nietzsche's view on arts
D) offer the best way to combine arts and
    entertainment
E) note the steady rise of entertainment

37

In line 3, "kept aloof from the traffic for fame" most nearly means that Nietzsche kept
A) arts above all the other subjects
B) himself away from becoming the popular artist
C) himself on top of the roof of all arts
D) many people away from him
E) his position between arts and fame

CONTINUE

38

The passage suggests that Nietzsche

A) was very religious person

B) believed in art, not the artists

C) called for a divorce Art from amusement

D) promoted art to be popular

E) treated art as gravely as religion

39

It can be inferred from the passage that the following chapter will discuss

A) Nietzsche's personal view of Art

B) the way modern European view on Art

C) a solution to separate Art from entertainment

D) European artists view on entertainment

E) the relations between Art and religion

40

The author's attitude towards the European's treatment of arts can be best described as

A) admonish

B) cheerful

C) polemic

D) serious

E) trivial

Test 8 Verbal Section   30 MINUTES, 60 QUESTIONS

Directions: the synonym questions ask you to find the most appropriate synonym to the question.

The analogy questions ask you to find the most appropriate analogy to the question.
Select the answer that best matches to the question.

Synonym Sample Question:

Q: SUPERIOR

   A higher rank

   B inferior

   C considerable

   D supermarket

   E supper

A) is the best answer because the synonym for superior is higher rank.

B) is incorrect because it applies the 'opposite concept.

C) and E) are irrelevant words.

D) is incorrect because it applies physical concept to mental concept

---

Test 8 Synonym questions 1 to 30

1.HACKNEYED

(A) Boring

(B) Interesting

(C) Hockey rules

(D) Surprise

(E) Requirement

2. IMPERATIVE

(A) unnecessary

(B) required

(C) king

(D) relations

(E) sadly

3. MUNDANE

(A) exciting

(B) boring

(C) Monday work

(D) weekly work

(E) tiredness

4. PLACID

(A) respect

(B) warlike

(C) peaceful

(D) placement

(E) organized

5. SPURIOUS

(A) real

(B) superior

(C) arrogant

(D) super

(E) fake

CONTINUE

6. STEALTHY

(A) disclose

(B) gaiety

(C) excited

(D) concealment

(E) stealing

7. URBANE

(A) polite

(B) rude

(C) country like

(D) modern

(E) wasteful

8. PERFIDY

(A) friendship

(B) loyal

(C) treachery

(D) fidelity

(E) professional

9. ADVENT

(A) departure

(B) arrival

(C) venture

(D) explore

(E) advertisement

10. ITINERANT

(A) staying

(B) ticketing

(C) international

(D) understand

(E) traveling

11. CACHE

(A) open

(B) place

(C) lazy

(D) hiding place

(E) spur

12. INCITE

(A) instigate

(B) ridiculous

(C) recital

(D) citation

(E) ratio

13. APPEASE

(A) peacemaker

(B) excessive

(C) shallow

(D) anger

(E) peace

14. DUPE

(A) truth

(B) bless

(C) peace

(D) deceive

(E) cheer

15. ACME

(A) malign

(B) mail

(C) bottom

(D) pinnacle

(E) foundation

CONTINUE ➡

16. DETER

(A) encourage

(B) humorous

(C) determination

(D) discourage

(E) literature

17. HOMILY

(A) deception

(B) lecture

(C) homely

(D) warm

(E) summon

18. EPICURE

(A) art of eating well

(B) manicure

(C) healing

(D) epidemic

(E) fast food

19. CAJOLE

(A) dissuade

(B) joyful

(C) excitement

(D) joint

(E) persuade

20. CHAGRIN

(A) money

(B) proud

(C) talkative

(D) Champaign

(E) humiliation

21. DOCILE

(A) tamed

(B) shock

(C) hard to control

(D) shark

(E) fish

22. VACILLATE

(A) waver

(B) dangerous

(C) difficult

(D) vaccine

(E) fixed

23. SAGE

(A) stupid

(B) wisdom

(C) aged

(D) saint

(E) ill judgment

24. BEQUEATH

(A) take back

(B) banquet

(C) generous

(D) question

(E) give

25. LAUD

(A) blame

(B) noisy

(C) long

(D) onerous

(E) praise

CONTINUE

26. CRASS

(A) stupid

(B) smart

(C) crack

(D) buttock

(E) revamp

27. PINNACLE

(A) enormous

(B) tiny

(C) lowest point

(D) top

(E) diligent

28. RECALCITRANT

(A) obedient

(B) easy

(C) height

(D) peak

(E) stubborn

29. SQUALID

(A) tidy

(B) bad

(C) dirty

(D) new

(E) scholarly

30. NEBULOUS

(A) clear

(B) exact

(C) incredible

(D) new concept

(E) opaque

Analogy Sample Question:

Q: River is to Ocean as:

A better is to good

B rain is to cloud

C father is to mother

D city is to country

E fork is to spoon

D is the correct answer. Just as the river is smaller than the Ocean, the city is smaller than the country. The pattern applied in this question is the Degree Pattern (small to big)

A) is incorrect because the word order is flipped over.

B) is incorrect because it applies the production pattern (cloud produces rain)

C), E) are incorrect because they apply the Antonym patterns.

Test 8 Analogy questions 31 to 60

31. Ears is to eyes as toes is to

(A) feet

(B) fingers

(C) body

(D) girls

(E) boy

CONTINUE

32. Engine is to car as

(A) heart is to human

(B) city is to building

(C) chair is to leg

(D) hat is to head

(E) ocean is to fish

33. Car plate is to name as

(A) study is to insurance

(B) fight is to win

(C) number is to name tag

(D) envelope is to stamp

(E) metal is to clothe

34. Butter is to bread as

(A) noodle is to soy source

(B) coffee is to bean

(C) soccer is to uniform

(D) movie is to actor

(E) girl is to boy

35. Hawaii is to islands as Sahara is to

(A) country

(B) wet

(C) camel

(D) desert

(E) sand

36. Rose is to flower as

(A) movie is to ticket

(B) art is to artist

(C) status is to exhibition

(D) music is to concert

(E) bee is to inset

37. Soccer is to field as

(A) child is to mom

(B) student is to practice

C) boxer is to fight

(D) hockey is to rink

(E) library is to book

38. Blood is to human as moist is to

(A) wet

(B) gloomy

(C) sky

(D) cloud

(E) dry

39. Rain is to monsoon as wind is to

(A) breeze

(B) hurricane

(C) earthquake

(D) volcano

(E) camping

40. Mirror is to reflection as

(A) coffee is to sleep

(B) old is to young

(C) bicycle is ride

(D) hospital is to doctor

(E) banana is to eat

41. Chicken is to bird as tiger is to

(A) endangered animal

(B) fast

(C) cage

(D) mammal

(E) furious

CONTINUE

42. Stare is to glimpse as dime is to

(A) dome

(B) money

(C) cent

(D) dollar

(E) quarter

43. God is to dying as

(A) win is to luck

(B) poor is money

(C) thief is to jail

(D) cure is to medicine

(E) human is to immortal

44. Sky is to the Ocean as

(A) evil is to god

(B) team is to locker room

(C) movie is to Hollywood

(D) boy is to girl

(E) mountain is to ridges

45. Human is to civilized as dog is to

(A) typed

(B) domesticated

(C) learned

(D) skilled

(E) wild

46. Paris is to beautiful city as

(A) European is to 14 billion populations

(B) snow is to winter

(C) fat person is to lazy

(D) hallway is to stair

(E) happy is to hilarious

47. Christianity is to belief as Biology is

(A) difficult

(B) organism

(C) living cells

(D) study subject

(E) lab

48. Vaccination is to flu as

(A) work is to study

(B) bat is to soccer

(C) school is to teacher

(D) study is to exam

(E) medicine is to disease

49. Striker is to baseball catcher as Champion is

(A) ring

(B) trophy

(C) challenger

(D) money

(E) match

50. knowledge is to A+ as speed is

(A) 20 kilograms

(B) gas

(C) slow

(D) automobile

(E) drive

51. Seven is to sandwich as sunny is to

(A) good meal

(B) rest

(C) shadow

(D) Sunday

(E) rainy

CONTINUE

52. Sally is to sell as shell is to

(A) fish

(B) coastline

(C) ocean

(D) shame

(E) proud

53. Eject is to project as percentile is to

(A) paint

(B) heal

(C) projectile

(D) reject

(E) plan

54. Despair is to repair as

(A) twin is to triplet

(B) team is to staff

(C) sad is to sorrow

(D) sand is to ocean

(E) believe is to grieve

55 Folk is to fork as dingy to

(A) table

(B) saving

(C) hinge

(D) gloomy

(E) sad

56. Borrow is to sorrow as far is to

(A) dinner

(B) concert

(C) jar

(D) student

(E) drive

57. East is to West as rain is to

(A) moist

(B) weather

(C) foggy

(D) snow

(E) umbrella

58. Gas is to gasoline as U.F.O. is

(A) hoax

(B) see

(C) alien

(D) acronym

(E) science

59. England is to isolated

(A) Japan is to Asia

(B) America is to 321.4 million

(C) Uganda is to poor

(D) Canada is to 2008 curling champion

(E) France is to Paris

60. Berger King is to junk food as

(A) diamond is to luxury

(B) father is to February born

(C) inspector is to badge

(D) cook's salary is to bi-weekly

(E) McDonald's is fast food

UNAUTHORIZED COPYING OR REUSE OF ANY PART OF THIS PAGE IS ILLEGAL

STOP

If you finish before time is called,
you may check your work on this section.

Do not turn to the next section.

Test 8

ABSOLUTE PATTERNS

TEST 8
READING SECTION

Please refer to the Reading Section Absolute Pattern Analysis next page

THE SYNONYM QUESTIONS	THE ANALOGY QUESTIONS
TEST 8 NO.1 ~ 30	TEST 8 NO. 31 ~ 60

Please refer to the Analogy Absolute Pattern Analysis in page. 444

1	A	16	D
2	B	17	B
3	B	18	A
4	C	19	E
5	E	20	E
6	D	21	A
7	A	22	A
8	C	23	B
9	B	24	E
10	E	25	E
11	D	26	A
12	A	27	D
13	E	28	E
14	D	29	C
15	D	30	E

Test 8

ABSOLUTE PATTERNS for the Reading Section

Q1. Pattern 3: Summary Question

Question Pattern: All of the followings are supported by the passage EXCEPT

Step 1	Step 2	Step 3
Keywords from the Passage	Keywords from Answer	Tone & Concept
Spiders, spoken of as bugs	A) Spiders, insects	Logical Conclusion

Incorrect Choices & Common Patterns		
Evidence	Incorrect keywords	Tone & Concept
Spiders, thousand-legs, crawfishes and even earth-worms are often spoken of as bugs	B) bugs', 'insects' not, interchangeably.	They are all written correctly.
	C) Insects largest group	
	D) Insects, bugs different	
	E) blood-sucking insects, bugs	

Q2. Pattern 3: Summary Question

Question Pattern: The phrase mentioned describes
Question Keywords: in line 13, "only three pairs of legs"

Step 1	Step 2	Step 3
Keywords from the Passage	Keywords from Answer	Tone & Concept
mature ones	D) only mature insect	Logical Conclusion

Incorrect Choices & Common Patterns		
Evidence	Incorrect keywords	Tone & Concept
mature ones have three and only three pairs of legs, one pair of feelers, one pair of large eyes, and one or two pairs of wings.	A) all mature bugs	Not Supported by the passage
	B) all insects	
	C) bugs and insects	
	E) get confused	

Q3. Pattern 3: Summary Question

Question Pattern: Which of the following does NOT comprise
Question Keywords: the part of insects' body?

Step 1	Step 2	Step 3
Keywords from the Passage	Keywords from Answer	Tone & Concept
one pair of large eyes,	A) Three pairs of eyes	Synonym

Incorrect Choices & Common Patterns		
Evidence	Incorrect keywords	Tone & Concept
...three and only three pairs of legs, one pair of feelers, one pair of large eyes, and one or two pairs of wings.	B) Three pairs of legs	They are all true statements.
	C) One pair of feelers	
	D) Two pairs of wings	
	E) One pair of ears	

Q4. Pattern 3: Summary Question

Question Pattern: Which of following statements is NOT supported by the passage?

Step 1	Step 2	Step 3
Keywords from the Passage	Keywords from Answer	Tone & Concept
Spiders, are often spoken of as bugs	B) insects, spiders	Logical Conclusion

Incorrect Choices & Common Patterns		
Evidence	Incorrect keywords	Tone & Concept
Spiders, thousand-legs, crawfishes and even earth-worms are often spoken of as bugs	A) insects as well as bugs	These are all supported by the passage.
	C) bugs, spiders	
	D) Vast majority, insect	
	E) general nature	

Q5. Pattern 3: Summary Question

Question Pattern: Which of the following
Question Keywords: animal can be classified as both an insect and a bug?

Step 1	Step 2	Step 3
Keywords from the Passage	Keywords from Answer	Tone & Concept
insects <u>includes the sap and blood-sucking</u>	A) Mosquito	Logical Conclusion

Incorrect Choices & Common Patterns		
Evidence	Incorrect keywords	Tone & Concept
Insects are commonly spoken of as "bugs." This term, however, is properly used only when referring to the one order of insects <u>which includes the sap and blood-sucking insects</u> such as the chinch bug, bed-bug, squash bug, and the like	B) Spider	these are all bugs
	C) Thousand-legs	
	D) Crawfishes	
	E) Earth-warms	

Q6. Pattern 5: Word-In-Context Question

Question Keywords: In line 16, "abdomen" refers to which part of insects?

Step 1	Step 2	Step 3
Keywords from the Passage	Keywords from Answer	Tone & Concept
The body s divided, a head, thorax and abdomen.	A) stomach	Abdomen = stomach

Incorrect Choices & Common Patterns		
Evidence	Incorrect keywords	Tone & Concept
The body is divided into a head, thorax and abdomen.	B) head	
	C) tail	
	D) legs	
	E) reproduction organ	

Q7. Pattern 3: Summary Question

Question Keywords: Lines 20 ("Oh! of course...admitted Rose.") suggests that Rose admits

Step 1	Step 2	Step 3
Keywords from the Passage	Keywords from Answer	Tone & Concept
Having a red hair is a <u>genetic inheritance</u>	E) genetic inheritance	Synonym

Incorrect Choices & Common Patterns		
Evidence	Incorrect keywords	Tone & Concept
It generally crops out once in a <u>generation,</u> Having a red hair is a <u>genetic inheritance</u> for which Rose admits.	A) personality	Not Supported by the passage
	B) social status	
	C) hair color	
	D) family tradition	

Q8. Pattern 3: Summary Question

Question Pattern: Throughout the passage,
Question Keywords: Rudolf emphasizes primarily which of the following about himself?

Step 1	Step 2	Step 3
Keywords from the Passage	Keywords from Answer	Tone & Concept
sufficient for my wants	C) resourcefulness	Logical Conclusion

Incorrect Choices & Common Patterns		
Evidence	Incorrect keywords	Tone & Concept
(C) <u>I have an income nearly sufficient for my wants</u> (no one's income is ever quite sufficient, you know),	A) profligacy	(A) I wonder when in the world you're going to do anything, Rudolf?" <u>said my brother's wife.</u>
	B) familiarity	
	D) relationship	
	E) unsuccessful marriage	

Q9. Pattern 6: Understanding Structure of the Passage

Question Pattern: The parenthetical phrase in lines 10-11 (and there can't be…to the fact) primarily serves

Step 1	Step 2	Step 3
Keywords from the Passage	Keywords from Answer	Tone & Concept
and therefore there can be no harm in referring	D) a justification	Logical Conclusion

Incorrect Choices & Common Patterns		
Evidence	Incorrect keywords	Tone & Concept
This remark of mine rather annoyed Rose, for everybody knows (and therefore there can be no harm in referring to the fact)	A) lament	Rudolf tries to justify his remarks that might have annoyed Rose. The other choices are Not Supported by the passage
	B) new theory	
	C) challenge	
	E) state an exception	

Q10. Pattern 7: Understanding Attitude / Tone

Question Pattern: Compared to, contains more
Question Keywords: Rose's, Robert's remark "So does…both." (line 22)

Step 1	Step 2	Step 3
Keywords from the Passage	Keywords from Answer	Tone & Concept
"So does the nose.	E) humorous tone	humorous comment

Incorrect Choices & Common Patterns		
Evidence	Incorrect keywords	Tone & Concept
"It generally crops out once in a generation," said my brother. "So does the nose. Rudolf has got them both."	A) apologetic	Just imagine a person with a red nose.
	B) assertive	
	C) analytic	
	D) invocative	

Q11. Pattern 7: Understanding Attitude / Tone

Question Pattern: Which of the following best reveals

Question Keywords: Rose's mood when she said "Oh! of course... his hair," (line 20)

Step 1	Step 2	Step 3
Keywords from the Passage	Keywords from Answer	Tone & Concept
"Oh! of course he can't help his hair	A) remorse	feeling guilty
Incorrect Choices & Common Patterns		
Evidence	Incorrect keywords	Tone & Concept
"Oh! of course he can't help his hair," admitted Rose.	B) fear	The tone contains the feeling of guilt.
	C) appreciation	
	D) celebration	
	E) bafflement	

Q12. Pattern 5: Word-In-Context Question

Question Pattern: most nearly refers to   **Question Keywords:** In line 20, "crops"

Step 1	Step 2	Step 3
Keywords from the Passage	Keywords from Answer	Tone & Concept
It generally crops out once in a generation	C) occurring	Synonym
Incorrect Choices & Common Patterns		
Evidence	Incorrect keywords	Tone & Concept
"It generally crops out once in a generation," said my brother.	A) farming	The best replacement for the word "Crops" is "occurring"
	B) harvesting	
	D) remaining	
	E) showing	

Q13. Pattern 2: Main Idea Question

Question Pattern: The passage as a whole

Step 1	Step 2	Step 3
Keywords from the Passage	Keywords from Answer	Tone & Concept
A wish to save time, trouble and money	C) simplistic, fundamental	Logical Conclusion

Incorrect Choices & Common Patterns		
Evidence	Incorrect keywords	Tone & Concept
A wish to save time, trouble and money to inexperienced housekeepers and cooks, and to bring the enjoyments and indulgences of society, were my motives for publishing this book.	A) over practicality B) creativity D) scientific E) bestseller	A), B), D) are Opposite E) is not mentioned C) This book is for the housekeepers and for those who favor simple and fundamental meal.

Q14. Pattern 2: Main Idea Question

Question Keywords: The author of the cookbook focused her main readers to be

Step 1	Step 2	Step 3
Keywords from the Passage	Keywords from Answer	Tone & Concept
even by the amateur, who is unacquainted	B) mothers	Logical Conclusion

Incorrect Choices & Common Patterns		
Evidence	Incorrect keywords	Tone & Concept
Line 13: I have endeavored to describe each, in so plain and circumstantial a manner, as I hope will be easily understood, even by the amateur, who is unacquainted with the practical part of culinary concerns.	A) cookbook editors C) fastidious stomach D) restaurant owners E) experienced chef	Not Supported by the passage

Q15. Pattern 2: Main Idea Question

Question Pattern: The author's main point
Question Keywords: in the first paragraph, (lines 1-6) is that the cookbook

Step 1	Step 2	Step 3
Keywords from the Passage	Keywords from Answer	Tone & Concept
recipes bonâ fide register of practical facts	B) fine recipes	Synonym
Incorrect Choices & Common Patterns		
Evidence	Incorrect keywords	Tone & Concept
The following recipes are not a mere marrowless collection of shreds and patches, and cuttings and pastings but a bonâ fide register of practical facts	A) combined data	Not Supported by the passage
	C) professional chefs	
	D) universally respected	
	E) restaurant business	

Q16. Type 2: Inference Question [Pattern 1: Local Question] {Category A}

Question Pattern: implies
Question Keywords: "OLD HOUSEKEEPERS...attention" (lines 13-15) that the author's predecessors have considered the cookery should focus on

Step 1	Step 2	Step 3
Keywords from the Passage	Keywords from Answer	Tone & Concept
Old housekeepers may think tediously...	C) exquisite table	Logical Conclusion
Incorrect Choices & Common Patterns		
Evidence	Incorrect keywords	Tone & Concept
Old housekeepers may think I have been tediously minute on many points which may appear trifling: my predecessors seem to have considered the rudiments of cookery quite unworthy of attention.	A) some little delicate	All these options are basically referring to the same comments
	B) everyday meal	
	D) common table	
	E) basic cooking process	

The answer is finding the opposite situation of "tediously minute" in the passage.

Q17. Pattern 3: Summary Question

Question Pattern: Which of the followings   **Question Keywords:** makes this cookbook unique?

Step 1	Step 2	Step 3
Keywords from the Passage	Keywords from Answer	Tone & Concept
having eaten each recipe	D) the author, ate all the recipes	Synonym

Incorrect Choices & Common Patterns		
Evidence	Incorrect keywords	Tone & Concept
the author has submitted to a labor no preceding cookery-book-maker, perhaps, ever attempted to encounter,--having eaten each recipe	A) not a mere marrowless	Minor Issue
	B) patches, cuttings, pastings	Minor Issue
	C) professional chefs	not stated
	E) from former books	Opposite

Q18. Type 3: Analogy Question [Pattern 1: Local Question] {Category A}

Question Pattern: Which of the following situation is analogous to the
Question Keywords: claim "moreover, the author...book" (lines 5-6)

Step 1	Step 2	Step 3
Keywords from the Passage	Keywords from Answer	Tone & Concept
writing the cookbook, eating the meal	D) A nurse is filling, checking	Logical Conclusion

Incorrect Choices & Common Patterns		
Evidence	Incorrect keywords	Tone & Concept
the nurse (COOKBOOK WRITER) is writing down the record (WRITING THE COOKBOOK) as she checks the patient's condition (EATING ALL THE MEALS ON THE BOOK)	B) detective's instinct	A) the chemistry teacher must offer a lecture based on his own experiment.
	A) students' experiment outcome	
	C) note from her grandmother	
	E) school instruction	

The logic employed in this question is the self-conduct without other people's assistance.

Choice B) instinct is different from practice like writing down the recipe.

Choice C) the mother is using her grandmother's recipe, not her own one.

Choice E) the boy was given the instruction from the school about his essay.

Q19. Pattern 3: Summary Question

Question Pattern: By saying that, the author
Question Keywords: " It is not intended to advise against marriage" (line 1),

Step 1	Step 2	Step 3
Keywords from the Passage	Keywords from Answer	Tone & Concept
It is not intended	D) defuses, objection	Logical Conclusion

Incorrect Choices & Common Patterns		
Evidence	Incorrect keywords	Tone & Concept
It is not intended to advise against marriage, nor to draw the line to show the contrasting view of author's later view on marriage. D) The author wants to remove a possible objection before initiates his opinion.	A) revokes	A), B) are Too extreme word usage C), E) are Not Supported by the passage E) "on his view" should change to "on other people's view"
	B) respects other's	
	C) admits, mixed view	
	E) suggests, alternative	

Q20. Pattern 3: Summary Question

Question Pattern: The author characterizes the main reason for
Question Keywords: unhappy marriage is rooted in

Step 1	Step 2	Step 3
Keywords from the Passage	Keywords from Answer	Tone & Concept
But, real trouble arises from a spiteful choice	C) hasty choice	Synonym

Incorrect Choices & Common Patterns		
Evidence	Incorrect keywords	Tone & Concept
But quite generally the real trouble arises from a spiteful choice or a hasty one., the author characterizes hasty choice becomes the catalysis of the unhappy marriage.	A) marry for mere beauty	A) is one of the reasons, not the primary reason.
	B) romantic marriage	
	D) unromantic marriage	
	E) parents' preference	

Q21. Pattern 3: Summary Question

Question Pattern: All the statements represent, EXCEPT
Question Keywords: "the real pleasures" in line 20 can be one of

Step 1	Step 2	Step 3
Keywords from the Passage	Keywords from Answer	Tone & Concept
"Don't marry for beauty merely	E) cosmetic surgery	Logical Conclusion

Incorrect Choices & Common Patterns		
Evidence	Incorrect keywords	Tone & Concept
"Don't marry for beauty merely. a wife's cosmetic surgery" would not bring the real pleasure.	A) buying a cookbook	Line 21: while the real pleasures of life may be found in a thousand ways outside of the beauty.
	B) same hobbies	
	C) helping a child	
	D) painting his wife's	

Q22. Pattern 3: Summary Question

Question Pattern: In the passage,
Question Keywords: the author views beauty in marriage as

Step 1	Step 2	Step 3
Keywords from the Passage	Keywords from Answer	Tone & Concept
Don't marry for beauty merely	C) less than a garden	Logical Conclusion

Incorrect Choices & Common Patterns		
Evidence	Incorrect keywords	Tone & Concept
Don't marry for beauty merely.	A) an admirable	Not Supported by the passage
	B) a grateful	
	D) too abstract	
	E) not only the requisite	

Q23. Pattern 3: Summary Question

Question Pattern: emphasizes the author's recognition of
Question Keywords: In line 14, the statement "it is well to treat it with exact candor"

Step 1	Step 2	Step 3
Keywords from the Passage	Keywords from Answer	Tone & Concept
it is well to treat it with exact candor	E) requires more honest	Logical Conclusion

Incorrect Choices & Common Patterns		
Evidence	Incorrect keywords	Tone & Concept
As marriage is the first question that every family will discuss, it is well to treat it with exact candor.	A) discovering beauty	A) is incorrect because the author does not give any value in beauty. B), C) are true statement but do not respond to the question.
	B) family interest	
	C) financial interest	
	D) happy marriage is impossible	

Q24. Pattern 3: Summary Question

Question Keywords: to prevent unhappy marriage, which, should be considered most?

Step 1	Step 2	Step 3
Keywords from the Passage	Keywords from Answer	Tone & Concept
The "yes or no" question is the vital	E) "yes" or "no" question	Synonym

Incorrect Choices & Common Patterns		
Evidence	Incorrect keywords	Tone & Concept
The "yes or no" question is the vital one for all young people to answer.	A) two families	A), B) are true statements but not the most valuables. C), D) are Opposite
	B) privacy	
	C) parents	
	D) external appearance	

Q25. Type 2: Inference Question [Pattern 1: Local Question] {Category A}

Question Pattern: The author's attitude toward based on
Question Keywords: "personification" in line 1 is

Step 1	Step 2	Step 3
Keywords from the Passage	Keywords from Answer	Tone & Concept
definition of this, <u>however, must be extended</u>	C) tentative acceptance	Logical Conclusion

Incorrect Choices & Common Patterns		
Evidence	Incorrect keywords	Tone & Concept
The definition of this, <u>however, must be extended</u> <u>from the mere representation of inanimate things</u> <u>as animate,</u> to include....	A) solid evidence B) logical argument D) disturbing misconception E) necessary speculation	C) The author believes the definition must be extended. Therefore, his view on animal myths is tentative.

Q26. Type 2: Inference Question [Pattern 1: Local Question] {Category A}

Question Pattern: The author mentions as an example of   **Question Keywords:** "personification" (line 1)

Step 1	Step 2	Step 3
Keywords from the Passage	Keywords from Answer	Tone & Concept
all myths	C) ubiquitous	ubiquitous means "all"

Incorrect Choices & Common Patterns		
Evidence	Incorrect keywords	Tone & Concept
At the foundation of <u>all myths</u> lies the <u>mental process</u> of personification,	A) dehumanizing B) gratification D) similar mentality E) similar physical	A) 'dehumanizing' is negative, while the passage is not necessarily negative. B) 'gratification' is too positive. D) It is about animal in myth, not people E) the word "physical" is incorrect

D) the word 'mentality' in the text refers to the mentality of an animated myth, not the regular people in all nations.

Q27. Type 2: Inference Question [Pattern 1: Local Question] {Category A}

Question Pattern: Which of the following pair most likely resemble the description of
Question Keywords: homonymy?

Step 1	Step 2	Step 3
Keywords from the Passage	Keywords from Answer	Tone & Concept
the sameness in sound of words with a difference	D) Boy and Boys	Logical Conclusion

Incorrect Choices & Common Patterns		
Evidence	Incorrect keywords	Tone & Concept
Again, many myths spring from homonymy, that is, the sameness in sound of words with a difference in signification.	A) Difficult and Easy	Illogical combinations
	B) Again and Repeat	
	C) Basic and Fundamental	
	E) Be and Bee	

Q28. Type 2: Inference Question [Pattern 1: Local Question] {Category A}

Question Pattern: The main reason for the statement that
Question Keywords: "They cannot say the boat moves" (line 9) is

Step 1	Step 2	Step 3
Keywords from the Passage	Keywords from Answer	Tone & Concept
cannot say "the boat moves" without	A) yet to be subjected to an animate object	Logical Conclusion

Incorrect Choices & Common Patterns		
Evidence	Incorrect keywords	Tone & Concept
They cannot say "the boat moves" without specifying whether the boat is an animate object or not,	B) without clear implication	Not Supported by the passage
	C) grammatical	
	D) didn't see the actual boat moving	
	E) all boats	

Q29. Pattern 3: Summary Question

Question Pattern: the author implies that , EXCEPT
Question Keywords: Aztec language has all the qualities

Step 1	Step 2	Step 3
Keywords from the Passage	Keywords from Answer	Tone & Concept
The sounds of words ,aided in myth	A) written, language	Logical Conclusion

Incorrect Choices & Common Patterns		
Evidence	Incorrect keywords	Tone & Concept
The sounds of words have aided greatly in myth building.	B) lack of grammatical	The main theme of the passage is about verbal language that is built upon the myth, not the written form of language.
	C) sounds of words	
	D) reliance on myth	
	E) homonymy	

Q30. Pattern 3: Summary Question

Question Keywords: The reference to "a serpent, a guest and twins" (line 17) primarily serves to

Step 1	Step 2	Step 3
Keywords from the Passage	Keywords from Answer	Tone & Concept
Again, many myths spring from homonymy,	C) homonymy	Logical Conclusion

Incorrect Choices & Common Patterns		
Evidence	Incorrect keywords	Tone & Concept
Again, many myths spring from homonymy, that is, the sameness in sound of words with difference in signification. wit, a serpent, a guest and twins…	A) imaginative nature	Not Supported by the passage
	B) disparage	
	D) alternative	
	E) extreme views	

UNAUTHORIZED COPYING OR REUSE OF ANY PART OF THIS PAGE IS ILLEGAL

Q31. Pattern 2: Main Idea Question

Question Pattern: The passage as a whole is primarily concerned with the

Step 1	Step 2	Step 3
Keywords from the Passage	Keywords from Answer	Tone & Concept
life that were not affected by the ugly belief.	B) pervasive impact	Logical Conclusion

Incorrect Choices & Common Patterns		
Evidence	Incorrect keywords	Tone & Concept
There were few aspects of sixteenth and seventeenth century life that were not affected by the ugly belief. *The underlined portions shows the pervasive impact of witchcraft in history.	A) modern historian	A), C) are too vague. D) The passage didn't mention what has been dishonest or earnest
	C) difficulties, debunking	
	D) earnest revelation	
	E) response	

Q32. Pattern 3: Summary Question

Question Keywords: "the ugly belief" mentioned in line 9 most nearly refers to the belief of those

Step 1	Step 2	Step 3
Keywords from the Passage	Keywords from Answer	Tone & Concept
life that were not affected by the ugly belief.	E) naïve people	Logical Conclusion

Incorrect Choices & Common Patterns		
Evidence	Incorrect keywords	Tone & Concept
There were few aspects of sixteenth and seventeenth life that were not affected by the ugly belief.	A) who practiced	Choice B is wrong because English witches themselves wouldn't say they are ugly.
	B) English witches	
	C) historians who deny	
	D) modern people	

Q33. Type 2: Inference Question [Pattern 1: Local Question] {Category A}

Question Pattern: The author mentions in order to point out   **Question Keywords:** "hopes" in lines 10

Step 1	Step 2	Step 3
Keywords from the Passage	Keywords from Answer	Tone & Concept
hopes of the men and women <u>ignorant denizens</u>	B) ignorance	Logical Conclusion

Incorrect Choices & Common Patterns		
Evidence	Incorrect keywords	Tone & Concept
it is impossible to understand the opinions, fears, and <u>hopes of the men and women </u>who lived in Elizabethan, without some knowledge of the part <u>played in that age by witchcraft. to the ignorant denizens of country villages.</u>	A) pervasiveness C) universal D) victims E) condolence	Denizen means citizen. The author defines the men and women in Elizabeth era were ignorant in believing such a practice.

Q34. Pattern 3: Summary Question

Question Pattern: In retrospect, the author believes that
Question Keywords: the study of witchcraft has not been properly treated as it should have been because

Step 1	Step 2	Step 3
Keywords from the Passage	Keywords from Answer	Tone & Concept
the belief in witchcraft is no longer existent	B) does not exist	Logical Conclusion

Incorrect Choices & Common Patterns		
Evidence	Incorrect keywords	Tone & Concept
There has been, of course, a reason for this neglect --the fact that the belief in witchcraft is no longer existent	A) was not all bad C) more pervasively D) psychology E) only in England	Not Supported by the passage

UNAUTHORIZED COPYING OR REUSE OF ANY PART OF THIS PAGE IS ILLEGAL

Q35. Pattern 3: Summary Question

Question Pattern: The passage provides information about EXCEPT

Question Keywords: witchcraft practiced in England in all the areas

Step 1	Step 2	Step 3
Keywords from the Passage	Keywords from Answer	Tone & Concept
Privy councilors , peasants, clergymen, justices	E) army	Not mentioned
Incorrect Choices & Common Patterns		
Evidence	Incorrect keywords	Tone & Concept
Privy councilors (D) anxious about their sovereign and thrifty peasants (C) worrying over their crops, clergymen (A) alert to detect the Devil in their own parishes, medical quacks eager to profit by the fear of evil women, justices (B) of the peace	A) church	These are all mentioned.
	B) court	
	C) farm	
	D) government body	

Q36. Pattern 2: Main Idea Question

Question Pattern: The primary purpose of the passage is to

Step 1	Step 2	Step 3
Keywords from the Passage	Keywords from Answer	Tone & Concept
a general examination of the condition of Art	B) general condition of Art	Synonym
Incorrect Choices & Common Patterns		
Evidence	Incorrect keywords	Tone & Concept
I shall now first attempt, from his standpoint, a general examination of the condition of Art at the present day,	A) art education	Too vague
	C) repudiate	Negative
	D) offer the best way	Too extreme word usage
	E) entertainment	Opposite

Q37. Pattern 3: Summary Question

Question Keywords: In line 3, "kept aloof from the traffic for fame" most nearly means that Nietzsche kept

Step 1	Step 2	Step 3
Keywords from the Passage	Keywords from Answer	Tone & Concept
"kept arts and fame to be mutually exclusive	B) away from popular	Logical Conclusion

Incorrect Choices & Common Patterns		
Evidence	Incorrect keywords	Tone & Concept
"kept arts and fame to be mutually exclusive" = kept arts and fame to be separate. Mutually exclusive means keep two entities separate.	A) all the other subjects	Not Supported by the passage
	C) himself on top	
	D) many people away	
	E) between arts and fame	

Q38. Type 2: Inference Question [Pattern 1: Local Question] {Category A}

Question Keywords: The passage suggests that Nietzsche

Step 1	Step 2	Step 3
Keywords from the Passage	Keywords from Answer	Tone & Concept
The religious solemnity, approaches	E) treated art as gravely as religion	Logical Conclusion

Incorrect Choices & Common Patterns		
Evidence	Incorrect keywords	Tone & Concept
The religious solemnity with which Nietzsche approaches this matter means that Nietzsche treated art as gravely as religion.	A) religious person	Choice C is true statement. However, this statement is not from Nietzsche, but from the author.
	B) believed in art, not the artists	
	C) divorce Art from amusement	
	D) promoted art to be popular	

Gravely means seriously. Nietzsche's view on art was as sacred as serving a religious principle.

UNAUTHORIZED COPYING OR REUSE OF ANY PART OF THIS PAGE IS ILLEGAL

Q39. Type 2: Inference Question [Pattern 1: Local Question] {Category A}

Question Pattern: It can be inferred from the passage that the following chapter will discuss

Step 1	Step 2	Step 3
Keywords from the Passage	Keywords from Answer	Tone & Concept
general examination of the condition of Art	B) view on Art	Logical Conclusion

Incorrect Choices & Common Patterns		
Evidence	Incorrect keywords	Tone & Concept
(A) Leaving the discussion of Nietzsche's personal view of Art to the next lecture, I shall now first attempt, from his standpoint, a general examination of the condition of Art at the present day,	A) Nietzsche's personal	A) is Opposite.
	C) entertainment	C), D) entertainment will not be the main topic.
	D) entertainment	
	E) religion	E) religion will not be the

Q40. Pattern 7: Understanding Attitude / Tone

Question Pattern: The author's attitude towards can be best described as
Question Keywords: the European's treatment to arts

Step 1	Step 2	Step 3
Keywords from the Passage	Keywords from Answer	Tone & Concept
them utterly unmoved, or to which they turn only	A) admonish	admonish = scorn gently

Incorrect Choices & Common Patterns		
Evidence	Incorrect keywords	Tone & Concept
in the minds of most people to-day, Art is a thing which either leaves them utterly unmoved, or to which they turn only when they are in need of distraction, of decoration	B) cheerful	Positive
	C) polemic	Too extreme word usage
	D) serious	Opposite
	E) trivial	Opposite

Test 8 ABSOLUTE PATTERNS for the Analogy Section

Q31. Absolute Pattern 7: Association (Characteristic) Pattern

B is the best answer

Both ears and eyes have two units each. Both toes and fingers have ten units each.

Q32. Absolute Pattern 8: Shape Pattern

A is the best answer

A car engine is in the center of a car so is the human heart in the human body.

Q33. Absolute Pattern 7: Association (Characteristic) Pattern

C is the best answer.

The number is the identification of car plate. The name is the identification of name tag.

Q34. Absolute Pattern 7: Association (Characteristic) Pattern

A is the best answer.

Butter is used for bread as soy source is used for noodle. (The same additive category)

Choice B is wrong because although coffee and bean are edible. The logic—what becomes what—does not correspond to the question. Choice D and E are out-of-category.

Q35. Absolute Pattern 7: Association (Characteristic) Pattern

D is the best answer

Hawaii is islands as Sahara is a desert.

Q36. Absolute Pattern 2: Part-Whole Pattern

E is the best answer

Rose is a part of the flower as bee is a part of the insect.

Q37. Absolute Pattern 6:Purpose (Job/Tool) Pattern

D is the best answer

We play soccer in the field, as we play hockey in the rink

Q38. Absolute Pattern 2: Part-Whole Pattern

D is the best answer

Blood is a part of human body as moist a part of the cloud.

Q39. Absolute Pattern 5: Degree Pattern

B is the best answer (weak to strong)

Monsoon is stronger than rain; the hurricane is stronger than the wind.

Choice A is reverse degree.

Q40. Absolute Pattern 6:Purpose (Job/Tool) Pattern

C is the best answer.

The purpose of a mirror is for reflection as the purpose of a bicycle is for a ride.

A is opposite to its effect.

Q41. Absolute Pattern 2: Part-Whole Pattern

D is the best answer

Choice A) "endangered animal" is incorrect because the question sentence describes the animal

category, not the list of endangered animal.

Q42. Absolute Pattern 5: Degree Pattern

C is the best answer.

The stare is more intense than the glimpse; dime is ten times of cent

D, E are reverse.

Q43. Absolute Pattern 7: Association (Characteristic) Pattern

E is the best answer

God is to immortal as a human is to dying.

Q44. Absolute Pattern 3: Antonym (Positive-Negative) Pattern

D is the best answer

The sky is opposite direction to the Ocean; a boy is opposite sex to a girl.

Q45. Absolute Pattern 7: Association (Characteristic) Pattern

B is the best answer

A human develops through civilization as dog develops through domestication.

The closest word that corresponds for the dog must be 'domesticated.'

Q46. Absolute Pattern 10: Subjective-Objective Pattern

C is the best answer

The question "Paris is to beautiful city" is a subjective view. Only choice (C) "fat person is to lazy" is subjective.

(A) European is to 14 billion populations and (B) snow is to winter are objective.

Q47. Absolute Pattern 13: Mental-Physical Pattern

A is the best answer.

Christianity is to belief is a mental concept; Biology is difficult is a mental concept.

All the remaining choices are a physical concept.

Q48. Absolute Pattern 6:Purpose (Job/Tool) Pattern

E is the best answer.

Vaccination is used to prevent flu as medicine is to disease.

(D) is not the same medicine category.

Q49. Absolute Pattern 12: Active-Passive Pattern

C is the best answer

A striker is an active role and a baseball pitcher" is a passive role. A champion takes a passive role to defend the title while a challenger should take the active role to get the title.

Q50. Absolute Pattern 9: Quantity-Quality Pattern

A is the best answer

Knowledge is to A+ " contains quantity (the measurable figure "A+).

The counterpart 55miles per hour must also contain the same quantity (the measurable figure 20 kilograms).

The remaining choices are all quality.

Q51. Absolute Pattern 11: Homophony Pattern

D is the best answer

The same sound.

Q52. Absolute Pattern 11: Homophony Pattern

D is the best answer.

Sally has the same sound as sell so does shell to shame.

Q53. Absolute Pattern 11: Homophony Pattern

C is the best answer.

Eject has the same sound as the project so does percentile to the projectile.

Q54. Absolute Pattern 11: Homophony Pattern

E is the best answer

Despair has the same sound as a repair so does believe to grieve.

Q55. Absolute Pattern 11: Homophony Pattern

C is the best answer

folk is to fork as dingy to (C) hinge

Q56. Absolute Pattern 11: Homophony Pattern

C is the best answer

Borrow and sorrow have the same sound, so does far and jar.

Q57. Absolute Pattern 3: Antonym (Positive-Negative) Pattern

D is the best answer

The East is the opposite direction to West" Rain reminds summer while snow reminds winter.

(A) moist (is production relationships)

(B) weather (is part-whole relationships)

(C) foggy (is an association relationships)

(E) umbrella (is tool relationships)

Q58. Absolute Pattern 15: Syntax Pattern

B is the best answer

Gas is the acronym for gasoline. U.F.O. is the acronym for Unidentified Flying Object.

Q59. Absolute Pattern 10: Subjective-Objective Pattern

C is the best answer.

"England is to isolated" is a subjective view. Choice (C) "Uganda is to poor" is a subjective view as well. The remaining choices (A) Japan is to Asia, (B) America is to 321.4 million, (D) Canada is to 2008 curling champion (E) France is to Paris are all objective (quantifiable data) view.

Q60. Absolute Pattern 10: Subjective-Objective Pattern

A is the best answer.

The question "Berger King is to junk food" is subjective view—especially from the owner of Berger King or stockholders' view. (A) diamond is to luxury is also subjective view because the level of luxury can't be identified or measured. .

(B) father is to February born; (C) inspector is to badge; (D) cook's salary is to bi-weekly; (E) McDonald's is fast food are all quantifiable (measurable) matter.

Published in 2018 by Rockridge edu. enterprise & services. inc.
ALL RIGHTS RESERVED.
COPYRIGHT @2016
BY SAN YOO

NO part of this book may be reproduced in any form, by phtosat, Microfilm, PDF or any other means, or incorporated into any information retrieval system, electronic or mechanical, without the written permission of the copyright owner

All inquiries should be addressed to:
Rockridge edu. enterprise & services inc.
869 SEYMOUR BLVD. NORTH VANCOUVER B.C. CANADA V7J 2J7
satvancouver@gmail.com

About the author

San, for over 20 years of his career, worked in various educational industries. From college entrance consulting to teaching standardized tests such as SAT / ACT / IELTS / TOEFL / LSAT/ GRE, he has been helping numerous students to enter their top choice universities.

In fact, favoritism of SSAT's high-level vocabularies and reading passages makes many Junior and high school students fearful and frustrated to SSAT. But, despite of this fact, SSAT most often than not follows unsurprising patterns—the patterns appear to be problematic and indeed are an albatross around many, may students' necks.

To create the questions and at the same time break the logics and patterns of SSAT Verbal questions based on its set-guidelines, San researched hundreds of SSAT tests released and published in the past 10 years.

Here, in this book, students can find how SSAT exploits (?) the students by depending on a scenario remarkably similar to that of many questions for several years.

San is currently living in North Vancouver, B.C. Canada, where he teaches—to further students' needs and realize their ambitions—and write books.

For enrollment through skype lesson, please contact to the author using his email: satvancouver@gmail.com

Dedicated to my wife, Eun Ju and my dog, Okong

30644321R00246

Made in the USA
Columbia, SC
11 November 2018